William Hine[?]
f[?] <P9-CMF-562>
Mary D. Crane
Decem 25 - 1913

Mitti [?] —

THREE PLAYS BY
GRANVILLE BARKER

Three Plays by Granville Barker

The Marrying of Ann Leete

The Voysey Inheritance

Waste

MITCHELL KENNERLEY
Publisher   New York

To the memory of my fellow-worker,
St. John Hankin.

The Marrying of Ann Leete

A COMEDY

1899

THE MARRYING OF ANN LEETE

The first three acts of the comedy pass in the garden at Markswayde, MR. CARNABY LEETE'S *house near Reading, during a summer day towards the close of the eighteenth century: the first act at four in the morning, the second shortly after mid-day, the third near to sunset. The fourth act takes place one day in the following winter; the first scene in the hall at Markswayde, the second scene in a cottage some ten miles off.*

This part of the Markswayde garden looks to have been laid out during the seventeenth century. In the middle a fountain; the centrepiece the figure of a nymph, now somewhat cracked, and pouring nothing from the amphora; the rim of the fountain is high enough and broad enough to be a comfortable seat.

The close turf around is in parts worn bare. This plot of ground is surrounded by a terrace three feet higher. Three sides of it are seen. From two corners broad steps lead down; stone urns stand at the bottom and top of the stone balustrades. The other two corners are rounded convexly into broad stone seats.

Along the edges of the terrace are growing rose trees, close together; behind these, paths; behind those, shrubs and trees. No landscape is to be seen. A big copper beech overshadows the seat on the left. A silver birch droops over the seat on the right. The trees far to the left indicate an orchard, the few to the right are more of the garden sort. It is the height of summer, and after a long drought the rose trees are dilapidated.

I

*It is very dark in the garden. Though there may be by
    now a faint morning light in the sky, it has not pen-
    etrated yet among these trees. It is very still, too.
    Now and then the leaves of a tree are stirred, as if
    in its sleep; that is all. Suddenly a shrill, fright-
    ened, but not tragical, scream is heard. After a
    moment* ANN LEETE *runs quickly down the steps and
    on to the fountain, where she stops, panting.* LORD
    JOHN CARP *follows her, but only to the top of the
    steps, evidently not knowing his way.* ANN *is a girl
    of twenty; he an English gentleman, nearer forty
    than thirty.*

LORD JOHN. I apologise.

ANN. Why is it so dark?

LORD JOHN. Can you hear what I'm saying?

ANN. Yes.

LORD JOHN. I apologise for having kissed you . . .
almost unintentionally.

ANN. Thank you. Mind the steps down.

LORD JOHN. I hope I'm sober, but the air . . .

ANN. Shall we sit for a minute? There are several
seats to sit on, somewhere.

LORD JOHN. This is a very dark garden.

   There is a slight pause.

ANN. You've won your bet.

LORD JOHN. So you did scream!

ANN. But it wasn't fair.

LORD JOHN. Don't reproach me.

ANN. Somebody's coming.

LORD JOHN. How d'you know?

ANN. I can h e a r somebody coming.

LORD JOHN. We're not sitting down.

   ANN'S *brother,* GEORGE LEETE, *comes to the top of
   the steps, and afterwards down them. Rather an
   old young man.*

GEORGE. Ann!

ANN. Yes.

GEORGE. My lord!

LORD JOHN. Here.

GEORGE. I can't see you. I'm sent to say we're all anxious to know what ghost or other bird of night or beast has frightened Ann to screaming point, and won you . . . the best in Tatton's stables—so he says now. He's quite annoyed.

LORD JOHN. The mare is a very good mare.

ANN. He betted it because he wanted to bet it; I didn't want him to bet it.

GEORGE. What frightened her?

ANN. I had rather, my lord, that you did not tell my brother why I screamed.

LORD JOHN. I kissed her.

GEORGE. Did you?

ANN. I had rather, Lord John, that you had not told my brother why I screamed.

LORD JOHN. I misunderstood you.

GEORGE. I've broke up the whist party. Ann, shall we return?

LORD JOHN. She's not here.

GEORGE. Ann!

    LADY COTTESHAM, ANN'S *sister, and ten years older, and* MR. DANIEL TATTON, *a well-living, middle-aged country gentleman, arrive together.* TATTON *carries a double candlestick . . . the lights out.*

MR. TATTON. Three steps?

SARAH. No . . . four.

LORD JOHN. Miss Leete.

    TATTON, *in the darkness, finds himself close to* GEORGE.

MR. TATTON. I am in a rage with you, my lord.

GEORGE. He lives next door.

MR. TATTON. My mistake. [*He passes on.*] Confess that she did it to please you.

LORD JOHN. Screamed!

MR. TATTON. Lost my bet. We'll say . . . won your bet . . . to please you. Was skeered at the dark . . . oh, fie!

LORD JOHN. Miss Leete trod on a toad.

MR. TATTON. I barred toads . . . here.

LORD JOHN. I don't think it.

MR. TATTON. I barred toads. Did I forget to? Well . . . it's better to be a sportsman.

SARAH. And whereabouts is she?

ANN. [*From the corner she has slunk to.*] Here I am, Sally.

MR. TATTON. Miss Ann, I forgive you. I'm smiling, I assure you, I'm smiling.

SARAH. We all laughed when we heard you.

MR. TATTON. Which reminds me, young George Leete, had you the ace?

GEORGE. King . . . knave . . . here are the cards, but I can't see.

MR. TATTON. I had the king.

ANN. [*Quietly to her sister.*] He kissed me.

SARAH. A man would.

GEORGE. What were trumps?

MR. TATTON. What were we playing . . . cricket?

ANN. [*As quietly again.*] D'you think I'm blushing?

SARAH. It's probable.

ANN. I am by the feel of me.

SARAH. George, we left Papa sitting quite still.

LORD JOHN. Didn't he approve of the bet?

MR. TATTON. He said nothing.

SARAH. Why, who doesn't love sport!

MR. TATTON. I'm the man to grumble. Back a woman's

pluck again . . . never. My lord . . . you weren't the one to go with her as umpire.

GEORGE. No . . . to be sure.

MR. TATTON. How was it I let that pass? Playing two games at once. Haven't I cause of complaint? But a man must give and take.

> *The master of the house, father of* GEORGE *and* SARAH COTTESHAM *and* ANN, MR. CARNABY LEETE, *comes slowly down the steps, unnoticed by the others. A man over fifty—à la Lord Chesterfield.*

GEORGE. [*To Lord John.*] Are you sure you're quite comfortable there?

LORD JOHN. Whatever I'm sitting on hasn't given way yet.

MR. TATTON. Don't forget that you're riding to Brighton with me.

LORD JOHN. To-morrow.

GEORGE. To-day. Well . . . the hour before sunrise is no time at all.

MR. TATTON. Sixty-five miles.

LORD JOHN. What are we all sitting here for?

MR. TATTON. I say people ought to be in bed and asleep.

CARNABY. But the morning air is delightful.

MR. TATTON. [*Jumping at the new voice.*] Leete! Now, had you the ace?

CARNABY. Of course.

MR. TATTON. We should have lost that, too, Lady Charlie.

SARAH. Bear up, Mr. Tat.

MR. TATTON. Come, a game of whist is a game of whist.

CARNABY. And so I strolled out after you all.

MR. TATTON. She trod on a toad.

CARNABY. [*Carelessly.*] Does she say so?

MR. TATTON. [*With mock roguishness.*] Ah!

> GEORGE *is on the terrace, looking to the left through*

the trees. TATTON *is sitting on the edge of the fountain.*

GEORGE.   Here's the sun . . . to show us ourselves.

MR. TATTON.   Leete, this pond is full of water!

CARNABY.   Ann, if you are there . . .

ANN.   Yes, Papa.

CARNABY.   Apologise profusely; it's your garden.

ANN.   Oh . . .

CARNABY.   Coat-tails, Tatton . . . or worse?

MR. TATTON.   [*Ruefully discovering damp spots about him.*]   Nothing vastly to matter.

LORD JOHN.   Hardy, well-preserved country gentleman.

MR. TATTON.   I bet I'm a younger man than you, my lord.

ANN.   [*Suddenly to the company generally.*]   I didn't tread upon any toad . . . I was kissed.

There is a pause of some discomfort.

SARAH.   Ann, come here to me.

LORD JOHN.   I apologised.

GEORGE.   [*From the terrace.*]   Are we to be insulted?

CARNABY.   My dear Carp, say no more.

There is another short pause. By this it is twilight, faces can be plainly seen.

SARAH.   Listen . . . the first bird.

MR. TATTON.   Oh, dear no, they begin to sing long before this.

CARNABY.   What is it now . . . a lark?

MR. TATTON.   I don't know.

ANN.   [*Quietly to* SARAH.]   That's a thrush.

SARAH.   [*Capping her.*]   A thrush.

CARNABY.   Charming.

MR. TATTON.   [*To* LORD JOHN.]   I don't see why you couldn't have told me how it was that she screamed.

CARNABY.   Our dear Tatton!   [*Sotto voce to his son.*] Hold your tongue, George.

MR. TATTON.　I did bar toads, and you said I didn't; and anyway, I had a sort of right to know.

LORD JOHN.　You know now.

SARAH.　I wonder if this seat is dry?

LORD JOHN.　There's been no rain for weeks.

SARAH.　The roads will be dusty for you, Mr. Tat.

MR. TATTON.　Just one moment. You don't mind me, Miss Ann, do you?

ANN.　I don't mind much.

MR. TATTON.　We said distinctly . . . To the orchard end of the garden and back, and if frightened—that's the word—so much as to scream . . . ! Now, what I want to know is . . .

LORD JOHN.　Consider the bet off.

MR. TATTON.　Certainly not. And we should have added . . . Alone.

CARNABY.　Tatton has persistence.

SARAH.　Mr. Tat, do you know where people go who take things seriously?

MR. TATTON.　Miss Leete, were you frightened when Lord John kissed you?

GEORGE.　Damnation!

CARNABY.　My excellent Tatton, much as I admire your searchings after truth, I must here parentally intervene, regretting, my dear Tatton, that my own carelessness of duennahood has permitted this—this . . . to occur.

　　After this, there is silence for a minute.

LORD JOHN.　Can I borrow a horse of you, Mr. Leete?

CARNABY.　My entire stable; and your Ronald shall be physicked.

SARAH.　Spartans that you are, to be riding!

LORD JOHN.　I prefer it to a jolting chaise.

MR. TATTON.　You will have my mare.

LORD JOHN.　[*Ignoring him.*] This has been a most enjoyable three weeks.

CARNABY. Four.

LORD JOHN. Is it four?

CARNABY. We bow to the compliment. Our duty to his Grace.

LORD JOHN. When I see him.

GEORGE. To our dear cousin.

MR. TATTON. [*To* LADY COTTESHAM.] Sir Charles at Brighton?

SARAH. [*Not answering.*] To be sure . . . we did discover . . . our mother was second cousin . . . once removed to you.

CARNABY. If the prince will be there . . . he is in waiting.

LORD JOHN. Any message, Lady Cottesham? . . . since we speak out of session.

SARAH. I won't trust you.

CARNABY. Or trouble you while I still may frank a letter. But my son-in-law is a wretched correspondent. Do you admire men of small vices? They make admirable husbands though their wives will be grumbling—Silence, Sarah—but that's a good sign.

SARAH. Papa is a connoisseur of humanity.

ANN. [*To the company as before.*] No, Mr. Tatton, I wasn't frightened when Lord John . . . kissed me. I screamed because I was surprised, and I'm sorry I screamed.

SARAH. [*Quietly to* ANN.] My dear Ann, you're a fool.

ANN. [*Quietly to* SARAH.] I will speak sometimes.

SARAH. Sit down again.

> *Again an uncomfortable silence, a ludicrous air about it this time.*

TATTON. Now, we'll say no more about that bet, but I was right.

LORD JOHN. Do you know, Mr. Tatton, that I have a temper to lose?

MR. TATTON.   What the devil does that matter to me, sir . . . my lord?

LORD JOHN.   I owe you a saddle and bridle.

MR. TATTON.   You'll oblige me by taking the mare.

LORD JOHN.   We'll discuss it to-morrow.

MR. TATTON.   I've said all I have to say.

GEORGE.   The whole matter's ridiculous!

MR. TATTON.   I see the joke.   Good-night, Lady Cottesham, and I kiss your hand.

SARAH.   Good morning, Mr. Tat.

MR. TATTON.   Good morning, Miss Ann, I . . .

SARAH.   [*Shielding her sister.*]   Good morrow is appropriate.

MR. TATTON.   I'll go by the fields.   [*To* CARNABY.]   Thank you for a pleasant evening.   Good morrow, George.   Do we start at mid-day, my lord?

LORD JOHN.   Any time you please.

MR. TATTON.   Not at all.   [*He hands the candlestick—of which he has never before left go—to* GEORGE.]   I brought this for a link.   Thank you.

CARNABY.   Mid-day will be midnight if you sleep at all now; make it two, or later.

MR. TATTON.   We put up at Guildford.   I've done so before.   I haven't my hat.   It's a day and a half's ride.

> TATTON *goes quickly up the other steps and away. It is now quite light.* GEORGE *stands by the steps,* LORD JOHN *is on one of the seats,* CARNABY *strolls round, now and then touching the rose trees,* SARAH *and* ANN *are on the other seat.*

GEORGE.   Morning!   These candles still smell.

SARAH.   How lively one feels and isn't!

CARNABY.   The flowers are opening.

ANN.   [*In a whisper.*]   Couldn't we go in?

SARAH.   Never run away.

ANN.   Everything looks so odd.

SARAH. What's o'clock . . . my lord?

LORD JOHN. Half after four.

ANN. [*To* SARAH.] My eyes are hot behind.

GEORGE. What ghosts we seem!

SARAH. What has made us spend such a night?

CARNABY. Ann incited me to it. [*He takes snuff.*]

SARAH. In a spirit of rebellion against good country habits . . .

ANN. [*To her sister again.*] Don't talk about me.

SARAH. They can see that you're whispering.

CARNABY. . . . Informing me now she was a woman and wanted excitement.

GEORGE. There's a curse.

CARNABY. How else d'ye conceive life for women?

SARAH. George is naturally cruel. Excitement's our education. Please vary it, though.

CARNABY. I have always held that to colour in the world-picture is the greatest privilege of the husband. Sarah.

SARAH. [*Not leaving* ANN's *side.*] Yes, Papa.

CARNABY. Sarah, when Sir Charles leaves Brighton . . .

SARAH *rises, but will not move further.*

CARNABY. [*Sweetly threatening.*] Shall I come to you? *But she goes to him now.*

CARNABY. By a gossip letter from town . . .

SARAH. [*Tensely.*] What is it?

CARNABY. You mentioned to me something of his visiting Naples.

SARAH. Very well. I detest Italy.

CARNABY. Let's have George's opinion.

He leads her towards GEORGE.

GEORGE. Yes?

CARNABY. Upon Naples.

GEORGE. I remember Naples.

CARNABY. Sarah, admire those roses.

SARAH. [*Cynically echoing her father.*] Let's have George's opinion.

> *Now* CARNABY *has drawn them both away, upon the terrace, and, the coast being clear,* LORD JOHN *walks towards* ANN, *who looks at him very scaredly.*

CARNABY. Emblem of secrecy among the ancients.

SARAH. Look at this heavy head, won't it snap off?

> *The three move out of sight.*

LORD JOHN. I'm sober now.

ANN. I'm not.

LORD JOHN. Uncompromising young lady.

ANN. And, excuse me, I don't want to . . . play.

LORD JOHN. Don't you wish me to apologise quietly, to you?

ANN. Good manners are all mockery, I'm sure.

LORD JOHN. I'm very much afraid you're a cynic.

ANN. I'm not trying to be clever.

LORD JOHN. Do I tease you?

ANN. Do I amuse you?

LORD JOHN. How dare I say so?

ANN. [*After a moment.*] I was not frightened.

LORD JOHN. You kissed me back.

ANN. Not on purpose. What do two people mean by behaving so . . . in the dark?

LORD JOHN. I am exceedingly sorry that I hurt your feelings.

ANN. Thank you, I like to feel.

LORD JOHN. And you must forgive me.

ANN. Tell me, why did you do it?

LORD JOHN. Honestly, I don't know. I should do it again.

ANN. That's not quite true, is it?

LORD JOHN. I think so.

ANN. What does it matter at all!

LORD JOHN. Nothing.

>GEORGE, SARAH *and then* CARNABY *move into sight and along the terrace.* LORD JOHN *turns to them.*

LORD JOHN. Has this place been long in your family, Mr. Leete?

CARNABY. Markswayde my wife brought us, through the Peters's . . . old Chiltern people . . . connections of yours, of course. There is no entail.

>LORD JOHN *walks back to* ANN.

SARAH. George, you assume this republicanism as you would—no, would not—a coat of latest cut.

CARNABY. Never argue with him . . . persist.

SARAH. So does he.

>*The three pass along the terrace.*

ANN. [*To* LORD JOHN.] Will you sit down?

LORD JOHN. It's not worth while. Do you know I must be quite twice your age?

ANN. A doubled responsibility, my lord.

LORD JOHN. I suppose it is.

ANN. I don't say so. That's a phrase from a book . . . sounded well.

LORD JOHN. My dear Miss Ann . . . [*He stops.*]

ANN. Go on being polite.

LORD JOHN. If you'll keep your head turned away.

ANN. Why must I?

LORD JOHN. There's lightning in the glances of your eye.

ANN. Do use vulgar words to me.

LORD JOHN. [*With a sudden fatherly kindness.*] Go to bed . . . you're dead tired. And good-bye . . . I'll be gone before you wake.

ANN. Good-bye.

>*She shakes hands with him, then walks towards her father, who is coming down the steps.*

ANN. Papa, don't my roses want looking to?

CARNABY. [*Pats her cheek.*] These?

ANN. Those.

CARNABY. Abud is under your thumb, horticulturally
speaking.

ANN. Where's Sally?

> *She goes on to* SARAH, *who is standing with* GEORGE
> *at the top of the steps.* CARNABY *looks* LORD JOHN
> *up and down.*

LORD JOHN. [*Dusting his shoulder.*] This cursed powder!

CARNABY. Do we respect innocence enough . . . any
of us?

> GEORGE *comes down the steps and joins them.*

GEORGE. Respectable politics will henceforth be useless
to me.

CARNABY. My lord, was his Grace satisfied with the
young man's work abroad, or was he not?

LORD JOHN. My father used to curse everyone.

CARNABY. That's a mere Downing Street custom.

LORD JOHN. And I seem to remember that a letter of
yours from . . . where were you in those days?

GEORGE. Paris . . . Naples . . . Vienna.

LORD JOHN. One place . . . once lightened a fit of gout.

CARNABY. George, you have in you the makings of a
minister.

GEORGE. No.

CARNABY. Remember the Age tends to the disreputable.

> GEORGE *moves away,* SARAH *moves towards them.*

CARNABY. George is something of a genius, stuffed with
theories and possessed of a curious conscience. But I am
fortunate in my children.

LORD JOHN. All the world knows it.

CARNABY. [*To* SARAH.] It's lucky that yours was a love
match, too. I admire you. Ann is 'to come,' so to speak.

SARAH. [*To* LORD JOHN.] Were you discussing affairs?

LORD JOHN. Not I.

GEORGE. Ann.

ANN. Yes, George.

*She goes to him; they stroll together up the steps
and along the terrace.*

SARAH.   I'm desperately fagged.

LORD JOHN.   [*Politely.*]   A seat.

SARAH.   Also tired of sitting.

CARNABY.   Let's have the Brighton news, Carp.

LORD JOHN.   If there's any.

CARNABY.   Probably I still command abuse.   Even my
son-in-law must, by courtesy, join in the cry . . . ah, poor
duty-torn Sarah!   You can spread abroad that I am as a
green bay tree.

CARNABY *paces slowly away from them.*

LORD JOHN.   Your father's making a mistake.

SARAH.   D'you think so?

LORD JOHN.   He's played the game once.

SARAH.   I was not then in the knowledge of things when
he left you.

LORD JOHN.   We remember it.

SARAH.   I should like to hear it.

LORD JOHN.   I have avoided this subject.

SARAH.   With him, yes.

LORD JOHN.   Oh! . . . why did I desert the army for
politics?

SARAH.   Better fighting.

LORD JOHN.   It sat so nobly upon him . . . the leaving
us for conscience sake when we were strongly in power.
Strange that six months later we should be turned out.

SARAH.   Papa was lucky.

LORD JOHN.   But this second time . . . ?

SARAH.   Listen.   This is very much a private quarrel
with Mr. Pitt, who hates Papa . . . gets rid of him.

LORD JOHN.   Shall I betray a confidence?

SARAH.   Better not.

LORD JOHN.   My father advised me to this visit.

SARAH.   Your useful visit.   More than kind of his Grace.

LORD JOHN. Yes . . . there's been a paragraph in the "Morning Chronicle," 'The Whigs woo Mr. Carnaby Leete.'

SARAH. We saw to it.

LORD JOHN. My poor father seems anxious to discover whether the Leete episode will repeat itself entirely. He is chronically unhappy in opposition. Are your husband and his colleagues trembling in their seats?

SARAH. I can't say.

LORD JOHN. Politics is a game for clever children, and women and fools. Will you take a word of warning from a soldier? Your father is past his prime.

CARNABY *paces back towards them.*

CARNABY. I'm getting to be old for these all-night sittings. I must be writing to your busy brother.

LORD JOHN. Arthur? . . . is at his home.

SARAH. Pleasantly sounding phrase.

CARNABY. His Grace deserted?

SARAH. Quite secretaryless!

LORD JOHN. Lady Arthur lately has been brought to bed. I heard yesterday.

SARAH. The seventh, is it not? Children require living up to. My congratulations.

LORD JOHN. Won't you write them?

SARAH. We are not intimate.

LORD JOHN. A good woman.

SARAH. Evidently. Where's Ann? We'll go in.

LORD JOHN. You're a mother to your sister.

SARAH. Not I.

CARNABY. My wife went her ways into the next world; Sarah hers into this; and our little Ann was left with a most admirable governess. One must never reproach circumstances. Man educates woman in his own good time.

LORD JOHN. I suppose she, or any young girl, is all heart.

CARNABY. What is it that you call heart . . . senti-
mentally speaking?

SARAH. Any bud in the morning.

LORD JOHN. That man Tatton's jokes are in shocking
taste.

CARNABY. Tatton is honest.

LORD JOHN. I'm much to blame for having won that bet.

CARNABY. Say no more.

LORD JOHN. What can Miss Ann think of me?

SARAH. Don't ask her.

CARNABY. Innocency's opinions are invariably enter-
taining.

LORD JOHN. Am I the first . . . ? I really beg your
pardon.

> GEORGE *and* ANN *come down the steps together.*

CARNABY. Ann, what do you think . . . that is to say—
and answer me truthfully . . . what at this moment is
your inclination of mind towards my lord here?

ANN. I suppose I love him.

LORD JOHN. I hope not.

ANN. I suppose I love you.

CARNABY. No . . no . . no . . no . . no . . no . . no.

SARAH. Hush, dear.

ANN. I'm afraid, Papa, there's something very ill-bred
in me.

> *Down the steps, and into the midst of them, comes*
> JOHN ABUD, *carrying his tools, among other things*
> *a twist of bass. A young gardener, honest, clean*
> *and common.*

ABUD. [*To* CARNABY.] I ask pardon, sir.

CARNABY. So early, Abud! . . . this is your territory.
So late . . . Bed.

> ANN *starts away up the steps;* SARAH *is following her.*

LORD JOHN. Good-bye, Lady Cottesham.

At this ANN *stops for a moment, but then goes straight on.*

SARAH.   A pleasant journey.

SARAH *departs, too.*

GEORGE.   [*Stretching himself.*]   I'm roused.

CARNABY.   [*To* ABUD.]   Leave your tools here for a few moments.

ABUD.   I will, sir.

ABUD *leaves them, going along the terrace and out of sight.*

CARNABY.   My head is hot.   Pardon me.

CARNABY *is sitting on the fountain rim; he dips his handkerchief in the water, and wrings it; then takes off his wig and binds the damp handkerchief round his head.*

CARNABY.   Wigs are most comfortable and old fashioned . . . unless you choose to be a cropped republican like my son.

GEORGE.   Nature!

CARNABY.   Nature grows a beard, sir.

LORD JOHN.   I've seen Turks.

CARNABY.   Horrible . . . horrible!   Sit down, Carp.

LORD JOHN *sits on the fountain rim,* GEORGE *begins to pace restlessly; he has been nursing the candlestick ever since* TATTON *handed it to him.*

CARNABY.   George, you look damned ridiculous strutting arm-in-arm with that candlestick.

GEORGE.   I am ridiculous.

CARNABY.   If you're cogitating over your wife and her expectations . . .

GEORGE *paces up the steps and away.   There is a pause.*

CARNABY.   D'ye tell stories . . . good ones?

LORD JOHN.   Sometimes.

CARNABY.   There'll be this.

LORD JOHN. I shan't.

CARNABY. Say no more. If I may so express myself, Carp, you have been taking us for granted.

LORD JOHN. How wide awake you are! I'm not.

CARNABY. My head's cool. Shall I describe your conduct as an unpremeditated insult?

LORD JOHN. Don't think anything of the sort.

CARNABY. There speaks your kind heart.

LORD JOHN. Are you trying to pick a quarrel with me?

CARNABY. As may be.

LORD JOHN. Why?

CARNABY. For the sake of appearances.

LORD JOHN. Damn all appearances.

CARNABY. Now I'll lose my temper. Sir, you have compromised my daughter.

LORD JOHN. Nonsense!

CARNABY. Villain! What's your next move?

For a moment LORD JOHN *sits with knit brows.*

LORD JOHN. [*Brutally.*] Mr. Leete, your name stinks.

CARNABY. My point of dis-ad-vantage!

LORD JOHN. [*Apologising.*] Please say what you like. I might have put my remark better.

CARNABY. I think not; the homely Saxon phrase is our literary dagger. Princelike, you ride away from Markswayde. Can I trust you not to stab a socially sick man? Why, it's a duty you owe to society . . . to weed out . . . us.

LORD JOHN. I'm not a coward. How?

CARNABY. A little laughter . . . in your exuberance of health.

LORD JOHN. You may trust me not to tell tales.

CARNABY. Of what . . . of whom?

LORD JOHN. Of here.

CARNABY. And what is there to tell of here?

LORD JOHN. Nothing.

CARNABY. But how your promise betrays a capacity for good-natured invention !

LORD JOHN. If I lie, call me out.

CARNABY. I don't deal in sentiment. I can't afford to be talked about otherwise than as I choose to be. Already the Aunt Sally of the hour; having under pressure of circumstances resigned my office; dating my letters from the borders of the Chiltern Hundreds . . . I am a poor politician, sir, and I must live.

LORD JOHN. I can't see that your family's infected . . . affected.

CARNABY. With a penniless girl you really should have been more circumspect.

LORD JOHN. I might ask to marry her.

CARNABY. My lord !

> *In the pause that ensues he takes up the twist of bass to play with.*

LORD JOHN. What should you say to that?

CARNABY. The silly child supposed she loved you.

LORD JOHN. Yes.

CARNABY. Is it a match?

LORD JOHN. [*Full in the other's face.*] What about the appearances of black-mail?

CARNABY. [*Compressing his thin lips.*] Do you care for my daughter?

LORD JOHN. I could . . . at a pinch.

CARNABY. Now, my lord, you are insolent.

LORD JOHN. Is this when we quarrel?

CARNABY. I think I'll challenge you.

LORD JOHN. That will look well.

CARNABY. You'll value that kiss when you've paid for it. Kindly choose Tatton as your second. I want his tongue to wag both ways.

LORD JOHN. I was forgetting how it all began.

CARNABY. George will serve me . . . protesting. His

principles are vile, but he has the education of a gentleman. Swords or . . . ? Swords. And at noon shall we
say? There's shade behind a certain barn, midway between this and Tatton's.

LORD JOHN. [*Not taking him seriously yet.*] What if
we both die horridly?

CARNABY. You are at liberty to make me a written
apology.

LORD JOHN. A joke's a joke.

> CARNABY *deliberately strikes him in the face with
> the twist of bass.*

LORD JOHN. That's enough.

CARNABY. [*In explanatory apology.*] My friend, you
are so obtuse. Abud!

LORD JOHN. Mr. Leete, are you serious?

CARNABY. Perfectly serious. Let's go to bed. Abud,
you can get to your work.

> *Wig in hand,* MR. LEETE *courteously conducts his
> guest towards the house.* ABUD *returns to his tools
> and his morning's work.*

THE SECOND ACT

*Shortly after mid-day, while the sun beats strongly
upon the terrace,* ABUD *is working dexterously at
the rose trees.* DR. REMNANT *comes down the steps,
hatted, and carrying a stick and a book. He is an
elderly man, with a kind manner; type of the eighteenth century casuistical parson. On his way he
stops to say a word to the gardener.*

DR. REMNANT.   Will it rain before nightfall?

ABUD.   About then, sir, I should say.

Down the other steps comes MRS. OPIE, *a prim, de-
corous, but well bred and unobjectionable woman.
She is followed by* ANN.

MRS. OPIE.   A good morning to you, Parson.

DR. REMNANT.   And to you, Mrs. Opie, and to Miss Ann.

ANN.   Good morning, Dr. Remnant. [*To* ABUD.] Have
you been here ever since . . . ?

ABUD.   I've had dinner, Miss.

ABUD'S *work takes him gradually out of sight.*

MRS. OPIE.   We are but just breakfasted.

DR. REMNANT.   I surmise dissipation.

ANN.   [*To* MRS. OPIE.] Thank you for waiting five
hours.

MRS. OPIE.   It is my rule to breakfast with you.

DR. REMNANT.   [*Exhibiting the book.*] I am come to
return, and to borrow.

ANN.   Show me.

DR. REMNANT.   Ballads by Robert Burns.

ANN.   [*Taking it.*] I'll put it back.

MRS. OPIE. [*Taking it from her.*] I've never heard of him.

DR. REMNANT. Oh, ma'am, a very vulgar poet!

GEORGE LEETE *comes quickly down the steps.*

GEORGE. [*To* REMNANT.] How are you?

DR. REMNANT. Yours, sir.

GEORGE. Ann.

ANN. Good morning, George.

GEORGE. Did you sleep well?

ANN. I always do . . . but I dreamt.

GEORGE. I must sit down for a minute. [*Nodding.*] Mrs. Opie.

MRS. OPIE. I wish you a good morning, sir.

GEORGE. [*To* ANN.] Don't look so solemn.

LADY COTTESHAM *comes quickly to the top of the steps.*

SARAH. Is Papa badly hurt?

ANN. [*Jumping up.*] Oh, what has happened?

GEORGE. Not badly.

SARAH. He won't see me.

His three children look at each other.

DR. REMNANT. [*Tacifully.*] May I go my ways to the library?

SARAH. Please do, Doctor Remnant.

DR. REMNANT. I flatly contradicted all that was being said in the village.

SARAH. Thoughtful of you.

DR. REMNANT. But tell me nothing.

DR. REMNANT *bows formally and goes.* GEORGE *is about to speak when* SARAH, *with a look at* MRS. OPIE, *says* . . .

SARAH. George, hold your tongue.

MRS. OPIE. [*With much hauteur.*] I am in the way.

At this moment DIMMUCK, *an old but unbenevolent-looking butler, comes to the top of the steps.*

DIMMUCK. The master wants Mrs. Opie.

MRS. OPIE. Thank you.

GEORGE. Your triumph!

MRS. OPIE is departing, radiant.

DIMMUCK. How was I to know you was in the garden?

MRS. OPIE. I am sorry to have put you to the trouble of a search, Mr. Dimmuck.

DIMMUCK. He's in his room.

And he follows her towards the house.

GEORGE. Carp fought with him at twelve o'clock.

The other two cannot speak from amazement.

SARAH. No!

GEORGE. Why, they didn't tell me, and I didn't ask. Carp was laughing. Tatton chuckled . . . afterwards.

SARAH. What had he to do?

GEORGE. Carp's second.

SARAH. Unaccountable children!

GEORGE. Feather parade . . . throw in . . . parry quarte: over the arm . . . put by: feint . . . flanconade and through his arm . . . damned easy. The father didn't wince or say a word. I bound it up . . . the sight of blood makes me sick.

After a moment SARAH turns to ANN.

SARAH. Yes, and you've been a silly child.

GEORGE. Ah, give me a woman's guess and the most unlikely reason to account for anything!

ANN. I hate that man. I'm glad Papa's not hurt. What about a surgeon?

GEORGE. No, you shall kiss the place well, and there'll be poetic justice done.

SARAH. How did you all part?

GEORGE. With bows and without a word.

SARAH. Coming home with him?

GEORGE. Not a word.

SARAH. Papa's very clever; but I'm puzzled.

GEORGE. Something will happen next, no doubt.

ANN. Isn't this done with?

SARAH. So it seems.

ANN. I should like to be told just what the game has been.

GEORGE. Bravo, Ann.

ANN. Tell me the rules . . . for next time.

SARAH. It would have been most advantageous for us to have formed an alliance with Lord John Carp, who stood here for his father and his father's party . . . now in opposition.

GEORGE. Look upon yourself—not too seriously—Ann, as the instrument of political destiny.

ANN. I'm afraid I take in fresh ideas very slowly. Why has Papa given up the Stamp Office?

SARAH. His colleagues wouldn't support him.

ANN. Why was that?

SARAH. They disapproved of what he did.

ANN. Did he do right . . . giving it up?

SARAH. Yes.

GEORGE. We hope so. Time will tell. An irreverent quipster once named him Carnaby Leech.

SARAH. I know.

GEORGE. I wonder if his true enemies think him wise to have dropped off the Stamp Office?

ANN. Has he quarrelled with Sir Charles?

SARAH. Politically.

ANN. Isn't that awkward for you?

SARAH. Not a bit.

GEORGE. Hear a statement that includes our lives. Markswayde goes at his death . . . see reversionary mortgage. The income's an annuity now. The cash in the house will be ours. The debts are paid . . . at last.

ANN. And there remains me.

GEORGE. Bad grammar. Meanwhile our father is a

tongue, which is worth buying, but I don't think he ought
to go over to the enemy . . . for the second time.

SARAH.   One party is as good as another; each works
for the same end, I should hope.

GEORGE.   I won't argue about it.

ANN.   I suppose that a woman's profession is marriage.

GEORGE.   My lord has departed.

ANN.   There'll be others to come.   I'm not afraid of
being married.

SARAH.   What did Papa want Mrs. Opie for?

ANN.   There'll be a great many things I shall want to
know about men now.

GEORGE.   Wisdom cometh with sorrow . . . oh, my sister.

SARAH.   I believe you two are both about as selfish as
you can be.

GEORGE.   I am an egotist . . . with attachments.

ANN.   Make use of me.

GEORGE.   Ann, you marry—when you marry—to please
yourself.

ANN.   There's much in life that I don't like, Sally.

SARAH.   There's much more that you will.

GEORGE.   I think we three have never talked together
before.

> ABUD, *who has been in sight on the terrace for a*
> *few moments, now comes down the steps.*

ABUD.   May I make so bold, sir, as to ask how is Mrs.
George Leete?

GEORGE.   She was well when I last heard.

ABUD.   Thank you, sir.

> *And he returns to his work.*

ANN.   I wonder will it be a boy or a girl?

GEORGE.   Poor weak woman.

SARAH.   Be grateful to her.

ANN.   A baby is a wonderful thing.

SARAH.   Babyhood in the abstract . . . beautiful.

ANN.   Even kittens . . .

> *She stops, and then in rather childish embarrass-*
> *ment, moves away from them.*

SARAH.   Don't shudder, George.

GEORGE.   I have no wish to be a father. Why?

SARAH.   It's a vulgar responsibility.

GEORGE.   My wayside flower!

SARAH.   Why pick it?

GEORGE.   Sarah, I love my wife.

SARAH.   That's easily said.

GEORGE.   She should be here.

SARAH.   George, you married to please yourself.

GEORGE.   By custom her rank is my own.

SARAH.   Does she still drop her aitches?

GEORGE.   Dolly . . .

SARAH.   Pretty name.

GEORGE.   Dolly aspires to be one of us.

SARAH.   Child-bearing makes these women blowzy.

GEORGE.   Oh heaven!

ANN.   [*Calling to* ABUD *on the terrace.*] Finish to-day,
Abud. If it rains . . .

> *She stops, seeing* MR. TETGEEN *standing at the top of*
> *the steps leading from the house. This is an in-*
> *tensely respectable, selfcontained-looking lawyer,*
> *but a man of the world, too.*

MR. TETGEEN.   Lady Cottesham.

SARAH.   Sir?

MR. TETGEEN.   My name is Tetgeen.

SARAH.   Mr. Tetgeen. How do you do?

MR. TETGEEN.   The household appeared to be in some
confusion, and I took the liberty to be my own messenger.
I am anxious to speak with you.

SARAH.   Ann, dear, ask if Papa will see you now.

> DIMMUCK *appears.*

DIMMUCK.   The master wants you, Miss Ann.

SARAH. Ask Papa if he'll see me soon.

ANN goes towards the house.

SARAH. Dimmuck, Mr. Tetgeen has been left to find his own way here.

DIMMUCK. I couldn't help it, my lady.

And he follows ANN.

SARAH. Our father is confined to his room.

GEORGE. By your leave.

Then GEORGE *takes himself off up the steps, and out of sight. The old lawyer bows to* LADY COTTESHAM, *who regards him steadily.*

MR. TETGEEN. From Sir Charles . . . a talking machine.

SARAH. Please sit.

He sits carefully upon the rim of the fountain, she upon the seat opposite.

SARAH. [*Glancing over her shoulder.*] Will you talk nonsense until the gardener is out of hearing? He is on his way away. You have had a tiring journey?

MR. TETGEEN. Thank you, no . . . by the night coach to Reading, and thence I have walked.

SARAH. The country is pretty, is it not?

MR. TETGEEN. It compares favorably with other parts.

SARAH. Do you travel much, Mr. Tetgeen? He has gone.

MR. TETGEEN. [*Deliberately, and sharpening his tone ever so little.*] Sir Charles does not wish to petition for a divorce.

SARAH. [*Controlling even her sense of humor.*] I have no desire to jump over the moon.

MR. TETGEEN. His scruples are religious. The case would be weak upon some important points, and there has been no public scandal . . . at the worst, very little.

SARAH. My good manners are, I trust, irreproachable, and you may tell Sir Charles that my conscience is my own.

MR. TETGEEN. Your husband's in the matter of . . .

SARAH.   Please say the word.

MR. TETGEEN.   Pardon me . . . not upon mere suspicion.

SARAH.   Now, is it good policy to suspect what is incapable of proof?

MR. TETGEEN.   I advise Sir Charles that, should you come to an open fight, he can afford to lose.

SARAH.   And have I no right to suspicions?

MR. TETGEEN.   Certainly.   Are they of use to you?

SARAH.   I have been a tolerant wife, expecting toleration.

MR. TETGEEN.   Sir Charles is anxious to take into consideration any complaints you may have to make against him.

SARAH.   I complain if he complains of me.

MR. TETGEEN.   For the first time, I think . . . formally.

SARAH.   Why not have come to me?

MR. TETGEEN.   Sir Charles is busy.

SARAH.   [*Disguising a little spasm of pain.*]   Shall we get to business?

MR. TETGEEN *now takes a moment to find his phrase.*

MR. TETGEEN.   I don't know the man's name.

SARAH.   This, surely, is how you might address a seduced housemaid!

MR. TETGEEN.   But Sir Charles and he, I understand, have talked the matter over.

The shock of this brings SARAH *to her feet, white with anger.*

SARAH.   Divorce me.

MR. TETGEEN.   [*Sharply.*]   Is there ground for it?

SARAH.   [*With a magnificent recovery of self control.*] I won't tell you that.

MR. TETGEEN.   I have said we have no case . . . that is to say, we don't want one; but any information is a weapon in store.

SARAH.   You did quite right to insult me.

MR. TETGEEN. As a rule, I despise such methods.

SARAH. It's a lie that they met . . . those two men?

MR. TETGEEN. It may be.

SARAH. It must be.

MR. TETGEEN. I have Sir Charles's word.

Now he takes from his pocket some notes, putting on his spectacles to read them.

SARAH. What's this . . . a written lecture?

MR. TETGEEN. We propose . . . first: that the present complete severance of conjugal relations shall continue. Secondly: that Lady Cottesham shall be at liberty to remove from South Audley Street and Ringham Castle all personal and private effects, excepting those family jewels which have merely been considered her property. Thirdly: Lady Cottesham shall undertake, formally, and in writing, not to molest—a legal term—Sir Charles Cottesham. [*Her handkerchief has dropped, here he picks it up and restores it to her.*] Allow me, my lady.

SARAH. I thank you.

MR. TETGEEN. [*Continuing.*] Fourthly: Lady Cottesham shall undertake . . . etc. . . . not to inhabit or frequent the city and towns of London, Brighthelmstone, Bath, The Tunbridge Wells, and York. Fifthly: Sir Charles Cottesham will, in acknowledgement of the maintenance of this agreement, allow Lady C. the sum of two hundred and fifty pounds per annum, which sum he considers sufficient for the upkeep of a small genteel establishment; use of the house known as Pater House, situate some seventeen miles from the Manor of Barton-le-Street, Yorkshire; coals from the mine adjoining; and from the home farm, milk, butter and eggs. [*Then he finds a further note.*] Lady Cottesham is not to play cards.

SARAH. I am a little fond of play.

MR. TETGEEN. There is no question of jointure.

SARAH. None. Mr. Tetgeen . . . I love my husband.

MR. TETGEEN.   My lady . . . I will mention it.

SARAH.   Such a humorous answer to this.   No . . . don't.   What is important?   Bread and butter . . . and eggs.   Do I take this?

MR. TETGEEN.   [*Handing her the paper.*]   Please.

SARAH.   [*With the ghost of a smile.*]   I take it badly.

MR. TETGEEN.   [*Courteously capping her jest.*]   I take my leave.

SARAH.   This doesn't call for serious notice?   I've done nothing legal by accepting it?

MR. TETGEEN.   There's no law in the matter; it's one of policy.

SARAH.   I might bargain for a bigger income.   [MR. TETGEEN *bows.*]   On the whole, I'd rather be divorced.

MR. TETGEEN.   Sir Charles detests scandal.

SARAH.   Besides, there's no case . . . is there?

MR. TETGEEN.   Sir Charles congratulates himself.

SARAH.   Sir Charles had best not bully me so politely . . . tell him.

MR. TETGEEN.   My lady!

SARAH.   I will not discuss this impertinence.   Did those two men meet and talk . . . chat together?   What d'you think of that?

MR. TETGEEN.   'Twas very practical.   I know that the woman is somehow the outcast.

SARAH.   A bad woman . . . an idle woman!   But I've tried to do so much that lay to my hands without ever questioning . . . !   Thank you, I don't want this retailed to my husband.   You'll take a glass of wine before you go?

MR. TETGEEN.   Port is grateful.

She takes from her dress two sealed letters.

SARAH.   Will you give that to Sir Charles . . . a letter he wrote me which I did not open.   This, my answer, which I did not send.

He takes the one letter courteously, the other she
puts back.

SARAH. I'm such a coward, Mr. Tetgeen.

MR. TETGEEN. May I say how sorry . . . ?

SARAH. Thank you.

MR. TETGEEN. And let me apologise for having expressed one opinion of my own.

SARAH. He wants to get rid of me. He's a bit afraid
of me, you know, because I fight . . . and my weapons
are all my own. This'll blow over.

MR. TETGEEN. [*With a shake of the head.*] You are to
take this offer as final.

SARAH. Beyond this?

MR. TETGEEN. As I hinted, I am prepared to advise
legal measures.

SARAH. I could blow it over . . . but I won't, perhaps.
I must smile at my husband's consideration in suppressing,
even to you . . . the man's name. Butter and eggs . . .
and milk. I should grow fat.

       ANN *appears suddenly.*

ANN. We go to Brighton to-morrow! [*And she comes*
excitedly to her sister.]

SARAH. Was that duel a stroke of genius?

ANN. All sorts of things are to happen.

SARAH. [*Turning from her to* MR. TETGEEN.] And
you'll walk as far as Reading?

MR. TETGEEN. Dear me, yes.

SARAH. [*To* ANN.] I'll come back.

       SARAH *takes* MR. TETGEEN *towards the house.* ANN
       seats herself. After a moment LORD JOHN CARP, *his*
       clothes dusty with some riding, appears from the oth-
       er quarter. She looks up to find him gazing at her.

LORD JOHN. Ann, I've ridden back to see you.

ANN. [*After a moment.*] We're coming to Brighton
to-morrow.

LORD JOHN. Good.

ANN. Papa's not dead.

LORD JOHN. [*With equal cheerfulness.*] That's good.

ANN. And he said we should be seeing more of you.

LORD JOHN. Here I am. I love you, Ann. [*He goes on his knees.*]

ANN. D'you want to marry me?

LORD JOHN. Yes.

ANN. Thank you very much; it'll be very convenient for us all. Won't you get up?

LORD JOHN. At your feet.

ANN. I like it.

LORD JOHN. Give me your hand.

ANN. No.

LORD JOHN. You're beautiful.

ANN. I don't think so. You don't think so.

LORD JOHN. I do think so.

ANN. I should like to say I don't love you.

LORD JOHN. Last night you kissed me.

ANN. Do get up, please.

LORD JOHN. As you wish.

> *Now he sits by her.*

ANN. Last night you were nobody in particular . . . to me.

LORD JOHN. I love you.

ANN. Please don't; I can't think clearly.

LORD JOHN. Look at me.

ANN. I'm sure I don't love you, because you're making me feel very uncomfortable, and that wouldn't be so.

LORD JOHN. Then we'll think.

ANN. Papa . . . perhaps you'd rather not talk about Papa.

LORD JOHN. Give yourself to me.

ANN. [*Drawing away from him.*] Four words! There

ought to be more in such a sentence . . . it's ridiculous.
I want a year to think about its meaning. Don't speak.

LORD JOHN. Papa joins our party.

ANN. That's what we're after . . . thank you.

LORD JOHN. I loathe politics.

ANN. Tell me something against them.

LORD JOHN. In my opinion your father's not a much
bigger blackguard—I beg your pardon—than the rest of us.

ANN. . . . Miserable sinners.

LORD JOHN. Your father turns his coat. Well . . . ?

ANN. I see nothing at all in that.

LORD JOHN. What's right and what's wrong?

ANN. Papa's right . . . for the present.

ANN. When shall we be married?

LORD JOHN. To-morrow?

ANN. [Startled.] If you knew that it isn't easy for me
to be practical you wouldn't make fun.

LORD JOHN. Why not to-morrow?

ANN. Papa——

LORD JOHN. Papa says yes . . suppose.

ANN. I'm very young . . not to speak of clothes. I
must have lots of new dresses.

LORD JOHN. Ask me for them.

ANN. Why do you want to marry me?

LORD JOHN. I love you.

ANN. It suddenly occurs to me that sounds unpleasant.

LORD JOHN. I love you.

ANN. Out of place.

LORD JOHN. I love you.

ANN. What if Papa were to die?

LORD JOHN. I want y o u.

ANN. I'm nothing . . I'm nobody . . I'm part of my
family.

LORD JOHN. I want you.

ANN. Won't you please forget last night?

LORD JOHN. I want you. Look straight at me.
   She looks, and stays fascinated.
LORD JOHN. If I say now that I love you——
ANN. I know it.
LORD JOHN. And love me?
ANN. I suppose so.
LORD JOHN. Make sure.
ANN. But I hate you, too .. I know that.
LORD JOHN. Shall I kiss you?
ANN. [*Helplessly.*] Yes.
   He kisses her full on the lips.
ANN. I can't hate you enough.
LORD JOHN. [*Triumphantly.*] Speak the truth now.
ANN. I feel very degraded.
LORD JOHN. Nonsense.
ANN. [*Wretchedly.*] This is one of the things which
don't matter.
LORD JOHN. Ain't you to be mine?
ANN. You want the right to behave like that as well
as the power.
LORD JOHN. You shall command me.
ANN. [*With a poor laugh.*] I rather like this, in a way.
LORD JOHN. Little coquette!
ANN. It does tickle my vanity.
   *For a moment he sits looking at her, then shakes
   himself to his feet.*
LORD JOHN. Now I must go.
ANN. Yes .. I want to think.
LORD JOHN. For Heaven's sake .. no!
ANN. I came this morning straight to where we were
last night.
LORD JOHN. As I hung about the garden my heart was
beating.
ANN. I shall like you better when you're not here.
LORD JOHN. We're to meet in Brighton?

ANN. I'm afraid so.

LORD JOHN. Good-bye.

ANN. There's just a silly sort of attraction between certain people, I believe.

LORD JOHN. Can you look me in the eyes and say you don't love me?

ANN. If I looked you in the eyes you'd frighten me again. I can say anything.

LORD JOHN. You're a deep child.

GEORGE LEETE *appears on the terrace.*

GEORGE. My lord!

LORD JOHN. [*Cordially.*] My dear Leete.

GEORGE. No . . I am not surprised to see you.

ANN. George, things are happening.

LORD JOHN. Shake hands.

GEORGE. I will not.

ANN. Lord John asks me to be married to him. Shake hands.

GEORGE. Why did you fight?

ANN. Why d i d you fight?

LORD JOHN. [*Shrugging.*] Your father struck me.

ANN. Now you've hurt him . . that's fair.

Then the two men do shake hands, not heartily.

GEORGE. We've trapped you, my lord.

LORD JOHN. I know what I want. I love your sister.

ANN. I don't like you . . but if you're good and I'm good we shall get on.

GEORGE. Why shouldn't one marry politically?

LORD JOHN. [*In* ANN's *ear.*] I love you.

ANN. No .. no .. no .. no .. no .. [*Discovering in this an echo of her father, she stops short.*]

GEORGE. We're a cold-blooded family.

LORD JOHN. I don't think so.

GEORGE. I married for love.

LORD JOHN. Who doesn't? But, of course, there should
be other reasons.

GEORGE. You won't receive my wife.

LORD JOHN. Here's your sister.

> LADY COTTESHAM *comes from the direction of the
> house.*

SARAH. Back again?

LORD JOHN. You see.

> *From the other side appears* MR. TATTON.

MR. TATTON. As you all seem to be here I don't mind
interrupting.

GEORGE. [*Hailing him.*] Well . . neighbour?

MR. TATTON. Come . . come . . what's a little fighting
more or less!

GEORGE. Bravo, English sentiment . . relieves a deal of
awkwardness.

> *The two shake hands.*

SARAH. [*Who by this has reached* LORD JOHN.] . .
And back so soon?

ANN. Lord John asks to marry me.

LORD JOHN. Yes.

MR. TATTON. I guessed so . . give me a bit of romance!

SARAH. [*Suavely.*] This is perhaps a little sudden, my
dear Lord John. Papa may naturally be a little shocked.

GEORGE. Not at all, Sarah.

MR. TATTON. How's the wound?

GEORGE. Not serious . . nothing's serious.

SARAH. You are very masterful, wooing sword in hand.

ANN. George and I have explained to Lord John that
we are all most anxious to marry me to him, and he
doesn't mind——

LORD JOHN. Being made a fool of. I love——

ANN. I will like you.

GEORGE. Charming cynicism, my dear Sarah.

MR. TATTON. Oh, Lord!

ANN. [*To her affianced.*] Good-bye now.

LORD JOHN. When do I see you?

ANN. Papa says soon.

LORD JOHN. Very soon, please. Tatton, my friend, Brighton's no nearer.

MR. TATTON. Lady Cottesham . . Miss Leete . . I kiss your hands.

LORD JOHN. [*Ebulliently clapping* GEORGE *on the back.*] Look more pleased. [*Then he bends over* LADY COTTESHAM'S *hand.*] Lady Charlie . . my service to you . . all. Ann. [*And he takes* ANN'S *hand to kiss.*]

ANN. If I can think better of all this, I shall. Good-bye. *She turns away from him. He stands for a moment considering her, but follows* TATTON *away through the orchard.* GEORGE *and* SARAH *are watching their sister, who then comments on her little affair with life.*

ANN. I'm growing up. [*Then with a sudden tremor.*] Sally, don't let me be forced to marry.

GEORGE. Force of circumstances, my dear Ann.

ANN. Outside things. Why couldn't I run away from this garden and over the hills . . ? I suppose there's something on the other side of the hills.

SARAH. You'd find yourself there . . and circumstances.

ANN. So I'm trapped as well as that Lord John.

SARAH. What's the injury?

ANN. I'm taken by surprise, and I know I'm ignorant, and I think I'm learning things backwards.

GEORGE. You must cheer up and say: John's not a bad sort.

SARAH. A man of his age is a young man.

ANN. I wish you wouldn't recommend him to me.

SARAH. Let's think of Brighton. What about your gowns?

ANN. I've nothing to wear.

SARAH. We'll talk to Papa.

GEORGE. The war-purse is always a long one.

SARAH. George . . be one of us for a minute.

GEORGE. But I want to look on, too, and laugh.

SARAH. [*Caustically.*] Yes . . that's your privilege . . except occasionally. [*Then to her sister.*] I wish you all the happiness of courtship days.

GEORGE. Arcadian expression!

ANN. I believe it means being kissed . . often.

SARAH. Have you not a touch of romance in you, little girl?

ANN. Am I not like Mr. Dan Tatton? He kisses dairy-maids and servants and all the farmers' daughters . . I beg your pardon, George.

GEORGE. [*Nettled.*] I'll say to you, Ann, that—in all essentials—one woman is as good as another.

SARAH. That is not so in the polite world.

GEORGE. When you consider it, no one l i v e s in the polite world.

ANN. Do they come outside for air, sooner or later?

SARAH. [*Briskly.*] Three best dresses you must have, and something very gay if you're to go near the Pavilion.

ANN. You're coming to Brighton, Sally?

SARAH. No.

ANN. Why not?

SARAH. I don't wish to meet my husband.

GEORGE. That man was his lawyer.

ANN. The political difference, Sally?

SARAH. Just that. [*Then with a deft turn of the subject.*] I don't say that yours is a pretty face, but I should think you would have charm.

GEORGE. For fashion's sake cultivate sweetness.

SARAH. You dance as well as they know how in Reading.

ANN. Yes . . I can twiddle my feet.

SARAH. Do you like dancing?

ANN.   I'd sooner walk.

GEORGE.   What . . and get somewhere!

ANN.   Here's George laughing.

SARAH.   He's out of it.

ANN.   Are you happy, George?

GEORGE.   Alas . . Dolly's disgraceful ignorance of etiquette damns us both from the beautiful drawing-room.

SARAH.   That laugh is forced.   But how can you . . .
look on?

There is a slight pause in their talk.   Then . . .

ANN.   He'll bully me with love.

SARAH.   Your husband will give you just what you ask
for.

ANN.   I hate myself, too.   I want to take people mentally.

GEORGE.   You want a new world . . you new woman.

ANN.   And I'm a good bit frightened of myself.

SARAH.   We have our places to fill in this.   My dear
child, leave futile questions alone.

GEORGE.   Neither have I any good advice to give you.

ANN.   I think happiness is a thing one talks too much
about.

*DIMMUCK appears.   And by now ABUD's work has
brought him back to the terrace.*

DIMMUCK.   The master would like to see your Ladyship
now.

SARAH.   I'll say we've had a visitor . . Guess.

GEORGE.   And you've had a visitor, Sarah.

ANN.   Papa will know.

SARAH.   Is he in a questioning mood?

ANN.   I always tell everything.

SARAH.   It saves time.

She departs towards the house.

DIMMUCK.   Mr. George.

GEORGE.   What is it?

DIMMUCK. He said No to a doctor when I haven't even mentioned the matter. Had I better send . . ?

GEORGE. Do . . if you care to waste the doctor's time.

DIMMUCK *gives an offended sniff and follows* LADY COTTESHAM.

ANN. I could sit here for days. George, I don't think I quite believe in anything I've been told yet.

GEORGE. What's that man's name?

ANN. John—John is a common name—John Abud.

GEORGE. Abud!

ABUD. Sir?

GEORGE. Come here.

ABUD *obediently walks towards his young master and stands before him.*

GEORGE. Why did you ask after the health of Mrs. George Leete?

ABUD. We courted once.

GEORGE. [*After a moment.*] Listen, Ann. Do you hate me, John Abud?

ABUD. No, sir.

GEORGE. You're a fine-looking fellow. How old are you?

ABUD. Twenty-seven, sir.

GEORGE. Is Once long ago?

ABUD. Two years gone.

GEORGE. Did Mrs. Leete quarrel with you?

ABUD. No, sir.

GEORGE. Pray tell me more.

ABUD. I was beneath her.

GEORGE. But you're a fine-looking fellow.

ABUD. Farmer Crowe wouldn't risk his daughter being unhappy.

GEORGE. But she was beneath me.

ABUD. That was another matter, sir.

GEORGE. I don't think you intend to be sarcastic.

ABUD. And . . being near her time for the first time, sir . . I wanted to know if she is in danger of dying yet.

GEORGE. Every precaution has been taken . . a nurse . . there is a physician near. I need not tell you . . but I do tell you.

ABUD. Thank you, sir.

GEORGE. I take great interest in my wife.

ABUD. We all do, sir.

GEORGE. Was it ambition that you courted her?

ABUD. I thought to start housekeeping.

GEORGE. Did you aspire to rise socially?

ABUD. I wanted a wife to keep house, sir.

GEORGE. Are you content?

ABUD. I think so, sir.

GEORGE. With your humble position?

ABUD. I'm a gardener, and there'll always be gardens.

GEORGE. Frustrated affections . . I beg your pardon. . . To have been crossed in love should make you bitter and ambitious.

ABUD. My father was a gardener and my son will be a gardener if he's no worse a man than I and no better.

GEORGE. Are you married?

ABUD. No, sir.

GEORGE. Are you going to be married?

ABUD. Not especially, sir.

GEORGE. Yes . . you must marry . . some decent woman; we want gardeners.

ABUD. Do you want me any more now, sir?

GEORGE. You have interested me. You can go back to your work.

ABUD *obeys.*

GEORGE. [*Almost to himself.*] I am hardly human.
He slowly moves away and out of sight.

ANN. John Abud.
He comes back and stands before her too.

ANN. I am very sorry for you.

ABUD. I am very much obligated to you, Miss.

ANN. Both those sayings are quite meaningless. Say something true about yourself.

ABUD. I'm not sorry for myself.

ANN. I won't tell. It's very clear you ought to be in a despairing state. Don't stand in the sun with your hat off.

ABUD. [*Putting on his hat.*] Thank you, Miss.

ANN. Have you nearly finished the rose-trees?

ABUD. I must work till late this evening.

ANN. Weren't you ambitious for Dolly's sake?

ABUD. She thought me good enough.

ANN. I'd have married her.

ABUD. She was ambitious for me.

ANN. And are you frightened of the big world?

ABUD. Fine things dazzle me sometimes.

ANN. But gardening is all that you're fit for?

ABUD. I'm afraid so, Miss.

ANN. But it's great to be a gardener . . to sow seeds and to watch flowers grow and to cut away dead things.

ABUD. Yes, Miss.

ANN. And you're in the fresh air all day.

ABUD. That's very healthy.

ANN. Are you very poor?

ABUD. I get my meals in the house.

ANN. Rough clothes last a long time.

ABUD. I've saved money.

ANN. Where do you sleep?

ABUD. At Mrs. Hart's . . at a cottage . . it's a mile off.

ANN. And you want no more than food and clothes and a bed and you earn all that with your hands.

ABUD. The less a man wants, Miss, the better.

ANN. But you mean to marry?

ABUD. Yes . . I've saved money.

ANN.　Whom will you marry? Would you rather not say? Perhaps you don't know yet?

ABUD.　It's all luck what sort of a maid a man gets fond of. It won't be a widow.

ANN.　Be careful, John Abud.

ABUD.　No . . I shan't be careful.

ANN.　You'll do very wrong to be made a fool of.

ABUD.　I'm safe, Miss; I've no eye for a pretty face.

　　DIMMUCK *arrives asthmatically at the top of the steps.*

DIMMUCK.　Where's Mr. George? Here's a messenger come post.

ANN.　Find him, Abud.

ABUD.　[*To* DIMMUCK.] From Dolly?

DIMMUCK.　Speak respectful.

ABUD.　It is from his wife?

DIMMUCK.　Go find him.

ANN.　[*As* ABUD *is immovable.*] Dimmuck . . . tell me about Mrs. George.

DIMMUCK.　She's doing well, Miss.

ABUD.　[*Shouting joyfully now.*] Mr. George! Mr. George!

ANN.　A boy or a girl, Dimmuck?

DIMMUCK.　Yes, Miss.

ABUD.　Mr. George! Mr. George!

DIMMUCK.　Ecod . . is he somewhere else?

　　DIMMUCK, *somewhat excited himself, returns to the house.*

ANN.　George!

ABUD.　Mr. George! Mr. George!

　　GEORGE *comes slowly along the terrace, in his hand an open book, which some people might suppose he was reading. He speaks with studied calm.*

GEORGE.　You are very excited, my good man.

ABUD.　She's brought you a child, sir,

ANN. Your child!

GEORGE. Certainly.

ABUD. Thank God, sir!

GEORGE. I will if I please.

ANN. And she's doing well.

ABUD. There's a messenger come post.

GEORGE. To be sure . . it might have been bad news.

And slowly he crosses the garden towards the house.

ABUD. [*Suddenly, beyond all patience.*] Run . . damn you!

*George makes one supreme effort to maintain his
dignity, but fails utterly. He gasps out . . .*

GEORGE. Yes, I will. [*And runs off as hard as he can.*]

ABUD. [*In an ecstasy.*] This is good. Oh, Dolly and God . . this is good!

ANN. [*Round eyed.*] I wonder that you can be pleased.

ABUD. [*Apologising . . without apology.*] It's life.

ANN. [*Struck.*] Yes, it is.

And she goes towards the house, thinking this over.

THE THIRD ACT

It is near to sunset. The garden is shadier than before.

> ABUD *is still working.* CARNABY LEETE *comes from the house, followed by* DR. REMNANT. *He wears his right arm in a sling. His face is flushed, his speech rapid.*

CARNABY. Parson, you didn't drink enough wine . . . damme, the wine was good.

DR. REMNANT. I am very grateful for an excellent dinner.

CARNABY. A good dinner, sir, is the crown to a good day's work.

DR. REMNANT. It may also be a comfort in affliction. Our philosophy does ill, Mr. Leete, when it despises the more simple means of contentment.

CARNABY. And which will be the better lover of a woman, a hungry or a well-fed man?

DR. REMNANT. A good meal digests love with it; for what is love but a food to live by . . but a hungry love will ofttimes devour its owner.

CARNABY. Admirable! Give me a man in love to deal with. Vous l'avez vu?

DR. REMNANT. Speak Latin, Greek or Hebrew to me, Mr. Leete.

CARNABY. French is the language of little things. My poor France! Ours is a little world, Parson . . . a man may hold it here. [*His open hand.*] Lord John Carp's a fine fellow.

DR. REMNANT.   Son of a Duke.

CARNABY.   And I commend to you the originality of his return.   At twelve we fight . . . at one-thirty he proposes marriage to my daughter.   D'ye see him humbly on his knees?   Will there be rain, I wonder?

DR. REMNANT.   We need rain . . Abud?

ABUD.   Badly, sir.

CARNABY.   Do we want a wet journey to-morrow! Where's Sarah?

DR. REMNANT.   Lady Cottesham's taking tea.

CARNABY.   [*To* ABUD, *with a sudden start.*]   And why the devil didn't you marry my daughter-in-law . . my own gardener?

GEORGE *appears dressed for riding.*

GEORGE.   Good-bye, sir, for the present.

CARNABY.   Boots and breeches!

GEORGE.   You shouldn't be about in the evening air with a green wound in your arm.   You drank wine at dinner. Be careful, sir.

CARNABY.   Off to your wife and the expected?

GEORGE.   Yes, sir.

CARNABY.   Riding to Watford?

GEORGE.   From there alongside the North Coach, if I'm in time.

CARNABY.   Don't founder my horse.   Will ye leave the glorious news with your grandfather at Wycombe?

GEORGE.   I won't fail to.   [*Then to* ABUD.]   We've been speaking of you.

ABUD.   It was never any secret, sir.

GEORGE.   Don't apologise.

Soon after this ABUD *passes out of sight.*

CARNABY.   Nature's an encumbrance to us, Parson.

DR. REMNANT.   One disapproves of flesh uninspired.

CARNABY.   She allows you no amusing hobbies . . always takes you seriously.

GEORGE. Good-bye, Parson.

DR. REMNANT. [*As he bows.*] Your most obedient.

CARNABY. And you trifle with damnable democracy, with pretty theories of the respect due to womanhood, and now the result . . . hark to it squalling.

DR. REMNANT. Being fifty miles off might not one say: The cry of the new-born?

CARNABY. Ill-bred babies squall. There's no poetic glamour in the world will beautify an undesired infant. . . George says so.

GEORGE. I did say so.

CARNABY. I feel the whole matter deeply.

　　GEORGE *half laughs.*

CARNABY. George, after days of irritability, brought to bed of a smile. That's a home thrust of a metaphor.

　　GEORGE *laughs again.*

CARNABY. Twins!

GEORGE. Yes, a boy and a girl . . . I'm the father of a boy and a girl.

CARNABY. [*In dignified, indignant horror.*] No one of you dared tell me that much!

　　SARAH *and* ANN *come from the house.*

GEORGE. You could have asked me for news of your grandchildren.

CARNABY. Twins is an insult.

SARAH. But you look very cheerful, George.

GEORGE. I am content.

SARAH. I'm surprised.

GEORGE. I am surprised.

SARAH. Now what names for them?

CARNABY. No family names, please.

GEORGE. We'll wait for a dozen years or so, and let them choose their own.

DR. REMNANT. But, sir, christening will demand——

CARNABY. Your son should have had my name, sir.

GEORGE. I know the rule . . as I have my grandfather's, which I take no pride in.

SARAH. George!

GEORGE. Not to say that it sounds his, not mine.

CARNABY. Our hopes of you were high once.

GEORGE. Sarah, may I kiss you? [*He kisses her cheek.*] Let me hear what you decide to do.

CARNABY. The begetting of you, sir, was a waste of time.

GEORGE. [*Quite pleasantly.*] Don't say that.

At the top of the steps ANN *is waiting for him.*

GEORGE. Thank you, sister Ann.

GEORGE. Thank you, sister Ann.

ANN. Why didn't you leave us weeks ago?

GEORGE. Why?

They pace away, arm-in-arm.

CARNABY. [*Bitterly.*] Glad to go! Brighton, Sarah.

SARAH. No, I shall not come, Papa.

CARNABY. Coward. [*Then to* REMNANT.] Good-night.

DR. REMNANT. [*Covering the insolent dismissal.*] With your kind permission I will take my leave. [*Then he bows to* SARAH.] Lady Cottesham.

SARAH. [*Curtseying.*] Doctor Remnant, I am yours.

CARNABY. [*Sitting by the fountain, stamping his foot.*] Oh, this cracked earth! Will it rain . . will it rain?

DR. REMNANT. I doubt now. That cloud has passed.

CARNABY. Soft, pellucid rain! There's a good word, and I'm not at all sure what it means.

DR. REMNANT. Per . . lucere . . . letting light through.

REMNANT *leaves them.*

CARNABY. Solt, pellucid rain! . . thank you. Brighton, Sarah.

SARAH. Ann needs new clothes.

CARNABY. See to it.

SARAH. I shall not be there.

She turns from him.

CARNABY.　Pretty climax to a quarrel!

SARAH.　Not a quarrel.

CARNABY.　A political difference.

SARAH.　Don't look so ferocious.

CARNABY.　My arm is in great pain and the wine's in my head.

SARAH.　Won't you go to bed?

CARNABY.　I'm well enough . . to travel. This marriage makes us safe, Sarah . . an anchor in each camp . . There's a mixed metaphor.

SARAH.　If you'll have my advice, Papa, you'll keep those plans clear from Ann's mind.

CARNABY.　John Carp is so much clay . . a man of forty ignorant of himself.

SARAH.　But if the Duke will not . .

CARNABY.　The Duke hates a scandal.

SARAH.　Does he detest scandal?

CARNABY.　The girl is well-bred and harmless . . why publicly quarrel with John and incense her old brute of a father? There's the Duke in a score of words. He'll take a little time to think it out so.

SARAH.　And I say: Do you get on the right side of the Duke once again—that's what we've worked for—and leave these two alone.

CARNABY.　Am I to lose my daughter?

SARAH.　Papa . . your food's intrigue.

CARNABY.　Scold at Society . . and what's the use?

SARAH.　We're over-civilized.

ANN *rejoins them now. The twilight is gathering.*

CARNABY.　My mother's very old . . . your grand-father's younger and seventy-nine . . he swears I'll never come into the title. There's little else.

SARAH.　You're feverish . . why are you saying this?

CARNABY.　Ann . . George . . George via Wycombe . . Wycombe Court . . Sir George Leete baronet, Justice of

the Peace, Deputy Lieutenant . . the thought's tumbled.
Ann, I first saw your mother in this garden . . there.

ANN.   Was she like me?

SARAH.   My age when she married.

CARNABY.   She was not beautiful . . then she died.

ANN.   Mr. Tatton thinks it a romantic garden.

CARNABY.   [*Pause.*] D'ye hear the wind sighing through
that tree?

ANN.   The air's quite still.

CARNABY.   I hear myself sighing . . when I first saw
your mother in this garden . . . that's how it was done.

SARAH.   For a woman must marry.

CARNABY.   [*Rises.*] You all take to it as ducks to water
. . but apple sauce is quite correct . . I must not mix
metaphors.

MRS. OPIE *comes from the house.*

SARAH.   Your supper done, Mrs. Opie?

MRS. OPIE.   I eat little in the evening.

SARAH.   I believe that saves digestion.

MRS. OPIE.   Ann, do you need me more to-night?

ANN.   Not any more.

MRS. OPIE.   Ann, there is gossip among the servants
about a wager . . .

ANN.   Mrs. Opie, that was . . . yesterday.

MRS. OPIE.   Ann, I should be glad to be able to contradict a reported . . embrace.

ANN.   I was kissed.

MRS. OPIE.   I am shocked.

CARNABY.   Mrs. Opie, is it possible that all these years
I have been nourishing a prude in my . . back drawing-
room?

MRS. OPIE.   I presume I am discharged of Ann's education; but as the salaried mistress of your household, Mr.
Leete, I am grieved not to be able to deny such a rumour
to your servants.

She sails back, righteously indignant.

CARNABY. Call out that you're marrying the wicked man . . comfort her.

SARAH. Mrs. Opie!

CARNABY. Consider that existence. An old maid . . so far as we know. Brevet rank . . missis. Not pleasant.

ANN. She wants nothing better . . at her age.

SARAH. How forgetful!

CARNABY. [*The force of the phrase growing.*] Brighton, Sarah.

SARAH. Now you've both read the love-letter which Tetgeen brought me.

CARNABY. Come to Brighton.

ANN. Come to Brighton, Sally.

SARAH. No. I have been thinking. I think I will accept the income, the house, coals, butter and eggs.

CARNABY. I give you a fortnight to bring your husband to his knees . . to your feet.

SARAH. I'm not sure that I could. My marriage has come naturally to an end.

CARNABY. Sarah, don't annoy me.

SARAH. Papa, you joined my bridegroom's political party . . now you see fit to leave it.

She glances at ANN, *who gives no sign, however.*

CARNABY. What have you been doing in ten years?

SARAH. Waiting for this to happen . . now I come to think.

CARNABY. Have ye the impudence to tell me that ye've never cared for your husband?

SARAH. I was caught by the first few kisses; but he . . .

CARNABY. Has he ever been unkind to you?

SARAH. Never. He's a gentleman through and through . . . quite charming to live with.

CARNABY. I see what more you expect. And he neither

drinks nor . . nor . . no one even could suppose your
leaving him.

SARAH. No. I'm disgraced.

CARNABY. Fight for your honour.

SARAH. You surprise me sometimes by breaking out
into cant phrases.

CARNABY. What is more useful in the world than
honour?

SARAH. I think we never had any . . we!

CARNABY. Give me more details. Tell me, who is this
man?

SARAH. I'm innocent'. . if that were all.

ANN. Sally, what do they say you've done?

SARAH. I cry out like any poor girl.

CARNABY. There must be no doubt that you're innocent.
Why not go for to force Charles into court?

SARAH. My innocence is not of the sort which shows
up well.

CARNABY. Hold publicity in reserve. No fear of the
two men arranging to meet, is there?

SARAH. They've met . . and they chatted about me.

CARNABY. [*After a moment.*] There's sound humour
in that.

SARAH. I shall feel able to laugh at them both from
Yorkshire.

CARNABY. God forbid! Come to Brighton . . we'll
rally Charles no end.

SARAH. Papa, I know there's nothing to be done.

CARNABY. Coward!

SARAH. Besides, I don't think I want to go back to my
happiness.

They are silent for a little.

CARNABY. How still! Look . . leaves falling already.
Can that man hear what we're saying?

SARAH. [*To* ANN.] Can Abud overhear?

ANN. I've never talked secrets in the garden before to-day. [*Raising her voice but a very little.*] Can you hear me, Abud?

No reply comes.

CARNABY. Evidently not. There's brains shown in a trifle.

SARAH. Does your arm pain you so much?

ANN. Sarah, this man that you're fond of and that's not your husband is not by any chance Lord John Carp?

SARAH. No.

ANN. Nothing would surprise me.

SARAH. You are witty . . but a little young to be so hard.

CARNABY. Keep to your innocent thoughts.

ANN. I must study politics.

SARAH. We'll stop talking of this.

ANN. No . . let me listen . . quite quietly.

CARNABY. Let her listen . . she's going to be married.

SARAH. Good luck, Ann.

CARNABY. I have great hopes of Ann.

SARAH. I hope she may be heartless. To be heartless is to be quite safe.

CARNABY. Now we detect a taste of sour grapes in your mouth.

SARAH. Butter and eggs.

CARNABY. We must all start early in the morning. Sarah will take you, Ann, round the Brighton shops . . fine shops. You shall have the money . . .

SARAH. I will not come with you.

CARNABY. [*Vexedly.*] How absurd . . how ridiculous . . to persist in your silly sentiment.

SARAH. [*Her voice rising.*] I'm tired of that world . . which goes on and on, and there's no dying . . . one grows into a ghost . . visible . . then invisible. I'm glad paint has gone out of fashion . . . the painted ghosts were very ill to see.

CARNABY. D'ye scoff at civilisation?

SARAH. Look ahead for me.

CARNABY. Banished to a hole in the damned provinces! But you're young yet, you're charming . . you're the wife . . and the honest wife of one of the country's best men. My head aches. D'ye despise good fortune's gifts? Keep as straight in your place in the world as you can. A monthly packet of books to Yorkshire . . no . . you never were fond of reading. Ye'd play patience . . cultivate chess problems . . kill yourself!

SARAH. When one world fails take another.

CARNABY. You have no more right to commit suicide than to desert the society you were born into. My head aches.

SARAH. George is happy.

CARNABY. D'ye dare to think so?

SARAH. No . . it's a horrible marriage.

CARNABY. He's losing refinement . . mark me . . he no longer polishes his nails.

SARAH. But there are the children now.

CARNABY. You never have wanted children.

SARAH. I don't want a little child.

CARNABY. She to be Lady Leete . . some day . . soon! What has he done for his family?

SARAH. I'll come with you. You are clever, Papa. And I know just what to say to Charles.

CARNABY. [*With a curious change of tone.*] If you study anatomy you'll find that the brain, as it works, pressing forward the eyes . . thought is painful. Never be defeated. Chapter the latest . . the tickling of the Carp. And my throat is dry . . shall I drink that water?

SARAH. No, I wouldn't.

CARNABY. Not out of my hand?

ANN. [*Speaking in a strange, quiet voice, after her long silence.*] I will not come to Brighton with you.

CARNABY. Very dry!

ANN. You must go back, Sally.

CARNABY. [*As he looks at her, standing stiffly.*] Now what is Ann's height . . five feet . . ?

ANN. Sally must go back, for she belongs to it . . but I'll stay here where I belong.

CARNABY. You've spoken three times, and the words are jumbling in at my ears meaninglessly. I certainly took too much wine at dinner . . or else . . . Yes . . Sally goes back . . and you'll go forward. Who stays here? Don't burlesque your sister. What's in the air . . what disease is this?

ANN. I mean to disobey you . . to stay here . . never to be unhappy.

CARNABY. So pleased!

ANN. I want to be an ordinary woman . . not clever . . not fortunate.

CARNABY. I can't hear.

ANN. Not clever. I don't believe in you, Papa.

CARNABY. I exist . . I'm very sorry.

ANN. I won't be married to any man. I refuse to be tempted . . I won't see him again.

CARNABY. Yes. It's raining.

SARAH. Raining!

CARNABY. Don't you stop it raining.

ANN. [*In the same level tones, to her sister now, who otherwise would turn, alarmed, to their father.*] And I curse you . . because, we being sisters, I suppose I am much what you were, about to be married; and I think, Sally, you'd have cursed your present self. I could become all that you are and more . . but I don't choose.

SARAH.   Ann, what is to become of you?

CARNABY.   Big drops . . big drops!

> *At this moment* ABUD *is passing towards the house, his work finished.*

ANN.   John Abud . . you mean to marry.   When you marry . . will you marry me?

> *A blank silence, into which breaks* CARNABY'S *sick voice.*

CARNABY.   Take me indoors.   I heard you ask the gardener to marry you.

ANN.   I asked him.

CARNABY.   I heard you say that you asked him.   Take me in . . but not out of the rain.

ANN.   Look .. he's straight-limbed and clear-eyed .. and I'm a woman.

SARAH.   Ann, are you mad?

ANN.   If we two were alone here in this garden, and everyone else in the world were dead . . what would you answer?

ABUD.   [*Still amazed.*]   Why . . yes.

CARNABY.   Then that's settled . . pellucid.

> *He attempts to rise, but staggers backwards and forwards.* SARAH *goes to him, alarmed.*

SARAH.   Papa! . . there's no rain yet.

CARNABY.   Hush, I'm dead.

ANN.   [*Her nerves failing her.*]   Oh . . oh . . oh . . !

SARAH.   Abud, don't ever speak of this.

ABUD.   No, my lady.

ANN.   [*With a final effort.*]   I mean it all.   Wait three months.

CARNABY.   Help me up steps . . son-in-law.

> CARNABY *has started to grope his way indoors. But he reels and falls, helpless.*

ABUD.   I'll carry him.

　　　Throwing down his tools ABUD *lifts the frail sick
　　　man and carries him towards the house.* SARAH
　　　follows.

ANN. [*Sobbing a little and weary.*]　Such a long day
it has been . . now ending.

　　　She follows too.

THE FOURTH ACT

*The hall at Markswayde is square; in decoration strictly
eighteenth century. The floor polished. Then comes six
feet of soberly painted wainscot and above the greenish
blue and yellowish green wall painted into panels. At
intervals are low relief pilasters; the capitals of these are
gilded. The ceiling is white and in the centre of it there
is a frosted glass dome through which a dull light strug-
gles. Two sides only of the hall are seen.*

*In the corner is a hat stand and on it are many cloaks
and hats and beneath it several pairs of very muddy boots.*

*In the middle of the left hand wall are the double doors
of the dining-room led up to by three or four stairs with
balusters, and on either side standing against the wall
long, formal, straight backed sofas.*

*In the middle of the right hand wall is the front door;
glass double doors can be seen and there is evidently a
porch beyond. On the left of the front door a small
window. On the right a large fireplace, in which a large
fire is roaring. Over the front door, a clock (the hands
pointing to half-past one.) Over the fireplace a family
portrait (temp. Queen Anne), below this a blunderbuss
and several horse-pistols. Above the sofa full-length
family portraits (temp. George I.) Before the front door
a wooden screen, of lighter wood than the wainscot, and
in the middle of it a small glass panel. Before this a
heavy square table on which are whips and sticks, a hat
or two and brushes; by the table a wooden chair. On*

*either side of the fire stand tall closed-in armchairs, and
between the fireplace and the door a small red-baize screen.*

*When the dining-room doors are thrown open another
wooden screen is to be seen.*

There are a few rugs on the floor, formally arranged.

MRS. OPIE *stands in the middle of the hall, holding
out a woman's brown cloak: she drops one side to
fetch out her handkerchief and apply it to her eye.*
DIMMUCK *comes in by the front door, which he
carefully closes behind him. He is wrapped in a
hooded cloak and carries a pair of boots and a newspaper. The boots he arranges to warm before the
fire. Then he spreads the Chronicle newspaper
upon the arm of a chair, then takes off his cloak and
hangs it upon a peg close to the door.*

DIMMUCK. Mrs. Opie . . will you look to its not
scorching?

MRS. OPIE *still mops her eyes.* DIMMUCK *goes
towards the dining-room door, but turns.*

DIMMUCK. Will you kindly see that the *Chronicle*
newspaper does not burn?

MRS. OPIE. I was crying.

DIMMUCK. I leave this to-morrow sennight . . thankful, ma'am, to have given notice in a dignified manner.

MRS. OPIE. I understand . . Those persons at table . .

DIMMUCK. You give notice.

MRS. OPIE. Mr. Dimmuck, this is my home.

LORD ARTHUR CARP *comes out of the dining-room.
He is a thinner and more earnest-looking edition of
his brother.* MRS. OPIE *turns a chair and hangs
the cloak to warm before the fire, and then goes
into the dining-room.*

LORD ARTHUR. My chaise round?

DIMMUCK. I've but just ordered it, my lord. Your
lordship's man has give me your boots.

LORD ARTHUR. Does it snow?

DIMMUCK. Rather rain than snow.

> LORD ARTHUR *takes up the newspaper.*

DIMMUCK. Yesterday's, my lord.

LORD ARTHUR. I've seen it. The mails don't hurry hereabouts. Can I be in London by the morning?

DIMMUCK. I should say you might be, my lord.

> LORD ARTHUR *sits by the fire, while* DIMMUCK *takes off his pumps and starts to put on his boots.*

LORD ARTHUR. Is this a horse called "Ronald?"

DIMMUCK. Which horse, my lord?

LORD ARTHUR. Which I'm to take back with me . . my brother left here. I brought the mare he borrowed.

DIMMUCK. I remember, my lord. I'll enquire.

LORD ARTHUR. Tell Parker . .

DIMMUCK. Your lordship's man?

LORD ARTHUR. . . He'd better ride the beast.

> SARAH *comes out of the dining-room. He stands up; one boot, one shoe.*

SARAH. Please put on the other.

LORD ARTHUR. Thank you . . I am in haste.

SARAH. To depart before the bride's departure?

LORD ARTHUR. Does the bride go with the bridegroom?

SARAH. She goes away.

LORD ARTHUR. I shall never see such a thing again.

SARAH. I think this entertainment is unique.

LORD ARTHUR. Any commissions in town?

SARAH. Why can't you stay to travel with us to-morrow and talk business to Papa by the way?

> DIMMUCK *carrying the pumps and after putting on his cloak goes out through the front door. When it is closed, her voice changes.*

SARAH. Why . . Arthur?

> *He does not answer. Then* MRS. OPIE *comes out of the dining-room to fetch the cloak. The two,*

with an effort, reconstruct their casual disjointed conversation.

SARAH. . . Before the bride's departure?

LORD ARTHUR. Does the bride go away with the bridegroom?

SARAH. She goes.

LORD ARTHUR. I shall never see such an entertainment again.

SARAH. We are quite unique.

LORD ARTHUR. Any commissions in town?

SARAH. Is she to go soon, too, Mrs. Opie?

MRS. OPIE. It is arranged they are to walk . . in this weather . . ten miles . . to the house.

SARAH. Cottage.

MRS. OPIE. Hut.

MRS. OPIE *takes the cloak into the dining-room. Then* SARAH *comes a little towards* LORD ARTHUR, *but waits for him to speak.*

LORD ARTHUR. [*A little awkwardly.*] You are not looking well.

SARAH. To our memory . . and beyond your little chat with my husband about me . . I want to speak an epitaph.

LORD ARTHUR. Charlie Cottesham behaved most honourably.

SARAH. And I think you did. Why have you not let me tell you so in your ear till now, to-day?

LORD ARTHUR. Sarah . . we had a narrow escape from . . .

SARAH. How's your wife?

LORD ARTHUR. Well . . thank you.

SARAH. Nervous, surely, at your travelling in winter?

LORD ARTHUR. I was so glad to receive a casual invitation from you and to come . . casually.

SARAH. Fifty miles.

LORD ARTHUR. Your father has been ill?

SARAH. Very ill through the autumn.

LORD ARTHUR. Do you think he suspects us?

SARAH. I shouldn't care to peep into Papa's innermost mind. You are to be very useful to him.

LORD ARTHUR. No.

SARAH. Then he'll go back to the government.

LORD ARTHUR. If he pleases . . if they please . . if you please.

SARAH. I am not going back to my husband. Arthur . . be useful to him.

LORD ARTHUR. No . . you are not coming to me. Always your father! [*After a moment.*] It was my little home in the country somehow said aloud you didn't care for me.

SARAH. I fooled you to small purpose.

LORD ARTHUR. I wish you had once made friends with my wife.

SARAH. If we . . this house I'm speaking of . . had made friends where we've only made tools and fools we shouldn't now be cursed as we are . . all. George, who is a cork, trying to sink socially. Ann is mad . . and a runaway.

LORD ARTHUR. Sarah, I've been devilish fond of you.

SARAH. Be useful to Papa. [*He shakes his head obstinately.*] Praise me a little. Haven't I worked my best for my family?

LORD ARTHUR. Suppose I could be useful to him now, would you, in spite of all, come to me . . no half measures?

SARAH. Arthur . . [*He makes a little passionate movement towards her, but she is cold.*] It's time for me to vanish from this world, because I've nothing left to sell.

LORD ARTHUR. I can't help him. I don't want you.

He turns away.

SARAH. I feel I've done my best.

LORD ARTHUR. Keep your father quiet.

SARAH. I mean to leave him.

LORD ARTHUR. What does he say to that?

SARAH. I've not yet told him.

LORD ARTHUR. What happens?

SARAH. To sell my jewels . . spoils of a ten years' war. Three thousand pound . . how much a year?

LORD ARTHUR. I'll buy them.

SARAH. And return them? You have almost the right to make such a suggestion.

LORD ARTHUR. Stick to your father. He'll care for you?

SARAH. No . . we all pride ourselves on our lack of sentiment.

LORD ARTHUR. You must take money from your husband.

SARAH. I have earned that and spent it.

LORD ARTHUR. [*Yielding once again to temptation.*] I'm devilish fond of you . . .

> *At that moment* ABUD *comes out of the dining-room. He is dressed in his best.* SARAH *responds readily to the interruption.*

SARAH. And you must give my kindest compliments to Lady Arthur and my . . affectionately . . to the children, and I'll let Papa know that you're going.

LORD ARTHUR. Letters under cover to your father?

SARAH. Papa will stay in town through the session, of course . . but they all tell me that seventy-five pounds a year is a comfortable income in . . Timbuctoo.

> *She goes into the dining-room.* ABUD *has selected his boots from the corner, and now stands with them in his hand, looking rather helpless. After a moment—*

LORD ARTHUR. I congratulate you, Mr. Abud.

ABUD. My lord . . I can't speak of myself.

> CARNABY *comes out of the dining-room. He is evidently by no means recovered from his illness. He*

stands for a moment with an ironical eye on JOHN
ABUD.

CARNABY. Son-in-law.

ABUD. I'm told to get on my boots, sir.

CARNABY. Allow me to assist you.

ABUD. I couldn't, sir.

CARNABY. Désolé!

Then he passes on. ABUD *sits on the sofa, furtively
puts on his boots, and afterwards puts his shoes in
his pockets.*

LORD ARTHUR. You were so busy drinking health to the
two fat farmers that I wouldn't interrupt you.

CARNABY. Good-bye. Describe all this to your brother
John.

LORD ARTHUR. So confirmed a bachelor!

CARNABY. Please say that we missed him.

LORD ARTHUR *hands him the newspaper.*

LORD ARTHUR. I've out-raced your *Chronicle* from London by some hours. There's a paragraph . . second col-
umn . . near the bottom.

CARNABY. [*Looking at it blindly.*] They print villain-
ously now-a-days.

LORD ARTHUR. Inspired.

CARNABY. I trust his Grace is well?

LORD ARTHUR. Gouty.

CARNABY. Now doesn't the social aspect of this case
interest you?

LORD ARTHUR. I object to feeding with the lower classes.

CARNABY. There's pride! How useful to note their
simple manners! From the meeting of extremes new
ideas spring . . new life.

LORD ARTHUR. Take that for a new social-political
creed, Mr. Leete.

CARNABY. Do I lack one?

LORD ARTHUR. Please make my adieux to the bride.

CARNABY. Appropriate . . . 'à Dieu' . . she enters Nature's cloister. My epigram.

LORD ARTHUR. But . . good heavens . . are we to choose to be toiling animals?

CARNABY. To be such is my daughter's ambition.

LORD ARTHUR. You have not read that.

CARNABY. [*Giving back the paper, vexedly.*] I can't see.

LORD ARTHUR. "The Right Honourable Carnaby Leete is, we are glad to hear, completely recovered and will return to town for the opening of Session."

CARNABY. I mentioned it.

LORD ARTHUR. "We understand that although there has been no reconciliation with the Government it is quite untrue that this gentleman will in any way resume his connection with the Opposition."

CARNABY. Inspired?

LORD ARTHUR. I am here from my father to answer any questions.

CARNABY. [*With some dignity and the touch of a threat.*] Not now, my lord.

DIMMUCK *comes in at the front door.*

DIMMUCK. The chaise, my lord.

CARNABY. I will conduct you.

LORD ARTHUR. Please don't risk exposure.

CARNABY. Nay, I insist.

LORD ARTHUR. Health and happiness to you both, Mr. Abud.

LORD ARTHUR *goes out, followed by* CARNABY, *followed by* DIMMUCK. *At that moment* MR. SMALLPEICE *skips excitedly out of the dining-room. A ferret-like little lawyer.*

MR. SMALLPEICE. Oh . . where is Mr. Leete?

Not seeing him MR. SMALLPEICE *skips as excitedly back into the dining-room.* DIMMUCK *returns and*

hangs up his cloak then goes towards ABUD, *whom
he surveys.*

DIMMUCK. Sir!

*With which insult he starts for the dining-room
reaching the door just in time to hold it open for*
SIR GEORGE LEETE *who comes out. He surveys* ABUD
for a moment, then explodes.

SIR GEORGE LEETE. Damn you . . stand in the presence
of your grandfather-in-law.

ABUD *stands up.* CARNABY *returns coughing, and*
SIR GEORGE *looks him up and down.*

SIR GEORGE LEETE. I shall attend your funeral.

CARNABY. My daughter Sarah still needs me.

SIR GEORGE LEETE. I wonder at you, my son.

CARNABY. Have you any money to spare?

SIR GEORGE LEETE. No.

CARNABY. For Sarah, my housekeeper; I foresee a busy
session.

ABUD *is now gingerly walking up the stairs.*

SIR GEORGE LEETE. Carnaby . . look at that.

CARNABY. Sound in wind and limb. Tread boldly,
son-in-law.

ABUD *turns, stands awkwardly for a moment and
then goes into the dining-room.*

SIR GEORGE LEETE. [*Relapsing into a pinch of snuff.*]
I'm calm.

CARNABY. Regard this marriage with a wise eye . . as
an amusing little episode.

SIR GEORGE LEETE. Do you?

CARNABY. And forget its oddity. Now that the hu-
miliation is irrevocable, is it a personal grievance to you?

SIR GEORGE LEETE. Give me a dinner a day for the rest
of my life and I'll be content.

CARNABY. Lately, one by one, opinions and desires
have been failing me . . a flicker and then extinction.

I shall shortly attain to being a most able critic upon life.

SIR GEORGE LEETE. Shall I tell you again? You came into this world without a conscience. That explains you and it's all that does. That such a damnable coupling as this should be permitted by God Almighty . . or that the law shouldn't interfere! I've said my say.

    MR. SMALLPEICE *again comes out of the dining-room.*

MR. SMALLPEICE. Mr. Leete.

CARNABY. [*Ironically polite.*] Mr. Shallpeice.

MR. SMALLPEICE. Mr. Crowe is proposing your health.

    MR. CROWE *comes out. A crop-headed beefy-looking farmer of sixty.*

MR. CROWE. Was.

CARNABY. There's a good enemy!

MR. CROWE. Get out of my road . . lawyer Smallpeice.

CARNABY. Leave enough of him living to attend to my business.

MR. SMALLPEICE. [*Wriggling a bow at* CARNABY.] Oh . . dear sir!

SIR GEORGE LEETE. [*Disgustedly to* MR. SMALLPEICE.] You!

MR. SMALLPEICE. Employed in a small matter . . as yet.

CARNABY. [*To* CROWE.] I hope you spoke your mind of me.

MR. CROWE. Not behind your back, sir.

    MRS. GEORGE LEETE *leads* LADY LEETE *from the dining-room.* LADY LEETE *is a very old, blind and decrepit woman.* DOLLY *is a buxom young mother; whose attire borders on the gaudy.*

CARNABY. [*With some tenderness.*] Well . . Mother . . dear?

MR. CROWE. [*Bumptiously to* SIR GEORGE LEETE.] Did my speech offend you, my lord?

SIR GEORGE LEETE. [*Sulkily.*] I'm a baronet.

LADY LEETE. Who's this here?

CARNABY. Carnaby.

DOLLY. Step down . . grandmother.

LADY LEETE. Who did ye say you were?

DOLLY. Mrs. George Leete.

LADY LEETE. Take me to the fire-side.

So CARNABY *and* DOLLY *lead her slowly to a chair by the fire where they carefully bestow her.*

MR. SMALLPEICE. [*To* FARMER CROWE.] He's leaving Markswayde, you know . . and me agent.

LADY LEETE. [*Suddenly bethinking her.*] Grace was not said. Fetch my chaplain . . at once.

MR. SMALLPEICE. I will run.

He runs into the dining-room.

DOLLY. [*Calling after with her country accent.*] Not parson Remnant . . t'other one.

LADY LEETE. [*Demanding.*] Snuff.

CARNABY. [*To his father.*] Sir . . my hand is a little unsteady.

SIR GEORGE *and* CARNABY *between them give* LADY LEETE *her snuff.*

MR. CROWE. Dolly . . ought those children to be left so long?

DOLLY. All right, father . . I have a maid.

LADY LEETE *sneezes.*

SIR GEORGE LEETE. She'll do that once too often altogether.

LADY LEETE. I'm cold.

DOLLY. I'm cold . . I lack my shawl.

CROWE. Call out to your man for it.

DOLLY. [*Going to the dining-room door.*] Will a gentleman please ask Mr. George Leete for my Cache-y-mire shawl?

MR. CROWE. [*To* CARNABY.] And I drank to the health of our grandson.

CARNABY. Now suppose George were to assume your name, Mr. Crowe?

> MR. TOZER *comes out of the dining-room. Of the worst type of eighteenth century parson, for which one may see Hogarth's 'Harlot's Progress.' He is very drunk.*

SIR GEORGE LEETE. [*In his wife's ear.*] Tozer!

LADY LEETE. When . . why!

SIR GEORGE LEETE. To say grace.

> LADY LEETE *folds her withered hands.*

MR. TOZER. [*Through his hiccoughs.*] Damn you all.

LADY LEETE. [*Reverently, thinking it is said.*] Amen.

MR. TOZER. Only my joke.

CARNABY. [*Rising to the height of the occasion.*] Mr. Tozer, I am indeed glad to see you, upon this occasion, so delightfully drunk.

MR. TOZER. Always a gen'elman . . by nature.

SIR GEORGE LEETE. Lie down . . you dog.

> GEORGE *comes out carrying the cashmere shawl.*

GEORGE. [*To his father.*] Dolly wants her father to rent Markswayde, sir.

MR. CROWE. Not me, my son. You're to be a farmer-baronet.

SIR GEORGE. Curse your impudence!

CARNABY. My one regret in dying would be to miss seeing him so.

> GEORGE *goes back into the dining-room.*

MR. CROWE. I am tickled to think that the man marrying your daughter wasn't good enough for mine.

CARNABY. And yet at fisticuffs I'd back John Abud against our son George.

> DR. REMNANT *has come out of the dining-room.* TOZER *has stumbled towards him and is wagging an argumentative finger.*

MR. TOZER. . . Marriage means enjoyment!

DR. REMNANT. [*Controlling his indignation.*] I repeat that I have found in my own copy of the prayer book no insistence upon a romantic passion.

MR. TOZER. My 'terpretation of God's word is 'bove criticism.

> MR. TOZER *reaches the door and falls into the dining-room.*

CARNABY. [*Weakly to* DR. REMNANT.] Give me your arm for a moment.

DR. REMNANT. I think Lady Cottesham has Mrs. John Abud prepared to start, sir.

CARNABY. I trust Ann will take no chill walking through the mud.

DR. REMNANT. Won't you sit down, sir?

CARNABY. No.

> *For some moments* CROWE *has been staring indignantly at* SIR GEORGE. *Now he breaks out.*

MR. CROWE. The front door of this mansion is opened to a common gardener and only then to me and mine!

SIR GEORGE LEETE. [*Virulently.*] Damn you and yours and damn them . . and damn you again for the worse disgrace.

MR. CROWE. Damn *you*, sir . . have you paid him to marry the girl?

> *He turns away, purple faced, and* SIR GEORGE *chokes impotently.* ABUD *and* MR. PRESTIGE *come out talking. He is younger and less assertive than* FARMER CROWE.

MR. PRESTIGE. [*Pathetically.*] All our family always has got drunk at weddings.

ABUD. [*In remonstrance.*] Please, uncle.

CARNABY. Mr. Crowe . . I have been much to blame for not seeking you sooner.

MR. CROWE. [*Mollified.*] Shake hands.

CARNABY. [*Offering his with some difficulty.*] My arm

is stiff . . from an accident. This is a maid's marriage, I assure you.

MR. PRESTIGE. [*Open mouthed to* DR. REMNANT.] One c o u l d hang bacon here!

DOLLY. [*Very high and mighty.*] The family don't.

CARNABY. [*To his father.*] And won't you apologise for your remarks to Mr. Crowe, sir?

LADY LEETE. [*Demanding.*] Snuff!

CARNABY. And your box to my mother, sir.

SIR GEORGE *attends to his wife.*

DOLLY. [*Anxiously to* DR. REMNANT.] Can a gentleman change his name?

MR. CROWE. Parson . . once noble always noble, I take it.

DR. REMNANT. Certainly . . but I hope you have money to leave them, Mr. Crowe.

DOLLY. [*To* ABUD.] John.

ABUD. Dorothy.

DOLLY. You've not seen my babies yet.

LADY LEETE *sneezes.*

SIR GEORGE LEETE. Carnaby . . d'ye intend to murder that Crowe fellow . . or must I?

MR. SMALLPEICE *skips from the dining-room.*

MR. SMALLPEICE. Mr. John Abud . .

MR. CROWE. [*To* DR. REMNANT *as he nods towards* CARNABY.] Don't tell me he's got over that fever yet.

MR. SMALLPEICE. . . The ladies say . . are you ready or are you not?

MR. PRESTIGE. I'll get thy cloak, John.

MR. PRESTIGE *goes for the cloak.* CARNABY *has taken a pistol from the mantel-piece and now points it at* ABUD.

CARNABY. He's fit for heaven!

GEORGE LEETE *comes from the dining-room, and, noticing his father's action, says sharply . .*

GEORGE.   I suppose you know that pistol's loaded.

Which calls everyone's attention. DOLLY *shrieks.*

CARNABY.   What if there had been an accident!

And he puts back the pistol. ABUD *takes his cloak from* PRESTIGE.

ABUD.   Thank you, uncle.

MR. PRESTIGE.   I'm a proud man, Mr. Crowe ..

CARNABY.   Pride!

GEORGE.   [*Has a sudden inspiration, and strides up to* ABUD.] Here ends the joke, my good fellow. Be off without your wife.

ABUD stares, as do the others. Only CARNABY *suddenly catches* REMNANT'S *arm.*

MR. PRESTIGE.   [*Solemnly.*] But it's illegal to separate them.

GEORGE.   [*Giving up.*] Mr. Prestige .. you are the backbone of England.

CARNABY.   [*To* REMNANT.] Where are your miracles?

MRS. PRESTIGE comes out. A motherly farmer's wife, a mountain of a woman.

MRS. PRESTIGE.   John .. kiss your aunt.

ABUD goes to her, and she obliterates him in an embrace.

GEORGE.   [*To his father.*] Sense of humour .. Sense of humour!

LADY LEETE.   Snuff.

But no one heeds her this time.

CARNABY.   It doesn't matter.

GEORGE.   Smile. Let's be helpless gracefully.

CARNABY.   There are moments when I'm not sure——

GEORGE.   It's her own life.

TOZER staggers from the dining-room drunker than ever. He falls against the baluster and waves his arms.

MR. TOZER.   Silence there for the corpse!

MR. CROWE. You beast!

MR. TOZER. Respect my cloth . . Mr. Prestige.

MR. CROWE. That's not my name.

MR. TOZER. I'll have you to know that I'm Sir George Leete's baronet's most boon companion and her la'ship never goes nowhere without me. [*He subsides into a chair.*]

LADY LEETE. [*Tearfully.*] Snuff.

> *From the dining-room comes* ANN; *her head bent. She is crossing the hall when* SARAH *follows, calling her.*

SARAH. Ann!

> ANN *turns back to kiss her. The rest of the company stand gazing.* SIR GEORGE *gives snuff to* LADY LEETE.

ANN. Good bye, Sally.

SARAH. [*In a whisper.*] Forget us.

GEORGE. [*Relieving his feelings.*] Good-bye, everybody . . good-bye, everything.

> ABUD *goes to the front door and opening it stands waiting for her. She goes coldly but timidly to her father, to whom she puts her face up to be kissed.*

ANN. Good-bye, Papa.

CARNABY. [*Quietly, as he kisses her cheek.*] I can do without you.

SIR GEORGE LEETE. [*Raging at the draught.*] Shut that door.

ANN. I'm gone.

> *She goes with her husband.* MRS. OPIE *comes hurriedly out of the dining-room, too late.*

MRS. OPIE. Oh!

DR. REMNANT. Run . . Mrs. Opie.

CARNABY. There has started the new century!

> MRS. OPIE *opens the front door to look after them.*

SIR GEORGE LEETE. [*With double energy.*] Shut that door.

> LADY LEETE *sneezes and then chokes. There is much commotion in her neighbourhood.*

SIR GEORGE. Now she's hurt again.

DOLLY. Water!

MR. CROWE. Brandy!

SARAH. [*Going.*] I'll fetch both.

GEORGE. We must all die . . some day.

MR. TOZER. [*Who has struggled up to see what is the matter.*] And go to——

DR. REMNANT. Hell. You do believe in that, Mr. Tozer.

MRS. OPIE. [*Fanning the poor old lady.*] She's better.

CARNABY. [*To his guests.*] Gentlemen . . punch.

> PRESTIGE *and* SMALLPEICE; MRS. PRESTIGE, GEORGE *and* DOLLY *move towards the dining-room.*

MR. PRESTIGE. [*To* SMALLPEICE.] You owe all this to me.

MR. CROWE. Dolly . . I'm going.

MRS. PRESTIGE. [*To her husband as she nods towards* CARNABY.] Nathaniel . . look at 'im.

GEORGE. [*To his father-in-law.*] Must we come too?

MRS. PRESTIGE. [*As before.*] I can't help it . . a sneerin' carpin' cavillin' devil!

MRS. OPIE. Markswayde is to let . . as I hear . . Mr. Leete?

CARNABY. Markswayde is to let.

> *He goes on his way to the dining-room meeting* SARAH *who comes out carrying a glass of water and a decanter of brandy.* SIR GEORGE LEETE *is comfortably warming himself at the fire.*

* * * * * * * * * * *

The living room of JOHN ABUD'S *new cottage has bare plaster walls and its ceilings and floor are of red*

*brick; all fresh looking but not new. In the middle
of the middle wall there is a latticed window, dimity
curtained; upon the plain shelf in front are several
flower-pots.*

*To the right of this, a door, cross beamed and with a large
lock to it besides the latch.*

*Against the right hand wall, is a dresser, furnished with
dishes and plates: below it is a common looking
grandfather clock; below this a small door which
when opened shows winding stairs leading to the
room above. In the left hand wall there is a door
which is almost hidden by the fireplace which juts
out below it. In the fireplace a wood fire is laid
but not lit. At right angles to this stands a heavy
oak settle opposite a plain deal table; just beyond
which is a little bench. On either side of the window is a Windsor armchair. Between the window
and the door hangs a framed sampler.*

*In the darkness the sound of the unlocking of a door and
of* ABUD *entering is heard. He walks to the table,
strikes a light upon a tinder-box and lights a candle
which he finds there.* ANN *is standing in the doorway.* ABUD *is in stocking feet.*

ABUD. Don't come further. Here are your slippers.

*He places one of the Windsor chairs for her on which
she sits while he takes off her wet shoes and puts
on her slippers which he found on the table. Then
he takes her wet shoes to the fireplace. She sits
still. Then he goes to the door and brings in his
own boots from the little porch and puts them in
the fireplace too. Then he locks the door and hangs
up the key beside it. Then he stands looking at
her; but she does not speak, so he takes the candle,
lifts it above his head and walks to the dresser.*

ABUD. [*Encouragingly.*] Our dresser . . Thomas Jupp

made that. Plates and dishes. Here's Uncle Prestige's clock.

ANN. Past seven.

ABUD. That's upstairs. Table and bench, deal. Oak settle . . solid.

ANN. Charming.

ABUD. Windsor chairs . . Mother's sampler.

ANN. Home.

ABUD. Is it as you wish? I have been glad at your not seeing it until to-night.

ANN. I'm sinking into the strangeness of the place.

ABUD. Very weary? It's been a long nine miles.

She does not answer. He goes and considers the flower-pots in the window.

ANN. I still have on my cloak.

ABUD. Hang it behind the door there . . no matter if the wet drips.

ANN. I can wipe up the puddle.

She hangs up her cloak. He selects a flower-pot and brings it to her.

ABUD. Hyacinth bulbs for the spring.

ANN. [*After a glance.*] I don't want to hold them.
He puts back the pot, a little disappointed.

ABUD. Out there's the scullery.

ANN. It's very cold.

ABUD. If we light the fire now that means more trouble in the morning.

She sits on the settle.

ANN. Yes, I am very weary.

ABUD. Go to bed.

ABUD. Not yet. [*After a moment.*] How much light one candle gives! Sit where I may see you.

He sits on the bench. She studies him curiously.

ANN. Well . . this is an experiment.

ABUD. [*With reverence.*] God help us both.

ANN. Amen. Some people are so careful of their lives.
If we fail miserably we'll hold our tongues . . won't we?

ABUD. I don't know . . I can't speak of this.

ANN. These impossible things which are done mustn't
be talked of . . that spoils them. We don't want to boast
of this, do we?

ABUD. I fancy nobody quite believes that we are married.

ANN. Here's my ring . . real gold.

ABUD. [*With a sudden fierce throw up of his head.*]
Never you remind me of the difference between us.

ANN. Don't speak to me so.

ABUD. Now I'm your better.

ANN. My master . . The door's locked.

ABUD. [*Nodding.*] I know that I must be . . or be a
fool.

ANN. [*After a moment.*] Be kind to me.

ABUD. [*With remorse.*] Always I will.

ANN. You are master here.

ABUD. And I've angered you?

ANN. And if I fail . . I'll never tell you . . to make a
fool of you. And you're trembling. [*She sees his hand,
which is on the table, shake.*]

ABUD. Look at that now.

ANN. [*Lifting her own.*] My white hands must redden.
No more dainty appetite . . no more pretty books.

ABUD. Have you learned to scrub?

ANN. Not this floor.

ABUD. Mother always did bricks with a mop. To-
morrow I go to work. You'll be left for all day.

ANN. I must make friends with the other women around.

ABUD. My friends are very curious about you.

ANN. I'll wait to begin till I'm seasoned.

ABUD. Four o'clock's the hour for getting up.

ANN. Early rising always was a vice of mine.

ABUD. Breakfast quickly . . . and I take my dinner with me.

ANN. In a handkerchief.

ABUD. Hot supper, please.

ANN. It shall be ready for you.

There is silence between them for a little. Then he says timidly.

ABUD. May I come near to you?

ANN. [*In a low voice.*] Come.

He sits beside her, gazing.

ABUD. Wife . . I never have kissed you.

ANN. Shut your eyes.

ABUD. Are you afraid of me?

ANN. We're not to play such games at love.

ABUD. I can't help wanting to feel very tender towards you.

ANN. Think of me . . not as a wife . . but as a mother of your children . . if it's to be so. Treat me so.

ABUD. You are a part of me.

ANN. We must try and understand it . . as a simple thing.

ABUD. But shall I kiss you?

ANN. [*Lowering her head.*] Kiss me.

But when he puts his arms round her she shrinks.

ANN. No.

ABUD. But I will. It's my right.

Almost by force he kisses her. Afterwards she clenches her hands, and seems to suffer.

ABUD. Have I hurt you?

She gives him her hand, with a strange little smile.

ANN. I forgive you.

ABUD. [*Encouraged.*] Ann . . we're beginning life together.

ANN. Remember . . work's enough . . no stopping to talk.

ABUD. I'll work for you.

ANN. I'll do my part . . something will come of it.

For a moment they sit together hand in hand. Then she leaves him and paces across the room. There is a slight pause.

ANN. Papa . . I said . . we've all been in too great a hurry getting civilised. False dawn. I mean to go back.

ABUD. He laughed.

ANN. So he saw I was of no use to him, and he's penniless, and he let me go. When my father dies what will he take with him? . . . for you do take your works with you into Heaven or Hell, I believe. Much wit. Sally is afraid to die. Don't you aspire like George's wife. I was afraid to live . . and now . . I am content.

She walks slowly to the window, and from there to the door, against which she places her ear. Then she looks round at her husband.

ANN. I can hear them chattering.

Then she goes to the little door and opens it. ABUD *takes up the candle.*

ABUD. I'll hold the light . . the stairs are steep.

He lights her up the stairs.

The Voysey Inheritance

1903-5

THE VOYSEY INHERITANCE

*The office of Voysey and Son is in the best part of Lincoln's
Inn. Its panelled rooms give out a sense of grand-
motherly comfort and security, very grateful at first
to the hesitating investor, the dubious litigant. Mr.
Voysey's own room, into which he walks about
twenty past ten of a morning, radiates enterprise besides. There is polish on everything; on the windows, on the mahogany of the tidily packed writing
table that stands between them, on the brasswork of
the fire-place in the other wall, on the glass of the
fire-screen which preserves only the pleasantness of
a sparkling fire, even on Mr. Voysey's hat as he takes
it off to place it on the little red curtained shelf behind the door. Mr. Voysey is sixty or more, and
masterful; would obviously be master anywhere
from his own home outwards, or wreck the situation
in his attempt. Indeed there is a buccaneering air
sometimes in the twist of his glance, not altogether
suitable to a family solicitor. On this bright October
morning, Peacey, the head clerk, follows just too
late to help him off with his coat, but in time to take
it and hang it up with a quite unnecessary subservi-
ence. Mr. Voysey is evidently not capable enough
to like capable men about him. Peacey, not quite
removed from Nature, has made some attempts to
acquire protective colouring. A very drunken client*

83

*might mistake him for his master. His voice very
easily became a toneless echo of Mr. Voysey's; later
his features caught a line or two from that mirror
of all the necessary virtues into which he was so
constantly gazing; but how his clothes, even when
new, contrive to look like old ones of Mr. Voysey's
is a mystery, and to his tailor a most annoying one.
And Peacey is just a respectful number of years his
master's junior. Relieved of his coat, Mr. Voysey
carries to his table the bunch of beautiful roses he is
accustomed to bring to the office three times a week,
and places them for a moment only near the bowl of
water there ready to receive them, while he takes up
his letters. These lie ready, too, opened mostly, one
or two private ones left closed and discreetly separate. By this time the usual salutations have
passed, Peacey's "Good morning, sir;" Mr. Voysey's
"Morning, Peacey." Then as he gets to his letters
Mr. Voysey starts his day's work.*

MR. VOYSEY. Any news for me?

PEACEY. I hear bad accounts of Alguazils preferred, sir.

MR. VOYSEY. Oh . . from whom?

PEACEY. Merrit and James's head clerk in the train this morning.

MR. VOYSEY. They looked all right on . . Give me the Times. [PEACEY *goes to the fire-place for the Times; it is warming there.* MR. VOYSEY *waves a letter, then places it on the table.*] Here, that's for you . . Gerrard Cross business. Anything else?

PEACEY. [*As he turns the Times to its Finance page.*] I've made the usual notes.

MR. VOYSEY. Thank'ee.

PEACEY. Young Benham isn't back yet.

MR. VOYSEY. Mr. Edward must do as he thinks fit about that. Alguazils, Alg—oh, yes.

He is running his eye down the columns. PEACEY
leans over the letters.

PEACEY. This is from Jackson, sir. Shall I take it?

MR. VOYSEY. From Jackson . . Yes. Alguazils. Mr.
Edward's here, I suppose?

PEACEY. No, sir.

MR. VOYSEY. [*His eye twisting with some sharpness.*]
What!

PEACEY. [*Almost alarmed.*] I beg pardon, sir.

MR. VOYSEY. Mr. Edward.

PEACEY. Oh, yes, sir, been in his room some time. I
thought you said Headley; he's not due back till Thursday.

MR. VOYSEY *discards the Times and sits to his desk*
and his letters.

MR. VOYSEY. Tell Mr. Edward I've come.

PEACEY. Yes, sir. Anything else?

MR. VOYSEY. Not for the moment. Cold morning, isn't
it?

PEACEY. Quite surprising, sir.

MR. VOYSEY. We had a touch of frost down at Chislehurst.

PEACEY. So early!

MR. VOYSEY. I want it for the celery. All right, I'll call
through about the rest of the letters.

PEACEY *goes, having secured a letter or two, and* MR.
VOYSEY, *having sorted the rest* (a *proportion into*
the waste paper basket) *takes up the forgotten roses*
and starts setting them into a bowl, with an artistic
hand. Then his son EDWARD *comes in.* MR. VOYSEY
gives him one glance and goes on arranging the
roses, but says cheerily . .

MR. VOYSEY. Good morning, my dear boy.

EDWARD *has little of his father in him, and that little*
is undermost. It is a refined face, but self-conscious-
ness takes the place in it of imagination and in sup-

*pressing traits of brutality in his character it looks
as if the young man had suppressed his sense of
humour, too. But whether or no, that would not be
much in evidence now, for* EDWARD *is obviously going through some experience which is scaring him
(there is no better word). He looks not to have
slept for a night or two, and his standing there,
clutching and unclutching the bundle of papers he
carries, his eyes on his father, half appealingly, but
half accusingly, too, his whole being altogether so
unstrung and desperate, makes* MR. VOYSEY'S *uninter-
rupted arranging of the flowers seem very calculated
indeed. At last the little tension of silence is broken.*

EDWARD. Father . .

MR. VOYSEY. Well?

EDWARD. I'm glad to see you.

*This is a statement of fact. He doesn't know that
the commonplace phrase sounds ridiculous at such a
moment.*

MR. VOYSEY. I see you've the papers there.

EDWARD. Yes.

MR. VOYSEY. You've been through them?

EDWARD. As you wished me . .

MR. VOYSEY. Well? [EDWARD *doesn't answer. Reference to the papers seems to overwhelm him with shame.*
MR. VOYSEY *goes on with cheerful impatience.*] Come,
come, my dear boy, you mustn't take it like this. You're
puzzled and worried, of course. But why didn't you come
down to me on Saturday night? I expected you . . I told
you to come. Then your mother was wondering, of course,
why you weren't with us for dinner yesterday.

EDWARD. I went through all the papers twice. I wanted
to make quite sure.

MR. VOYSEY. Sure of what? I told you to come to me.

EDWARD. [*He is very near crying.*] Oh, father!

MR. VOYSEY. Now look here, Edward, I'm going to ring, and dispose of these letters. Please pull yourself together. [*He pushes the little button on his table.*]

EDWARD. I didn't leave my rooms all day yesterday.

MR. VOYSEY. A pleasant Sunday! You must learn, whatever the business may be, to leave it behind you at the Office. Why, life's not worth living else.

> PEACEY *comes in to find* MR. VOYSEY *before the fire, ostentatiously warming and rubbing his hands.*

Oh, there isn't much else, Peacey. Tell Simmons that if he satisfies you about the details of this lease it'll be all right. Make a note for me of Mr. Grainger's address at Mentone. I shall have several letters to dictate to Atkinson. I'll whistle for him.

PEACEY. Mr. Burnett .. Burnett v. Marks had just come in, Mr. Edward.

EDWARD. [*Without turning.*] It's only fresh instructions. Will you take them?

PEACEY. All right.

> PEACEY *goes, lifting his eyebrow at the queerness of* EDWARD'S *manner. This* MR. VOYSEY *sees, returning to his table with a little scowl.*

MR. VOYSEY. Now sit down. I've given you a bad forty-eight hours, it seems. Well, I've been anxious about you. Never mind, we'll thresh the thing out now. Go through the two accounts. Mrs. Murberry's first .. how do you find it stands?

EDWARD. [*His feelings choking him.*] I hoped you were playing some trick on me.

MR. VOYSEY. Come, now.

> EDWARD *separates the papers precisely and starts to detail them; his voice quite toneless. Now and then his father's sharp comments ring out in contrast.*

EDWARD. We've got the lease of her present house, several agreements .. and here's her will. Here's also a sometime expired power of attorney over her securities and her property generally . . it was for six months.

MR. VOYSEY.   She was in South Africa.

EDWARD.   Here's the Sheffield mortgage and the Henry Smith mortgage with Banker's receipts . . hers to us for the interest up to date . . four and a half and five per cent. Then . . Fretworthy Bonds. There's a memorandum in your writing that they are at the Bank; but you didn't say what Bank.

MR. VOYSEY.   My own . . Stukeley's.

EDWARD.   [*Just dwelling on the words.*]   Your own. I marked that with a query. There's eight thousand five hundred in three and a half India stock. And there are her Banker's receipts for cheques on account of those dividends. I presume for those dividends.

MR. VOYSEY.   Why not?

EDWARD.   [*Gravely.*]   Because then, Father, there are Banker's half yearly receipts for sums amounting to an average of four hundred and twenty pounds a year. But I find no record of any capital to produce this.

MR. VOYSEY.   Go on. What do you find?

EDWARD.   Till about three years back there seems to have been eleven thousand in Queenslands which would produce—did produce exactly the same sum. But after January of that year I find no record of this.

MR. VOYSEY.   In fact, the Queenslands are missing?

EDWARD.   [*Hardly uttering the word.*]   Yes.

MR. VOYSEY.   From which you conclude?

EDWARD.   I concluded at first that you had not handed me all the papers connected with——

MR. VOYSEY.   Since Mrs. Murberry evidently gets another four twenty a year somehow; lucky woman.

EDWARD.   [*In agony.*]   Oh!

MR. VOYSEY.   Well, we'll return to the good lady later. Now let's take the other.

EDWARD. The Hatherley Trust.

MR. VOYSEY. Quite so.

EDWARD. [*With one accusing glance.*] Trust.

MR. VOYSEY. Go on.

EDWARD. Oh, father . .

His grief comes uppermost again, and MR. VOYSEY *meets it kindly.*

MR. VOYSEY. I know, my dear boy. I shall have lots to say to you. But let's get quietly through with these details first.

EDWARD. [*Bitterly now.*] Oh, this is simple enough. We're young Hatherley's only trustees till his coming of age in about five years' time. The property was eighteen thousand invested in Consols. Certain sums were to be allowed for his education; these have been and are still being paid. There is no record as to the rest of the capital.

MR. VOYSEY. None?

EDWARD. Yes . . I beg your pardon, sir. There's a memorandum to refer to the Bletchley Land Scheme.

MR. VOYSEY. That must be ten years ago. But he's credited with the interest on his capital?

EDWARD. On paper, sir. The balance was to be reinvested. There's a partial account in your hand writing. He's credited with the Consol interest.

MR. VOYSEY. Quite so.

EDWARD. I think I've heard you say that the Bletchley scheme paid seven and a half.

MR. VOYSEY. At one time. Have you taken the trouble to calculate what will be due from us to the lad?

EDWARD. Capital and compound interest . . . about twenty-six thousand pounds.

MR. VOYSEY. Yes, it's a large sum. In five years' time?

EDWARD. When he comes of age.

MR. VOYSEY. Well, that gives us, say four years and six months in which to think about it,

EDWARD *waits, hopelessly, for his father to speak again; then says . .*

EDWARD. Thank you for showing me these, sir. Shall I put them back in your safe now?

MR. VOYSEY. Yes, you'd better. There's the key. [ED-WARD *reaches for the bunch, his face hidden.*] Put them down. Your hand shakes . . why, you might have been drinking . . I'll put them away later. It's no use having hysterics, Edward. Look the trouble in the face.

EDWARD'S *only answer is to go to the fire, as far from his father as the room allows. And there he leans on the mantelpiece, his shoulders heaving.*

MR. VOYSEY. I'm sorry, my dear boy. I wouldn't tell you if I could help it.

EDWARD. I can't believe it. And that you should be telling it me.

MR. VOYSEY. Let your feelings go, and get that part of the business over. It isn't pleasant, I know. It isn't pleasant to inflict it on you.

EDWARD. How I got through that outer office this morning, I don't know. I came early, but some of them were here. Peacey came into my room; he must have seen there was something up.

MR. VOYSEY. That's no matter.

EDWARD. [*Able to turn to his father again; won round by the kind voice.*] How long has it been going on? Why didn't you tell me before? Oh, I know you thought you'd pull through; but I'm your partner . . I'm responsible, too. Oh, I don't want to shirk that . . don't think I mean to shirk that, father. Perhaps I ought to have discovered, but those affairs were always in your hands. I trusted . . I beg your pardon. Oh, it's us . . not you. Everyone has trusted us.

MR. VOYSEY. [*Calmly and kindly still.*] You don't seem to notice that I'm not breaking my heart like this.

EDWARD.   What's the extent of the mischief? When did
it begin? Father, what made you begin it?

MR. VOYSEY.   I didn't begin it.

EDWARD.   You didn't. Who, then?

MR. VOYSEY.   My father before me. [EDWARD *stares.*]
That calms you a little.

EDWARD.   I'm glad . . my dear father! [*And he puts
out his hand. Then just a doubt enters his mind.*] But
I . . it's amazing.

MR. VOYSEY.   [*Shaking his head.*]   My inheritance,
Edward.

EDWARD.   My dear father!

MR. VOYSEY.   I had hoped it wasn't to be yours.

EDWARD.   D'you mean to tell me that this sort of thing
has been going on for years? For more than thirty years!

MR. VOYSEY.   Yes.

EDWARD.   That's a little difficult to understand just at
first, sir.

MR. VOYSEY.   [*Sententiously.*]   We do what we must in
this world, Edward. I have done what I had to do.

EDWARD.   [*His emotion well cooled by now.*]   Perhaps
I'd better just listen quietly while you explain.

MR. VOYSEY.   [*Concentrating.*]   You know that I'm heavily into Northern Electrics.

EDWARD.   Yes.

MR. VOYSEY.   But you don't know how heavily. When I
discovered the Municipalities were organising the purchase, I thought, of course, the stock'd be up a hundred
and forty—a hundred and fifty in no time. Now Leeds
won't make up her quarrel with the other place . . there'll
be no bill brought in for ten years. I bought at ninety-
five. What are they now?

EDWARD.   Eighty-eight.

MR. VOYSEY.   Eighty-seven and a half. In ten years I
may be . . ! That's why you've had to be told.

EDWARD. With whose money are you so heavily into
Northern Electrics?

MR. VOYSEY. The firm's money.

EDWARD. Clients' money?

MR. VOYSEY. Yes.

EDWARD. [*Coldly.*] Well . . I'm waiting for your explanation, sir.

MR. VOYSEY. You seem to have recovered yourself pretty much.

EDWARD. No, sir. I'm trying to understand, that's all.

MR. VOYSEY. [*With a shrug.*] Children always think
the worst of their parents. I did of mine. It's a pity.

EDWARD. Go on, sir, go on. Let me know the worst.

MR. VOYSEY. There's no immediate danger. I should
think anyone could see that from the state of these accounts. There's no actual danger at all.

EDWARD. Is that the worst?

MR. VOYSEY. [*His anger rising.*] Have you studied
these two accounts, or have you not?

EDWARD. Yes, sir.

MR. VOYSEY. Well, where's the deficiency in Mrs. Murberry's income . . has she ever gone without a shilling?
What has young Hatherley lost?

EDWARD. He stands to lose——

MR. VOYSEY. He stands to lose nothing if I'm spared for
a little, and you will only bring a little common sense to
bear, and try to understand the difficulties of my position.

EDWARD. Father, I'm not thinking ill of you . . that is,
I'm trying not to. But won't you explain how you're
justified—?

MR. VOYSEY. In putting our affairs in order.

EDWARD. Are you doing that?

MR. VOYSEY. What else?

EDWARD. [*Starting patiently to examine the matter.*]
How bad were things when you first came to control them?

MR. VOYSEY. Oh, I forget.

EDWARD. You can't forget.

MR. VOYSEY. Well . . pretty bad.

EDWARD. Do you know how it was my grandfather began to——

MR. VOYSEY. Muddlement, muddlement! Then the money went, and what was he to do? He'd no capital, no credit, and was in terror of his life. My dear Edward, if I hadn't found it out he'd have confessed to the first man who came and asked for a balance sheet.

EDWARD. Well, what exact sum was he to the bad then?

MR. VOYSEY. I forget. Several thousands.

EDWARD. But surely it has not taken all these years to pay off——

MR. VOYSEY. Oh, hasn't it!

EDWARD. [*Making his point.*] But how does it happen, sir, that such a comparatively recent trust as young Hatherley's has been broken into?

MR. VOYSEY. Well, what could be safer than to use that money? There's a Consol investment, and not a sight wanted of either capital or interest for five years.

EDWARD. [*Utterly beaten.*] Father, are you mad?

MR. VOYSEY. Certainly not. My practice is to reinvest my clients' money when it is entirely under my control. The difference between the income this money has to bring to them and the income it is actually bringing to me I utilise in my endeavour to fill up the deficit in the firm's accounts . . in fact, to try and put things straight. Doesn't it follow that the more low interest bearing capital I can use, the better . . the less risky things I have to put it into. Most of young Hatherley's Consol capital is out on mortgage at four and a half and five . . safe as safe can be.

EDWARD. But he should have the benefit.

MR. VOYSEY. He has the amount of his consol interest.

EDWARD. Are the mortgages in his name?

MR. VOYSEY. Some of them . . some of them. That's a technical matter. With regard to Mrs. Murberry . . those Fretworthy Bonds at my bank . . I've raised five thousand on them. I can release her Bonds to-morrow if she wants them.

EDWARD. Where's the five thousand.

MR. VOYSEY. I don't know . . It was paid into my private account. Yes, I do remember. Some of it went to complete a purchase . . that and two thousand more out of the Skipworth fund.

EDWARD. But, my dear father——

MR. VOYSEY. Well?

EDWARD. [*Summing it all up very simply.*] It's not right.

MR. VOYSEY *considers his son for a moment with a pitying shake of the head.*

MR. VOYSEY. Oh . . why is it so hard for a man to see clearly beyond the letter of the law! Will you consider a moment, Edward, the position in which I found myself? Was I to see my father ruined and disgraced without lifting a finger to help him? . . not to mention the interest of the clients. I paid back to the man who would have lost most by my father's mistakes every penny of his money. He never knew the danger he'd been in . . never passed an uneasy moment about it. It was I who lay awake. I have now somewhere a letter from that man to my father thanking him effusively for the way in which he'd conducted some matter. It comforted my poor father. Well, Edward, I stepped outside the letter of the law to do that. Was that right or wrong?

EDWARD. In its result, sir, right.

MR. VOYSEY. Judge me by the result. I took the risk of failure . . I should have suffered. I could have kept clear of the danger if I'd liked.

EDWARD. But that's all past. The thing that concerns me is what you are doing now.

MR. VOYSEY. [*Gently reproachful now.*] My boy, you must trust me a little. It's all very well for you to come in at the end of the day and criticise. But I, who have done the day's work, know how that work had to be done. And here's our firm, prosperous, respected, and without a stain on its honour. That's the main point, isn't it? And I think that achievement should earn me the right to be trusted a little . . shouldn't it?

EDWARD. [*Quite irresponsive to this pathetic appeal.*] Look here, sir, I'm dismissing from my mind all prejudice about speaking the truth . . acting upon one's instructions, behaving as any honest firm of solicitors must behave . .

MR. VOYSEY. You need not. I tell no unnecessary lies. If a man of any business ability gives me definite instructions about his property, I follow them.

EDWARD. Father, no unnecessary lies!

MR. VOYSEY. Well, my friend, go and tell Mrs. Murberry that four hundred and twenty pounds of her income hasn't for the last eight years come from the place she thinks it's come from, and see how happy you'll make her.

EDWARD. But is that four hundred and twenty a year as safe to come to her as it was before you meddled with the capital?

MR. VOYSEY. I see no reason why——

EDWARD. What's the security?

MR. VOYSEY. [*Putting his coping stone on the argument.*] My financial ability.

EDWARD. [*Really not knowing whether to laugh or cry.*] Why, it seems as if you were satisfied with this state of things.

MR. VOYSEY. Edward, you really are most unsympathetic and unreasonable. I give all I have to the firm's work . . my brain . . my energies . . my whole life. I can't turn

my abilities into hard cash at par . . I wish I could. Do
you suppose that if I could establish every one of these people with a separate and consistent bank balance to-morrow
that I shouldn't do it? Do you suppose that it's a pleasure
. . that it's relaxation to have these matters continually on
one's mind? Do you suppose—?

EDWARD. [*Thankfully able to meet anger with anger.*]
I find it impossible to believe that you couldn't somehow
have put things to rights by now.

MR. VOYSEY. Oh, do you? Somehow!

EDWARD. In thirty years the whole system must either
have come hopelessly to grief . . or during that time there
must have been opportunities——

MR. VOYSEY. Well, if you're so sure, I hope that when
I'm under ground you may find them.

EDWARD. I !

MR. VOYSEY. And put everything right with a stroke of
the pen, if it's so easy !

EDWARD. I !

MR. VOYSEY. You're my partner and my son, and you'll
inherit the business.

EDWARD. [*Realising at last that he has been led to the
edge of this abyss.*] Oh, no, father.

MR. VOYSEY. Why else have I had to tell you all this?

EDWARD. [*Very simply.*] Father, I can't. I can't possibly. I don't think you've any right to ask me.

MR. VOYSEY. Why not, pray?

EDWARD. It's perpetuating the dishonesty.

MR. VOYSEY *hardens at the unpleasant word.*

MR. VOYSEY. You don't believe that I've told you the
truth.

EDWARD. I wish to believe it.

MR. VOYSEY. It's no proof . . that I've earned these
twenty or thirty people their incomes for the last—how
many years?

EDWARD. Whether what you have done and are doing is wrong or right . . I can't meddle in it.

For the moment MR. VOYSEY *looks a little dangerous.*

MR. VOYSEY. Very well. Forget all I've said. Go back to your room. Get back to your own mean drudgery. My life's work—my splendid life's work—ruined! What does that matter?

EDWARD. Whatever did you expect of me?

MR. VOYSEY. [*Making a feint at his papers.*] Oh, nothing, nothing. [*Then he slams them down with great effect.*] Here's a great edifice built up by years of labour and devotion and self-sacrifice . . a great arch you may call it . . a bridge which is to carry our firm to safety with honour. [*This variation of Disraeli passes unnoticed.*] My work! And now, as I near the end of my life, it still lacks the key-stone. Perhaps I am to die with my work just incomplete. Then is there nothing that a son might do? Do you think I shouldn't be proud of you, Edward . . that I shouldn't bless you from—wherever I may be, when you completed my life's work . . with perhaps just one kindly thought of your father?

In spite of this oratory, the situation is gradually impressing EDWARD.

EDWARD. What will happen if I . . if I desert you?

MR. VOYSEY. I'll protect you as best I can.

EDWARD. I wasn't thinking of myself, sir.

MR. VOYSEY. [*With great nonchalance.*] Well, I shan't mind the exposure, you know. It won't make me blush in my coffin . . and you're not so foolish, I hope, as to be thinking of the feelings of your brothers and sisters. Considering how simple it would have been for me to go to my grave in peace and quiet, and let you discover the whole thing afterwards, the fact that I didn't, that I have taken some thought for the future of all of you might perhaps have convinced you that I . . ! But there . . consult your own safety.

> EDWARD *has begun to pace the room, indecision growing upon him.*

EDWARD. This is a queer thing to have to make up one's mind about, isn't it, father?

MR. VOYSEY. [*Watching him closely, and modulating his voice.*] My dear boy, I understand the shock to your feelings that this disclosure must have been.

EDWARD. Yes, I thought this morning that next week would see us in the dock together.

MR. VOYSEY. And I suppose if I'd broken down, and begged your pardon for my folly, you'd have done anything for me, gone to prison smiling, eh?

EDWARD. I suppose so.

MR. VOYSEY. Yes, it's easy enough to forgive. I'm sorry I can't go in sack cloth and ashes to oblige you. [*Now he begins to rally his son; easy in his strength.*] My dear Edward, you've lived a quiet, humdrum life up to now, with your books and your philosophy and your agnosticism and your ethics of this and your ethics of that . . dear me, these are the sort of garden oats which young men seem to sow now-a-days ! . . and you've never before been brought face to face with any really vital question. Now don't make a fool of yourself just through inexperience. Try and give your mind freely and unprejudicedly to the consideration of this very serious matter. I'm not angry at what you've said to me. I'm quite willing to forget it. And it's for your own sake, and not for mine, Edward, that I do beg you to—to—to be a man, and try and take a practical common sense view of the position you find yourself in. It's not a pleasant position, I know, but it's unavoidable.

EDWARD. You should have told me before you took me into partnership. [*Oddly enough, it is this last flicker of rebellion which breaks down* MR. VOYSEY'S *caution. Now he lets fly with a vengeance.*]

MR. VOYSEY. Should I be telling you at all if I could possibly help it? Don't I know that you're about as fit for this job as a babe unborn? Haven't I been worrying over that for these last three years? But I'm in a corner . . and I won't see all this work of mine come to smash simply because of your scruples. If you're a son of mine you'll do as I tell you. Hadn't I the same choice to make? . . and this is a safer game for you than it was for me then. D'you suppose I didn't have scruples? If you run away from this, Edward, you're a coward. My father was a coward, and he suffered for it to the end of his days. I was sick-nurse to him here more than partner. Good Lord! . . of course it's pleasant and comfortable to keep within the law . . then the law will look after you. Otherwise you have to look pretty sharp after yourself. You have to cultivate your own sense of right and wrong; deal your own justice. But that makes a bigger man of you, let me tell you. How easily . . how easily could I have walked out of my father's office and left him to his fate; no one would have blamed me! But I didn't. I thought it my better duty to stay and . . yes, I say it with all reverence . . to take up my cross. Well, I've carried that cross pretty successfully. And what's more, it's made a happy man of me . . a better, stronger man than skulking about in shame and in fear of his life ever made of my poor dear father. [*Relieved at having let out the truth, but doubtful of his wisdom in doing so, he changes his tone.*] I don't want what I've been saying to influence you, Edward. You are a free agent . . and you must decide upon your own course of action. Now don't let's discuss the matter any more for the moment.

EDWARD *looks at his father with clear eyes.*

EDWARD. Don't forget to put these papers away.

*He restores them to their bundles and hands them
back; it is his only comment.* MR. VOYSEY *takes them
and his meaning in silence.*

MR. VOYSEY.   Are you coming down to Chislehurst soon?
We've got Hugh and his wife, and Booth and Emily, and
Christopher for two or three days, till he goes back to
school.

EDWARD.   How is Chris?

MR. VOYSEY.   All right again now . . grows more like
his father. Booth's very proud of him. So am I.

EDWARD.   I think I can't face them all just at present.

MR. VOYSEY.   Nonsense.

EDWARD.   [*A little wave of emotion going through him.*]
I feel as if this thing were written on my face. How I
shall get through business I don't know!

MR. VOYSEY.   You're weaker than I thought, Edward.

EDWARD.   [*A little ironically.*] A disappointment to you,
father?

MR. VOYSEY.   No, no.

EDWARD.   You should have brought one of the others
into the firm . . Trenchard or Booth.

MR. VOYSEY.   [*Hardening.*] Trenchard! [*He dismisses
that.*] Well, you're a better man than Booth. Edward,
you mustn't imagine that the whole world is standing on
its head merely because you've had an unpleasant piece of
news. You come down to Chislehurst to-night . . well,
say to-morrow night. It'll be good for you . . stop your
brooding . . that's your worst vice, Edward. You'll find
the household as if nothing had happened. Then you'll
remember that nothing really has happened. And pres-
ently you'll get to see that nothing need happen, if you
keep your head. I remember times, when things have
seemed at their worst, what a relief it's been to me . . my
romp with you all in the nursery just before your bed
time. Do you remember?

EDWARD. Yes. I cut your head open once with that gun.

MR. VOYSEY. [*In a full glow of fine feeling.*] And, my dear boy, if I knew that you were going to inform the next client you met of what I've just told you . .

EDWARD. [*With a shudder.*] Oh, father!

MR. VOYSEY. . . And that I should find myself in prison to-morrow, I wouldn't wish a single thing I've ever done undone. I have never wilfully harmed man or woman. My life's been a happy one. Your dear mother has been spared to me. You're most of you good children, and a credit to what I've done for you.

EDWARD. [*The deadly humour* of this too much for him.*] Father!

MR. VOYSEY. Run along now, run along. I must finish my letters and get into the City.

He might be scolding a schoolboy for some trifling fault. EDWARD *turns to have a look at the keen, un-embarrassed face.* MR. VOYSEY *smiles at him and proceeds to select from the bowl a rose for his buttonhole.*

EDWARD. I'll think it over, sir.

MR. VOYSEY. Of course you will. And don't brood, Edward, don't brood.

So EDWARD *leaves him; and having fixed the rose to his satisfaction, he rings his table telephone and calls through it to the listening clerk.*

Send Atkinson to me, please. [*Then he gets up, keys in hand, to lock away Mrs. Murberry's and the Hatherley trust papers.*]

THE SECOND ACT

The VOYSEY *dining-room at Chislehurst, when children and*
grandchildren are visiting, is dining-table and very
little else. And at this moment in the evening, when
five or six men are sprawling back in their chairs,
and the air is clouded with smoke, it is a very typ-
ical specimen of the middle-class English domestic
temple; the daily sacrifice consummated, the acolytes
dismissed, the women safely in the drawing-room,
and the chief priests of it taking their surfeited ease
round the dessert-piled altar. It has the usual red-
papered walls (like a reflection, they are, of the un-
derdone beef so much consumed within them); the
usual varnished woodwork, which is known as
grained oak; there is the usual hot, mahogany furni-
ture; and, commanding point of the whole room,
there is the usual black-marble sarcophagus of a
fireplace. Above this hangs one of the two or three
oil paintings, which are all that break the red pat-
tern of the walls, the portrait painted in 1880 of an
undistinguished looking gentleman aged sixty; he is
shown sitting in a more graceful attitude than it
could ever have been comfortable for him to assume.
MR. VOYSEY'S *father it is, and the brass plate at the*
bottom of the frame tells us that the portrait was a
presentation one. On the mantelpiece stands, of
course, a clock; at either end a china vase filled with
paper spills. And in front of the fire—since that is

the post of vantage, stands at this moment MAJOR
BOOTH VOYSEY. *He is the second son, of the age that
it is necessary for a Major to be, and of an appearance that many ordinary Majors in ordinary regiments are.   He went into the army because he
thought it would be like a schoolboy's idea of it;
and, being there, he does his little all to keep it so.
He stands astride, hands in pockets, coat-tails
through his arms, cigar in mouth, moustache brist-
ling.   On either side of him sits at the table an old
gentleman; the one is* MR. EVAN COLPUS, *the vicar of
their parish, the other* MR. GEORGE BOOTH, *a friend of
long standing, and the Major's godfather.* MR. COL-
PUS *is a harmless enough anachronism, except for
the waste of £400 a year in which his stipend in-
volves the community.   Leaving most of his paro-
chial work to an energetic curate, he devotes his
serious attention to the composition of two sermons
a week.   They deal with the difficulties of living the
Christian life as experienced by people who have
nothing else to do.   Published in series from time
to time, these form suitable presents for bedridden
parishioners.* MR. GEORGE BOOTH, *on the contrary, is
as gay an old gentleman as can be found in Chislehurst.   An only son; his father left him at the age
of twenty-five a fortune of a hundred thousand
pounds (a plum, as he called it).   At the same time
he had the good sense to dispose of his father's business, into which he had been most unwillingly introduced five years earlier, for a like sum before he
was able to depreciate its value. It was* MR. VOYSEY'S
*invaluable assistance in this transaction which first
bound the two together in great friendship.   Since
that time Mr. Booth has been bent on nothing but
enjoying himself.   He has even remained a bachelor*

*with that object. Money has given him all he wants,
therefore he loves and reverences money; while his
imagination may be estimated by the fact that he
has now reached the age of sixty-five still possess-
ing more of it than he knows what to do with. At
the head of the table, meditatively cracking walnuts,
sits* MR. VOYSEY. *He has his back there to the conservatory door—you know it is the conservatory
door because there is a curtain to pull over it, and
because half of it is frosted glass with a purple key
pattern round the edge. On* MR. VOYSEY'S *left is*
DENIS TREGONING, *a nice enough young man. And
at the other end of the table sits* EDWARD, *not smoking, not talking, hardly listening, very depressed.
Behind him is the ordinary door of the room, which
leads out into the dismal, draughty hall. The Major's voice is like the sound of a cannon through
the tobacco smoke.*

MAJOR BOOTH VOYSEY. Of course I'm hot and strong
for conscription . .

MR. GEORGE BOOTH. My dear boy, the country'd never
stand it. No Englishman——

MAJOR BOOTH VOYSEY. [*Dropping the phrase heavily
upon the poor old gentleman.*] I beg your pardon. If we
. . the Army . . say to the country . . Upon our honour,
conscription is necessary for your safety . . what answer
has the country? What? [*He pauses defiantly.*] There
you are . . none!

TREGONING. Booth will imagine because one doesn't
argue that one has nothing to say. You ask the country.

MAJOR BOOTH VOYSEY. Perhaps I will. Perhaps I'll
chuck the Service and go into the House. [*Then falling
into the sing song of a favourite phrase.*] I'm not a conceited man . . but I believe that if I speak out upon a
subject I understand, and only upon that subject, the House

will l i s t e n . . and if others followed my example we should be a far more business-like and go-ahead community.

> *He pauses for breath, and* MR. BOOTH *seizes the opportunity.*

MR. GEORGE BOOTH. If you think the gentlemen of England will allow themselves to be herded with a lot of low fellers and made to carry guns—!

MAJOR BOOTH VOYSEY. [*Obliterating him once more.*] Just one moment. Have you thought of the physical improvement which conscription would bring about in the manhood of the country? What England wants is Chest! [*He generously inflates his own.*] Chest and Discipline. I don't care how it's obtained. Why, we suffer from a lack of it in our homes——

MR. VOYSEY. [*With the crack of a nut.*] Your godson talks a deal, don't he? You know, when Booth gets into a club he gets on the committee . . gets on any committee to enquire into anything . . and then goes on at 'em just like this. Don't you, Booth?

> BOOTH *knuckles under easily enough to his father's sarcasm.*

MAJOR BOOTH VOYSEY. Well, sir, people tell me I'm a useful man on committees.

MR. VOYSEY. I don't doubt it . . your voice must drown all discussion.

MAJOR BOOTH VOYSEY. You can't say I don't listen to you, sir.

MR. VOYSEY. I don't . . and I'm not blaming you. But I must say I often think what a devil of a time the family will have with you when I'm gone. Fortunately for your poor mother, she's deaf.

MAJOR BOOTH VOYSEY. And wouldn't you wish me, sir, as eldest son . . . Trenchard not counting . . .

MR. VOYSEY. [*With the crack of another nut.*] Tren-

chard not counting. By all means, bully them. Get up
your subjects a bit better, and then bully them. I don't
manage things that way myself, but I think it's your best
chance . . if there weren't other people present I'd say
your only chance, Booth.

MAJOR BOOTH VOYSEY. [*With some discomfort.*] Ha!
If I were a conceited man, sir, I could trust you to take it
out of me.

MR. VOYSEY. [*As he taps* MR. BOOTH *with the nut crack-
ers.*] Help yourself, George, and drink to your godson's
health. Long may he keep his chest notes! Never heard
him on parade, have you?

TREGONING. I notice military men must display themselves . . that's why Booth acts as a firescreen. I believe
that after mess that position is positively rushed.

MAJOR BOOTH VOYSEY. [*Cheering to find an opponent
he can tackle.*] If you want a bit of fire, say so, you suck-
ing Lord Chancellor. Because I mean to allow you to be
my brother-in-law you think you can be impertinent.

> *So* TREGONING *moves to the fire, and that changes
> the conversation.*

MR. VOYSEY. By the bye, Vicar, you were at Lady Mary's
yesterday. Is she giving us anything towards that window?

MR. COLPUS. Five pounds more; she has promised me
five pounds.

MR. VOYSEY. Then how will the debt stand?

MR. COLPUS. Thirty-three . . no, thirty-two pounds.

MR. VOYSEY. We're a long time clearing it off.

MR. COLPUS. [*Gently querulous.*] Yes, now that the
window is up, people don't seem so ready to contribute as
they were.

TREGONING. We must mention that to Hugh!

MR. COLPUS. [*Tactful at once.*] Not that the work is
not universally admired. I have heard Hugh's design
praised by quite competent judges. But certainly I feel

now it might have been wiser to have delayed the unveiling until the money was forthcoming.

TREGONING. Never deliver goods to the Church on credit.

MR. COLPUS. Eh? [TREGONING *knows he is a little hard of hearing.*]

MR. VOYSEY. Well, as it was my wish that my son should do the design, I suppose in the end I shall have to send you a cheque.

MAJOR BOOTH VOYSEY. Anonymously.

MR. COLPUS. Oh, that would be——

MR. VOYSEY. No, why should I? Here, George Booth, you shall halve it with me.

MR. GEORGE BOOTH. I'm damned if I do.

MR. COLPUS. [*Proceeding, conveniently deaf.*] You remember that at the meeting we had of the parents and friends to decide on the positions of the names of the poor fellows and the regiments and coats of arms and so on . . when Hugh said so violently that he disapproved of the war and made all those remarks about land-lords and Bibles and said he thought of putting in a figure of Britannia blushing for shame or something . . I'm beginning to fear that may have created a bad impression.

MAJOR BOOTH VOYSEY. Why should they mind . . what on earth does Hugh know about war? He couldn't tell a battery horse from a bandsman. I don't pretend to criticise art. I think the window'd be very pretty if it wasn't so broken up into bits.

MR. GEORGE BOOTH. [*Fortified by his "damned" and his last glass of port.*] These young men are so ready with their disapproval. Criticism starts in the cradle nowadays. When I was young, people weren't always questioning this and questioning that.

MAJOR BOOTH VOYSEY. Lack of discipline.

MR. GEORGE BOOTH. [*Hurrying on.*] The way a man

now even stops to think what he's eating and drinking.
And in religious matters . . Vicar, I put it to you . .
there's no uniformity at all.

MR. COLPUS. Ah . . I try to keep myself free from the
disturbing influences of modern thought.

MR. GEORGE BOOTH. Young men must be forming their
own opinions about this and their opinions about that.
You know, Edward, you're worse even than Hugh is.

EDWARD. [*Glancing up mildly at this sudden attack.*]
What have I done, Mr. Booth?

MR. GEORGE BOOTH. [*Not the readiest of men.*] Well . .
aren't you one of those young men who go about the
world making difficulties?

EDWARD. What sort of difficulties?

MR. GEORGE BOOTH. [*Triumphantly.*] Just so . . I
never can make out. Surely when you're young you can
ask the advice of your elders and when you grow up you
find Laws . . lots of laws divine and human laid down
for our guidance. [*Well in possession of the conversation
he spreads his little self.*] I look back over a fairly long
life and . . perhaps I should say by Heaven's help . . I
find nothing that I can honestly reproach myself with.
And yet I don't think I ever took more than five minutes
to come to a decision upon any important point. One's
private life is, I think, one's own affair . . I should allow
no one to pry into that. But as to worldly things . . well,
I have come into several sums of money and my capital
is still intact . . ask your father. [MR. VOYSEY *nods
gravely.*] I've never robbed any man. I've never lied
over anything that mattered. As a citizen I pay my
taxes without grumbling very much. Yes, and I sent
conscience money too upon one occasion. I consider
that any man who takes the trouble can live the life of a
gentleman. [*And he finds that his cigar is out.*]

MAJOR BOOTH VOYSEY. [*Not to be outdone by this display of virtue.*] Well, I'm not a conceited man, but——

TREGONING. Are you sure, Booth?

MAJOR BOOTH VOYSEY. Shut up. I was going to say when my young cub of a brother-in-law-to-be interrupted me, that T r a i n i n g, for which we all have to be thankful to you, Sir, has much to do with it. [*Suddenly he pulls his trousers against his legs.*] I say, I'm scorching! D'you want another cigar, Denis?

TREGONING. No, thank you.

MAJOR BOOTH VOYSEY. I do.

> *And he glances round, but* TREGONING *sees a box on the table and reaches it. The Vicar gets up.*

MR. COLPUS. M-m-m-must be taking my departure.

MR. VOYSEY. Already!

MAJOR BOOTH VOYSEY. [*Frowning upon the cigar box.*] No, not those. Where are the Ramon Allones? What on earth has Honor done with them?

MR. VOYSEY. Spare time for a chat with Mrs. Voysey before you go. She has ideas about a children's tea fight.

MR. COLPUS. Certainly I will.

MAJOR BOOTH VOYSEY. [*Scowling helplessly around.*] My goodness! . . one can never find anything in this house.

MR. COLPUS. I won't say good-bye then.

> *He is sliding through the half opened door when* ETHEL *meets him flinging it wide. She is the younger daughter, the baby of the family, but twenty-three now.*

MR. VOYSEY. I say, it's cold again to-night! An ass of an architect who built this place . . such a draught between these two doors.

> *He gets up to draw the curtain. When he turns* COLPUS *has disappeared, while* ETHEL *has been followed into the room by* ALICE MAITLAND, *who shuts*

the door after her. MISS ALICE MAITLAND *is a
young lady of any age to thirty. Nor need her
appearance alter for the next fifteen years; since
her nature is healthy and well-balanced. She possesses indeed the sort of athletic chastity which is
a characteristic charm of Northern spinsterhood.
It mayn't be a pretty face, but it has alertness and
humour; and the resolute eyes and eyebrows are a
more innocent edition of* MR. VOYSEY'S, *who is her
uncle.* ETHEL *goes straight to her father* [*though
her glance is on* DENIS *and his on her*] *and chirps,
birdlike, in her spoiled-child way.*

ETHEL.   We think you've stayed in here quite long
enough.

MR. VOYSEY.   That's to say, Ethel thinks Denis has been
kept out of her pocket much too long.

ETHEL.   Ethel wants billiards . . not proper billiards . .
snooker or something.   Oh, Papa, what a dessert you've
eaten.   Greedy pig!

ALICE *is standing behind* EDWARD, *considering his
hair-parting apparently.*

ALICE.   Crack me a filbert, please, Edward . . I had
none.

EDWARD.   [*Jumping up, rather formally, well-mannered.*]
I beg your pardon, Alice.   Won't you sit down?

ALICE.   No.

MR. VOYSEY.   [*Taking* ETHEL *on his knee.*]   Come here,
puss.   Have you made up your mind yet what you want
for a wedding present?

ETHEL.   [*Rectifying a stray hair in his beard.*]   After
mature consideration, I decide on a cheque.

MR. VOYSEY.   Do you!

ETHEL.   Yes, I think that a cheque will give most scope
to your generosity.   Of course, if you desire to add any
trimmings in the shape of a piano or a Turkey carpet you

may . . and Denis and I will be very grateful. But I think I'd let yourself go over a cheque.

MR. VOYSEY. You're a minx.

ETHEL. What is the use of having money if you don't spend it on me?

MAJOR BOOTH VOYSEY. [*Giving up the cigar search.*] Here, who's going to play?

MR. GEORGE BOOTH. [*Pathetically as he gets up.*] Well, if my wrist will hold out . .

MAJOR BOOTH VOYSEY. [*To* TREGONING.] No, don't you bother to look for them. [*He strides from the room, his voice echoing through the hall.*] Honor, where are those Ramon Allones?

ALICE. [*Calling after.*] She's in the drawing-room with Auntie and Mr. Colpus.

MR. VOYSEY. Now I should suggest that you and Denis go and take off the billiard table cover. You'll find folding it up is a very excellent amusement.

> *He illustrates his meaning with his table napkin and by putting together the tips of his forefingers, roguishly.*

ETHEL. I am not going to blush. I do kiss Denis . . occasionally . . when he asks me.

MR. GEORGE BOOTH. [*Teasing her.*] You are blushing.

ETHEL. I am not. If you think we're ashamed of being in love, we're not, we're very proud of it. We will go and take off the billiard table cover and fold it up . . and then you can come in and play. Denis, my dear, come along solemnly, and if you flinch I'll never forgive you. [*She marches off and reaches the door before her defiant dignity breaks down; then suddenly—*] Denis, I'll race you.

> *And she flashes out.* DENIS, *loyal, but with no histrionic instincts, follows her rather sheepishly.*

DENIS. Ethel, I can't after dinner.

MR. VOYSEY.   Women play that game better than men.
A man shuffles through courtship with one eye on her
relations.

> *The Major comes stalking back, followed in a fear-
> ful flurry by his elder sister,* HONOR.   *Poor* HONOR
> [*her female friends are apt to refer to her as Poor*
> HONOR] *is a phenomenon common to most large
> families.   From her earliest years she has been bot-
> tle washer to her brothers.   While they were expen-
> sively educated, she was grudged schooling; her
> highest accomplishment was meant to be mending
> their clothes.   Her fate is a curious survival of the
> intolerance of parents towards her sex until the
> vanity of their hunger for sons had been satisfied.
> In a less humane society she would have been ex-
> posed at birth.   But if a very general though pat-
> ronising affection, accompanied by no consideration
> at all, can bestow happiness,* HONOR *is not unhappy
> in her survival.   At this moment, however, her life
> is a burden.*

MAJOR BOOTH VOYSEY.   Honor, they are not in the dining-
room.

HONOR.   But they must be!   Where else can they be?

> *She has a habit of accentuating one word in each
> sentence, and often the wrong one.*

MAJOR BOOTH VOYSEY.   That's what you ought to know.

MR. VOYSEY.   [*As he moves towards the door.*]   Well . .
will you have a game?

MR. GEORGE BOOTH.   I'll play you fifty up, not more.   I'm
getting old.

MR. VOYSEY.   [*Stopping at a dessert dish.*]   Yes, these
are good apples of Bearman's.   I think six of my trees
are spoilt this year.

HONOR.   Here you are, Booth.

She triumphantly discovers the discarded box, at which the Major becomes pathetic with indignation.

MAJOR BOOTH VOYSEY. Oh, Honor, don't be such a fool. These are what we've been smoking. I want the Ramon Allones.

HONOR. I don't know the difference.

MAJOR BOOTH VOYSEY. No, you don't; but you might learn.

MR. VOYSEY. [*In a voice like the crack of a very fine whip.*] Booth.

MAJOR BOOTH VOYSEY. [*Subduedly.*] What is it, sir?

MR. VOYSEY. Look for your cigars yourself. Honor, go back to your reading and your sewing, or whatever you were fiddling at, and fiddle in peace.

MR. VOYSEY departs, leaving the room rather hushed. MR. BOOTH has not waited for this parental display. Then ALICE insinuates a remark very softly.

ALICE. Have you looked in the Library?

MAJOR BOOTH VOYSEY. [*Relapsing to an injured mutter.*] Where's Emily?

HONOR. Upstairs with little Henry; he woke up and cried.

MAJOR BOOTH VOYSEY. Letting her wear herself to rags over the child . . !

HONOR. Well, she won't let me go.

MAJOR BOOTH VOYSEY. Why don't you stop looking for those cigars?

HONOR. If you don't mind, I want a reel of blue silk now I'm here.

MAJOR BOOTH VOYSEY. I daresay they are in the Library. What a house!

He departs.

HONOR. Booth is so trying.

ALICE. Honor, why do you put up with it?

HONOR. Someone has to.

ALICE. [*Discreetly nibbling a nut which EDWARD has*

cracked for her.] I'm afraid I think Master Major Booth ought to have been taken in hand early . . with a cane.

HONOR. [*As she vaguely burrows into corners.*] Papa did. But it's never prevented him booming at us . . oh, ever since he was a baby. Now he's flustered me so I simply can't think where this blue silk is.

ALICE. All the Pettifers desired to be remembered to you, Edward.

HONOR. I must do without it. [*But she goes on looking.*] I think, Alice, that we're a very difficult family . . except perhaps Edward.

EDWARD. Why except me?

HONOR. [*Who has only excepted out of politeness to present company.*] Well, you may be difficult . . to yourself. [*Then she starts to go, threading her way through the disarranged chairs.*] Mr. Colpus will shout so loud at Mother, and she hates people to think she's so very deaf. I thought Mary Pettifer looking old . . [*And she talks herself out of the room.*]

ALICE. [*After her.*] She's getting old.

Now ALICE *does sit down; as if she'd be glad of her tête-à-tête.*

ALICE. I was glad not to spend August abroad for once. We drove into Cheltenham to a dance . . carpet. I golfed a lot.

EDWARD. How long were you with them?

ALICE. Not a fortnight. It doesn't seem three months since I was here, does it?

EDWARD. I'm down so very little.

ALICE. I'm here a disgraceful deal.

EDWARD. You know they're always pleased.

ALICE. Well, being a homeless person! But what a cart-load to descend all at once . . yesterday and to-day. The Major and Emily . . Emily's not at all well. Hugh and Mrs. Hugh. And me. Are you staying?

EDWARD. No. I must get a word with my father . .

ALICE. A business life is not healthy for you, Edward. You look more like half-baked pie-crust than usual.

EDWARD. [*A little enviously.*] You're very well.

ALICE. I'm always well, and nearly always happy.

MAJOR BOOTH *returns. He has the right sort of cigar in his mouth, and is considerably mollified.*

ALICE. You found them?

MAJOR BOOTH VOYSEY. Of course, they were there. Thank you very much, Alice. Now I want a knife.

ALICE. I must present you with a cigar-cutter, Booth.

MAJOR BOOTH VOYSEY. I hate 'em. [*He eyes the dessert disparagingly.*] Nothing but silver ones.

EDWARD *hands him a carefully opened pocket knife.* Thank you, Edward. And I must take one of the candles. Something's gone wrong with the library ventilator and you never can see a thing in that room.

ALICE. Is Mrs. Hugh there?

MAJOR BOOTH VOYSEY. Writing letters. Things are neglected, Edward, unless one is constantly on the look out. The Pater only cares for his garden. I must speak seriously to Honor.

He has returned the knife, still open, and now having lit his cigar at the candle he carries this off.

ALICE. Honor has the patience of a . . of an old maid.

EDWARD. Her mission in life isn't a pleasant one. [*He gives her a nut, about the fifteenth.*] Here; 'scuse fingers.

ALICE. Thank you. [*Looking at him, with her head on one side and her face more humorous than ever.*] Edward, why have you given up proposing to me?

He starts, flushes; then won't be outdone in humour.

EDWARD. One can't go on proposing for ever.

ALICE. [*Reasonably.*] Why not? Have you seen anyone you like better?

EDWARD. No.

ALICE. Well . . I miss it.

EDWARD. What satisfaction did you find in refusing me?

ALICE. [*As she weighs the matter.*] I find satisfaction in feeling that I'm wanted.

EDWARD. Without any intention of giving yourself . . throwing yourself away.

ALICE. [*Teasing his sudden earnestness.*] Ah, now you come from mere vanity to serious questions.

EDWARD. Mine were always serious questions to you.

ALICE. That's a fault I find in you, Edward; all questions are serious to you. I call you a perfect little pocket-guide to life . . all questions and answers; what to eat, drink and avoid, what to believe and what to say . . all in the same type, the same importance attached to each.

EDWARD. [*Sententiously.*] Well . . everything matters.

ALICE. [*Making a face.*] D'you plan out every detail of your life . . every step you take . . every mouthful?

EDWARD. That would be waste of thought. One must lay down principles.

ALICE. I prefer my plan, I always do what I know I want to do. Crack me another nut.

EDWARD. Haven't you had enough?

ALICE. I k n o w I want one more.

> *He cracks another, with a sigh which sounds ridiculous in that connection.*

EDWARD. Well, if you've never had to decide anything very serious . .

ALICE. [*With great gravity.*] Everything's serious.

EDWARD. Everything isn't vital.

ALICE. [*Skilfully manœuvring the subject.*] I've answered vital questions. I knew that I didn't want to marry you . . each time.

EDWARD. Oh, then you didn't just make a rule of saying no.

ALICE. As you proposed . . on principle? No, I al-

ways gave you a fair chance. I'll give you one now if
you like.

> *He rouses himself to play up to this outrageous
> piece of flirting.*

EDWARD. I'm not to be caught.

ALICE. Edward, how rude you are. [*She eats her nut
contentedly.*]

EDWARD. Do other men propose to you?

ALICE. Such a thing may have happened . . when I
was young. Perhaps it might even now if I were to
allow it.

EDWARD. You encourage me shamelessly.

ALICE. It isn't everyone who proposes on principle.
As a rule a man does it because he can't help himself.
And then to be said no to . . hurts.

> *They are interrupted by the sudden appearance of
> MRS. HUGH VOYSEY, a brisk, bright little woman,
> in an evening gown, which she has bullied a cheap
> dressmaker into making look exceedingly smart.
> BEATRICE is as hard as nails and as clever as paint.
> But if she keeps her feelings buried pretty deep it
> is because they are precious to her; and if she is im-
> patient with fools it is because her own brains have
> had to win her everything in the world, so perhaps
> she does overvalue them a little. She speaks always
> with great decision and little effort.*

BEATRICE. I believe I could write important business
letters upon an island in the middle of Fleet Street. But
while Booth is poking at a ventilator with a billiard cue
. . no, I can't.

> *She goes to the fireplace, waving her half finished
> letter.*

ALICE. [*Soothingly.*] Didn't you expect Hugh back to
dinner?

BEATRICE. Not specially . . He went to rout out some things from his studio. He'll come back in a filthy mess.

ALICE. Now if you listen . . Booth doesn't enjoy making a fuss by himself . . you'll hear him rout out Honor.

They listen. But what happens is that BOOTH *appears at the door, billiard cue in hand, and says solemnly . .*

MAJOR BOOTH VOYSEY. Edward, I wish you'd come and have a look at this ventilator, like a good fellow.

Then he turns and goes again, obviously with the weight of an important matter on his shoulders. With the ghost of a smile EDWARD *gets up and follows him.*

ALICE. If I belonged to this family I should hate Booth.

With which comment she joins BEATRICE *at the fireplace.*

BEATRICE. A good day's shopping?

ALICE. 'M. The baby bride and I bought clothes all the morning. Then we had lunch with Denis and bought furniture.

BEATRICE. Nice furniture?

ALICE. It'll be very good and very new. They neither of them know what they want. [*Then suddenly throwing up her chin and exclaiming.*] When it's a question of money I can understand it . . but if one can provide for oneself or is independent why get married! Especially having been brought up on the sheltered life principle . . one may as well make the most of its advantages . . one doesn't go falling in love all over the place as men seem to . . most of them. Of course with Ethel and Denis it's different. They've both been caught young. They're two little birds building their nests and it's all ideal. They'll soon forget they've ever been apart.

Now HONOR *flutters into the room, patient but wild eyed.*

HONOR. Mother wants last week's Notes and Queries. Have you seen it?

BEATRICE. [*Exasperated at the interruption.*] No.

HONOR. It ought not to be in here. [*So she proceeds to look for it.*] She's having a long argument with Mr. Colpus over Oliver Cromwell's relations.

ALICE. [*Her eyes twinkling.*] I thought Auntie didn't approve of Oliver Cromwell.

HONOR. She doesn't and she's trying to prove that he was a brewer or something. I suppose someone has taken it away.

So she gives up the search and flutters out again.

ALICE. This is a most unrestful house.

REATRICE. I once thought of putting the Voyseys into a book of mine. Then I concluded they'd be as dull there as they are anywhere else.

ALICE. They're not duller than most other people.

BEATRICE. But how very dull that is!

ALICE. They're a little noisier and perhaps not quite so well mannered. But I love them.

BEATRICE. I don't. I should have thought Love was just what they couldn't inspire.

ALICE. Of course, Hugh is unlike any of the others.

BEATRICE. He has most of their bad points. I don't love Hugh.

ALICE. [*Her eyebrows up, though she smiles.*] Beatrice, you shouldn't say so.

BEATRICE. It sounds affected, doesn't it? Never mind; when he dies I'll wear mourning . . but not weeds; I bargained against that when we were engaged.

ALICE. [*Her face growing a little thoughtful.*] Beatrice, I'm going to ask questions. You were in love with Hugh when you married him?

BEATRICE. Well . . I married him for his money.

ALICE. He hadn't much.

BEATRICE. I had none . . and I wanted to write books.
Yes, I loved him.

ALICE. And you thought you'd be happy?

BEATRICE. [*Considering carefully.*]   No, I didn't.   I
hoped he'd be happy.

ALICE. [*A little ironical.*] Did you think your writing
books would make him so?

BEATRICE. My dear Alice, wouldn't you feel it a very
degrading thing to have your happiness depend upon somebody else?

ALICE. [*After pausing to find her phrase.*] There's a
joy of service.

BEATRICE. [*Ironical herself now.*] I forgot . . you've
four hundred a year?

ALICE. What has that to do with it?

BEATRICE. [*Putting her case very precisely.*] I've had
to earn my own living, consequently there isn't one thing
in my life that I have ever done quite genuinely for its
own sake . . but always with an eye towards bread-and-
butter, pandering to the people who were to give me that.
Happiness has been my only independence.

> *The conservatory door opens, and through it come*
> MR. VOYSEY *and* MR. BOOTH, *in the midst of a discus-*
> *sion.*

MR. VOYSEY. Very well, man, stick to the shares and
risk it.

MR. GEORGE BOOTH. No, of course, if you seriously advise me——

MR. VOYSEY. I never advise greedy children. I let 'em
overeat 'emselves, and take the consequences——

ALICE. [*Shaking a finger.*] Uncle Trench, you've been
in the garden without a hat, after playing billiards in that
hot room.

MR. GEORGE BOOTH. We had to give up . . my wrist
was bad. They've started pool.

BEATRICE. Is Booth going to play?

MR. VOYSEY. We left him instructing Ethel how to hold a cue.

BEATRICE. Perhaps I can finish my letter.

Off she goes. ALICE *is idly following with a little paper her hand has fallen on behind the clock.*

MR. VOYSEY. Don't run away, my dear.

ALICE. I'm taking this to Auntie . . Notes and Queries . . she wants it.

MR. GEORGE BOOTH. Damn . . this gravel's stuck to my shoe.

MR. VOYSEY. That's a new made path.

MR. GEORGE BOOTH. Now don't you think it's too early to have put in those plants?

MR. VOYSEY. No. We're getting frost at night already.

MR. GEORGE BOOTH. I should have kept that bed a good ten feet further from the tree.

MR. VOYSEY. Nonsense. The tree's to the north of it. This room's cold. Why don't they keep the fire up! [*He proceeds to put coals on it.*]

MR. GEORGE BOOTH. You were too hot in that billiard room. You know, Voysey . . about those Alguazils?

MR. VOYSEY. [*Through the rattling of the coals.*] What?

MR. GEORGE BOOTH. [*Trying to pierce the din.*] Those Alguazils.

MR. VOYSEY, *with surprising inconsequence, points a finger at the silk handkerchief across* MR. BOOTH'S *shirt front.*

MR. VOYSEY. What d'you put your handkerchief there for?

MR. GEORGE BOOTH. Measure of precau— [*At that moment he sneezes.*] Damn it . . if you've given me a chill dragging me round your infernal garden——

MR. VOYSEY. [*Slapping him on the back.*] You're an old crook.

MR. GEORGE BOOTH. Well, I'll be glad of this winter in Egypt. [*He returns to his subject.*] And if you think seriously that I ought to sell out of the Alguazils before I go . . ? [*He looks with childlike enquiry at his friend, who is apparently yawning slightly.*] Why can't you take them in charge? . . and I'll give you a power of attorney or whatever it is . . and you can sell out if things look bad.

> At this moment PHŒBE, *the middle aged parlour-maid, comes in, tray in hand. Like an expert fisherman,* MR. VOYSEY *once more lets loose the thread of the conversation.*

MR. VOYSEY. D'you want to clear?

PHŒBE. It doesn't matter, sir.

MR. VOYSEY. No, go on . . go on.

> So MARY, *the young housemaid, comes in as well, and the two start to clear the table. All of which fidgets poor* MR. BOOTH *considerably. He sits shrivelled up in his armchair by the fire; and now* MR. VOYSEY *attends to him.*

MR. VOYSEY. What d'you want with high interest at all . . you never spend half your income?

MR. GEORGE BOOTH. I like to feel that my money is doing some good in the world. These mines are very useful things, and forty-two per cent. is pleasing.

MR. VOYSEY. You're an old gambler.

MR. GEORGE BOOTH. [*Propitiatingly.*] Ah, but then I've you to advise me. I always do as you tell me in the end, now you can't deny that.

MR. VOYSEY. The man who don't know must trust in the man who does! [*He yawns again.*]

MR. GEORGE BOOTH. [*Modestly insisting.*] There's five thousand in Alguazils—what else could we put it into?

MR. VOYSEY. I can get you something at four and a half.

MR. GEORGE BOOTH. Oh, Lord . . that's nothing.

MR. VOYSEY. [*With a sudden serious friendliness.*] I

wish, my dear George, you'd invest more on your own account. You know—what with one thing and the other—I've got control of practically all you have in the world. I might be playing old Harry with it for all you know.

MR. GEORGE BOOTH. [*Overflowing with confidence.*] My dear feller . . if I'm satisfied! Ah, my friend, what'll happen to your firm when you depart this life! . . not before my time, I hope, though.

MR. VOYSEY. [*With a little frown.*] What d'ye mean?

MR. GEORGE BOOTH. Edward's no use.

MR. VOYSEY. I beg your pardon . . very sound in business.

MR. GEORGE BOOTH. May be . . but I tell you he's no use. Too many principles, as I said just now. Men have confidence in a personality, not in principles. Where would you be without the confidence of your clients?

MR. VOYSEY. [*Candidly.*] True!

MR. GEORGE BOOTH. He'll never gain that.

MR. VOYSEY. I fear you dislike Edward.

MR. GEORGE BOOTH. [*With pleasant frankness.*] Yes, I do.

MR. VOYSEY. That's a pity.

MR. GEORGE BOOTH. [*With a flattering smile.*] Well, he's not his father and never will be. What's the time?

MR. VOYSEY. [*With inappropriate thoughtfulness.*] Twenty to ten.

MR. GEORGE BOOTH. I must be trotting.

MR. VOYSEY. It's very early.

MR. GEORGE BOOTH. Oh, and I've not said a word to Mrs. Voysey . .

> *As he goes to the door he meets* EDWARD, *who comes in apparently looking for his father; at any rate catches his eye immediately, while* MR. BOOTH *obliviously continues.*

MR. GEORGE BOOTH. Will you stroll round home with me?

MR. VOYSEY. I can't.

MR. GEORGE BOOTH. [*Mildly surprised at the short reply.*] Well, good night. Good night, Edward.

He trots away.

MR. VOYSEY. Leave the rest of the table, Phœbe.

PHŒBE. Yes, sir.

MR. VOYSEY. You can come back in ten minutes.

PHŒBE *and* MARY *depart and the door is closed. Alone with his son* MR. VOYSEY *does not move; his face grows a little keener, that's all.*

MR. VOYSEY. Well, Edward?

EDWARD *starts to move restlessly about, like a cowed animal in a cage; silently for a moment or two. Then when he speaks, his voice is toneless and he doesn't look at his father.*

EDWARD. I should like you now, sir, if you don't mind, to drop with me all these protestations about putting the firm's affairs straight, and all your anxieties and sacrifices to that end. I see now, of course . . what a cleverer man than I could have seen yesterday . . that for some time, ever since, I suppose, you recovered from the first shock and got used to the double dealing, this hasn't been your object at all. You've used your clients' capital to produce your own income . . to bring us up and endow us with. Booth's ten thousand pounds; what you are giving Ethel on her marriage . . It's odd it never struck me yesterday that my own pocket money as a boy was probably withdrawn from some client's account. You've been very generous to us all, Father. I suppose about half the sum you've spent on us would have put things right.

MR. VOYSEY. No, it would not.

EDWARD. [*Appealing for the truth.*] Oh . . at some time or other!

MR. VOYSEY. Well, if there have been good times there have been bad times. At present the three hundred a year I'm to allow your sister is going to be rather a pull.

EDWARD. Three hundred a year . . and yet you've never attempted to put a single account straight. Since it isn't lunacy, sir . . I can only conclude that you enjoy being in this position.

MR. VOYSEY. I have put accounts absolutely straight . . at the winding up of a trust for instance . . at great inconvenience too. And to all appearances they've been above suspicion. What's the object of all this rodomontade, Edward?

EDWARD. If I'm to remain in the firm, it had better be with a very clear understanding of things as they are.

MR. VOYSEY. [*Firmly, not too anxiously.*] Then you do remain?

EDWARD. [*In a very low voice.*] Yes, I remain.

MR. VOYSEY. [*Quite gravely.*] That's wise of you . . I'm very glad. [*And he is silent for a moment.*] And now we needn't discuss the impractical side of it any more.

EDWARD. But I want to make one condition. And I want some information.

MR. VOYSEY. [*His sudden cheerfulness relapsing again.*] Well?

EDWARD. Of course no one has ever discovered . . and no one suspects this state of things?

MR. VOYSEY. Peacey knows.

EDWARD. Peacey!

MR. VOYSEY. His father found out.

EDWARD. Oh. Does he draw hush money?

MR. VOYSEY. [*Curling a little at the word.*] It is my custom to make a little present every Christmas. Not a cheque . . notes in an envelope. [*He becomes benevolent.*] I don't grude the money . . Peacey's a devoted fellow.

EDWARD. Naturally this would be a heavily taxed industry. [*Then he smiles at his vision of the mild old clerk.*] Peacey! There's another thing I want to ask, sir. Have you ever under stress of circumstances done worse than just make use of a client's capital? You boasted to me yesterday that no one had ever suffered in pocket because of you. Is that absolutely true?

MR. VOYSEY *draws himself up, dignified and magniloquent.*

MR. VOYSEY. My dear Edward, for the future my mind is open to you, you can discover for yourself how matters stand to-day. But I decline to gratify your curiosity as to what is over and done with.

EDWARD. [*With entire comprehension.*] Thank you, sir. The condition I wish to make is that we should really do what we have pretended to be doing . . try and put the accounts straight.

MR. VOYSEY. [*With a little polite shrug.*] I've no doubt you'll prove an abler man of business than I.

EDWARD. One by one.

MR. VOYSEY. Which one will you begin with?

EDWARD. I shall begin, Father, by halving the salary I draw from the firm.

MR. VOYSEY. I see . . Retrenchment and Reform.

EDWARD. And I think you cannot give Ethel this five thousand pounds dowry.

MR. VOYSEY. [*Shortly, with one of the quick twists of his eye.*] I have given my word to Denis.

EDWARD. The money isn't yours to give.

MR. VOYSEY. [*In an indignant crescendo.*] I should not dream of depriving Ethel of what, as my daughter, she has every right to expect. I am surprised at your suggesting such a thing.

EDWARD. [*Pale and firm.*] I'm set on this, Father.

MR. VOYSEY. Don't be such a fool, Edward.   What

would it look like . . suddenly to refuse without rhyme or reason? What would old Tregoning think?

EDWARD. [*Distressed.*] You could give them a reason.

MR. VOYSEY. Perhaps you'll invent one.

EDWARD. If need be, Ethel should be told the truth.

MR. VOYSEY. What!

EDWARD. I know it would hurt her.

MR. VOYSEY. And Denis told too, I suppose?

EDWARD. Father, it is my duty to do whatever is necessary to prevent this.

MR. VOYSEY. It'll be necessary to tell the nearest policeman. It is my duty to pay no more attention to these scruples of yours than a nurse pays to her child's tantrums. Understand, Edward, I don't want to force you to continue my partner. Come with me gladly or don't come at all.

EDWARD. [*Dully.*] It is my duty to be of what use I can to you, sir. Father, I want to save you if I can.

> *He flashes into this exclamation of almost broken-hearted affection.* MR. VOYSEY *looks at his son for a moment and his lip quivers. Then he steels himself.*

MR. VOYSEY. Thank you! I have saved myself quite satisfactorily for the last thirty years, and you must please believe that by this time I know my own business best.

EDWARD. [*Hopelessly.*] Let the money come some other way. How is your own income regulated?

MR. VOYSEY. I have a bank balance and a cheque book, haven't I? I spend what I think well to spend. What's the use of earmarking this or that as my own? You say none of it is my own. I might say it's all my own. I think I've earned it.

EDWARD. [*Anger coming on him.*] That's what I can't forgive. If you'd lived poor . . if you'd really devoted your skill to your clients' good and not to your aggrandisement . . then, even though things were only as they are

now, I could have been proud of you. But, Father, own
the truth to me, at least . . that's my due from you, considering how I'm placed by all you've done. Didn't you
simply seize this opportunity as a means to your own end,
to your own enriching?

MR. VOYSEY. [*With a sledge hammer irony.*] Certainly.
I sat that morning in my father's office, studying the hel-
met of the policeman in the street below, and thinking
what a glorious path I had happened on to wealth and honour and renown. [*Then he begins to bully* EDWARD *in the
kindliest way.*] My dear boy, you evidently haven't begun
to grasp the A B C of my position. What has carried me
to victory? The confidence of my clients. What has
earned that confidence? A decent life, my integrity, my
brains? No, my reputation for wealth . . that, and nothing else. Business now-a-days is run on the lines of the
confidence trick. What makes old George Booth so glad
to trust me with every penny he possesses? Not affection
. . he's never cared for anything in his life but his collection of prints. No; he imagines that I have as big a stake
in the country, as he calls it, as he has, and he's perfectly
happy.

EDWARD. [*Stupefied, helpless.*] So he's involved!

MR. VOYSEY. Of course he's involved, and he's always
after high interest, too . . it's little one makes out of him.
But there's a further question here, Edward. Should I
have had confidence in myself if I'd remained a poor man?
No, I should not. You must either be the master of money
or its servant. And if one is not opulent in one's daily life
one loses that wonderful . . financier's touch. One must
be confident oneself . . and I saw from the first that I
must inspire confidence. My whole public and private life
has tended to that. All my surroundings . . you and your
brothers and sisters that I have brought into, and up, and

put out in the world so worthily . . you in your turn inspire confidence.

EDWARD. Not our worth, not our abilities, nor our virtues, but the fact that we travel first class and ride in hansoms.

MR. VOYSEY. [*Impatiently.*] Well, I haven't organised Society upon a basis of wealth.

EDWARD. Is every single person who trusts you involved in your system?

MR. VOYSEY. What new hole are you finding to pick in my conduct?

EDWARD. My mind travelled naturally from George Booth, with his big income, to old Nursie, with her savings which she brought you to invest. You've let those be, at least.

MR. VOYSEY. I never troubled to invest them . . it wasn't worth while.

EDWARD. Father!

MR. VOYSEY. D'you know what she brought me? . . five hundred pounds.

EDWARD. That's damnable.

MR. VOYSEY. Indeed. I give her seventy-five pounds a year for it. Would you like to take charge of that account, Edward? I'll give you five hundred to invest to-morrow.

> EDWARD, *hopelessly beaten, falls into an almost comic*
> *state of despair.*

EDWARD. My dear Father, putting every moral question aside . . it's all very well your playing Robin Hood in this magnificent manner; but have you given a moment's thought to the sort of inheritance you'll be leaving me?

MR. VOYSEY. [*Pleased for the first time.*] Ah! That is a question you have every right to ask.

EDWARD. If you died to-morrow, could we pay eight shillings in the pound . . or seventeen . . or five? Do you know?

MR. VOYSEY. And my answer is, that by your help I
have every intention, when I die, of leaving a will behind
me of property to you all running into six figures. D'you
think I've given my life and my talents to this money
making for a less result than that? I'm fond of you all . .
and I want you to be proud of me .. and I mean that the
name of Voysey shall be carried high in the world by my
children and grandchildren. Don't you be afraid, Edward.
Ah, you lack experience, my boy . . you're not full grown
yet . . your impulses are a bit chaotic. You emotionalise
over your work, and you reason about your emotions. You
must sort yourself. You must realise that money making
is one thing, and religion another, and family-life a third
. . and that if we apply our energies whole-heartedly to
each of these in turn, and realise that different laws govern each, that there is a different end to be served, a different ideal to be striven for in each——

> *His coherence is saved by the sudden appearance of
> his wife, who comes round the door, smiling be-
> nignly. Not in the least put out, in fact, a little
> relieved, he greets her with an affectionate shout,
> for she is very deaf.*

MR. VOYSEY. Hullo, Mother!

MRS. VOYSEY. Oh, there you are, Trench. I've been
deserted.

MR. VOYSEY. George Booth gone?

MRS. VOYSEY. Are you talking business? Perhaps you
don't want me.

MR. VOYSEY. No, no . . no business.

MRS. VOYSEY. [*Who has not looked for his answer.*] I
suppose the others are in the billiard room.

MR. VOYSEY. [*Vociferously.*] We're not talking business, old lady.

EDWARD. I'll be off, sir.

MR. VOYSEY. [*Genial as usual.*] Why don't you stay? I'll come up with you in the morning.

EDWARD. No, thank you, sir.

MR. VOYSEY. Then I shall be up about noon to-morrow.

EDWARD. Good-night, Mother.

MRS. VOYSEY *places a plump, kindly hand on his arm and looks up affectionately.*

MRS. VOYSEY. You look tired.

EDWARD. No, I'm not.

MRS. VOYSEY. What did you say?

EDWARD. [*Too weary to repeat himself.*] Nothing, Mother dear.

He kisses her cheek, while she kisses the air.

MR. VOYSEY. Good-night, my boy.

Then he goes. MRS. VOYSEY *is carrying her Notes and Queries. This is a dear old lady, looking older, too, than probably she is. Placid describes her. She has had a life of little joys and cares, has never measured herself against the world, never even questioned the shape and size of the little corner of it in which she lives. She has loved an indulgent husband, and borne eight children, six of them surviving, healthy. That is her history.*

MRS. VOYSEY. George Booth went some time ago. He said he thought you'd taken a chill walking round the garden.

MR. VOYSEY. I'm all right.

MRS. VOYSEY. D'you think you have?

MR. VOYSEY. [*In her ear.*] No.

MRS. VOYSEY. You should be careful, Trench. What did you put on?

MR. VOYSEY. Nothing.

MRS. VOYSEY. How very foolish! Let me feel your hand. You are quite feverish.

MR. VOYSEY. [*Affectionately.*] You're a fuss-box, old
lady.

MRS. VOYSEY. [*Coquetting with him.*] Don't be rude,
Trench.

> HONOR *descends upon them. She is well into that
> nightly turmoil of putting everything and every-
> body to rights which always precedes her bed-time.
> She carries a shawl which she clasps round her
> mother's shoulders, her mind and gaze already on
> the next thing to be done.*

HONOR. Mother, you left your shawl in the drawing-
room. Can they finish clearing?

MR. VOYSEY. [*Arranging the folds of the shawl with
real tenderness.*] Now who's careless!

> PHŒBE *comes into the room.*

HONOR. Phœbe, finish here and then you must bring in
the tray for Mr. Hugh.

MRS. VOYSEY. [*Having looked at the shawl, and* HONOR,
and connected the matter in her mind.] Thank you, Honor.
You'd better look after your Father; he's been walking
round the garden without his cape.

HONOR. Papa!

MR. VOYSEY. Phœbe, you get that little kettle and boil
it, and brew me some hot whiskey and water. I shall be
all right.

HONOR. [*Fluttering more than ever.*] I'll get it.
Where's the whiskey? And Hugh coming back at ten
o'clock with no dinner. No wonder his work goes wrong.
Here it is. Papa, you do deserve to be ill.

> *Clasping the whiskey decanter, she is off again.*
> MRS. VOYSEY *sits at the dinner table and adjusts
> her spectacles. She returns to Notes and Queries,
> one elbow firmly planted and her plump hand
> against her plump cheek. This is her favourite at-
> titude; and she is apt, when reading, to soliloquise*

*in her deaf woman's voice. At least, whether she
considers it soliloquy or conversation, is not easy to
discover.* MR. VOYSEY *stands with his back to the
fire, grumbling and pulling faces.*

MRS. VOYSEY. This is a very perplexing correspondence
about the Cromwell family. One can't deny the man had
good blood in him . . his grandfather Sir Henry, his
uncle Sir Oliver . . and it's difficult to discover where
the taint crept in.

MR. VOYSEY. There's a pain in my back. I believe I
strained myself putting in all those strawberry plants.

MARY, *the house parlour maid, carries in a tray of
warmed-up dinner for* HUGH *and plants it on the
table.*

MRS. VOYSEY. Yes, but then how was it he came to
disgrace himself so? I believe the family disappeared.
Regicide is a root and branch curse. You must read this
letter signed C. W. A. . . it's quite interesting. There's
a misprint in mine about the first umbrella maker . . now
where was it . . [*And so the dear lady will ramble on
indefinitely.*]

THE THIRD ACT

*The dining-room looks very different in the white light
of a July noon. Moreover on this particular day,
it isn't even its normal self. There is a peculiar
luncheon spread on the table. The embroidered
cloth is placed cornerwise and on it are decanters of
port and sherry; sandwiches, biscuits and an uncut
cake; two little piles of plates and one little pile of
napkins. There are no table decorations and indeed
the whole room has been made as bare and as tidy
as possible. Such preparations denote one of the
recognised English festivities, and the appearance
of* PHŒBE, *the maid, who has just completed them,
the set solemnity of her face and the added touches
of black to her dress and cap, suggest that this is
probably a funeral. When* MARY *comes in the fact
that she has evidently been crying and that she decorously does not raise her voice above an unpleasant whisper makes it quite certain.*

MARY.   Phœbe, they're coming . . and I forgot one of
the blinds in the drawing room.

PHŒBE.   Well, pull it up quick and make yourself
scarce. I'll open the door.

MARY *got rid of,* PHŒBE *composes her face still
more rigorously into the aspect of formal grief and
with a touch to her apron as well goes to admit the
funeral party. The first to enter are* MRS. VOYSEY
and MR. BOOTH, *she on his arm; and the fact that*

> *she is in widow's weeds makes the occasion clear.*
> *The little old man leads his old friend very tenderly.*

MR. GEORGE BOOTH.   Will you come in here?

MRS. VOYSEY.   Thank you.

> *With great solicitude he puts her in a chair; then*
> *takes her hand.*

MR. GEORGE BOOTH.   Now I'll intrude no longer.

MRS. VOYSEY.   You'll take some lunch?

MR. GEORGE BOOTH.   No.

MRS. VOYSEY.   Not a glass of wine?

MR. GEORGE BOOTH.   If there's anything I can do just send round.

MRS. VOYSEY.   Thank you.

> *He reaches the door, only to be met by the Major*
> *and his wife. He shakes hands with them both.*

MR. GEORGE BOOTH.   My dear Emily! My dear Booth!

> EMILY *is a homely, patient, pale little woman of*
> *about thirty-five. She looks smaller than usual in*
> *her heavy black dress and is meeker than usual on*
> *an occasion of this kind. The Major, on the other*
> *hand, though his grief is most sincere, has an ir-*
> *resistible air of being responsible for, and indeed*
> *rather proud of the whole affair.*

BOOTH.   I think it all went off as he would have wished.

MR. GEORGE BOOTH.   [*Feeling that he is called on for praise.*]   Great credit . . great credit.

> *He makes another attempt to escape and is stopped*
> *this time by* TRENCHARD VOYSEY, *to whom he is ex-*
> *tending a hand and beginning his formula. But*
> TRENCHARD *speaks first.*

TRENCHARD.   Have you the right time?

MR. GEORGE BOOTH.   [*Taken aback and fumbling for his watch.*]   I think so . . I make it fourteen minutes to one. [*He seizes the occasion.*]   Trenchard, as a very old and dear friend of your father's, you won't mind me saying how glad I was that you were present to-day. Death closes all. Indeed . . it must be a great regret to you that you did not see him before . . before . .

TRENCHARD. [*His cold eye freezing this little gush.*] I don't think he asked for me.

MR. GEORGE BOOTH. [*Stoppered.*] No? No! Well . . well . . .

> *At this third attempt to depart he actually collides with someone in the doorway. It is* HUGH VOYSEY.

MR. GEORGE BOOTH. My dear Hugh . . I won't intrude. *Quite determined to escape, he grasps his hand, gasps out his formula and is off.* TRENCHARD *and* HUGH, *eldest and youngest son, are as unlike each other as it is possible for* VOYSEYS *to be, but that isn't very unlike.* TRENCHARD *has in excelsis the cocksure manner of the successful barrister;* HUGH *the rather sweet though querulous air of diffidence and scepticism belonging to the unsuccessful man of letters, or artist. The self-respect of* TRENCHARD'S *appearance is immense, and he cultivates that air of concentration upon any trivial matter, or even upon nothing at all, which will some day make him an impressive figure upon the Bench.* HUGH *is always vague, searching Heaven or the corners of the room for inspiration, and even on this occasion his tie is abominably crooked. The inspissated gloom of this assembly, to which each member of the family, as he arrives, adds his share, is unbelievable. Instinct apparently leads them to reproduce as nearly as possible the appearance and conduct of the corpse on which their minds are fixed.* HUGH *is depressed partly at the inadequacy of his grief:* TRENCHARD *conscientiously preserves an air of the indifference which he feels;* BOOTH *stands statuesque at the mantelpiece; while* EMILY *is by* MRS. VOYSEY, *whose face in its quiet grief is, nevertheless, a mirror of many happy memories of her husband.*

BOOTH. I wouldn't hang over her, Emily.

EMILY. No, of course not.

Apologetically, she sits by the table.

TRENCHARD. I hope your wife is well, Hugh?

HUGH. Thank you, Trench; I think so. Beatrice is in America . . on business.

TRENCHARD. Really!

There comes in a small, well groomed, bullet headed boy in Etons. This is the Major's eldest son. Looking scared and solemn, he goes straight to his mother.

EMILY. Now be very quiet, Christopher . .

Then DENIS TREGONING appears.

TRENCHARD. Oh, Tregoning, did you bring Honor back?

DENIS. Yes.

BOOTH. [*At the table.*] A glass of wine, Mother.

MRS. VOYSEY. What?

BOOTH hardly knows how to turn his whisper decorously into enough of a shout for his mother to hear. But he manages it.

BOOTH. Have a glass of wine?

MRS. VOYSEY. Sherry, please.

While he pours it out with an air of its being medicine on this occasion, and not wine at all, EDWARD comes quickly into the room, his face very set, his mind obviously on other matters than the funeral. No one speaks to him for the moment, and he has time to observe them all. TRENCHARD is continuing his talk to DENIS.

TRENCHARD. Give my love to Ethel. Is she ill that——

TREGONING. Not exactly, but she couldn't very well be with us. I thought perhaps you might have heard. We're expecting . .

*He hesitates with the bashfulness of a young hus-
band.* TRENCHARD *helps him out with a citizen's
bow of respect for a citizen's duty.*

TRENCHARD. Indeed. I congratulate you. I hope all
will be well. Please give my love . . my best love to Ethel.

BOOTH. [*In an awful voice.*] Lunch, Emily?

EMILY. [*Scared.*] I suppose so, Booth, thank you.

BOOTH. I think the boy had better run away and play
. . [*He checks himself on the word.*] Well, take a book,
and keep quiet; d'ye hear me, Christopher?

CHRISTOPHER, *who looks incapable of a sound, gazes
at his father with round eyes.* EMILY *whispers
"Library" to him, and adds a kiss in acknowledg-
ment of his good behaviour. After a moment he
slips out, thankfully.*

EDWARD. How's Ethel, Denis?

TREGONING. A little smashed, of course, but no harm
done.

ALICE MAITLAND *comes in, brisk and businesslike, a
little impatient of this universal cloud of mourning.*

ALICE. Edward, Honor has gone to her room. I want
to take her some food and make her eat it. She's very
upset.

EDWARD. Make her drink a glass of wine, and say it is
necessary she should come down here. And d'you mind
not coming back yourself, Alice?

ALICE. [*Her eyebrows up.*] Certainly, if you wish.

BOOTH. [*Overhearing.*] What's this? What's this?

*Alice gets her glass of wine, and goes. The Major
is suddenly full of importance.*

BOOTH. What is this, Edward?

EDWARD. I have something to say to you all.

BOOTH. What?

EDWARD. Well, Booth, you'll hear when I say it.

BOOTH. Is it business? . . because I think this is scarcely the time for business.

EDWARD. Why?

BOOTH. Do you find it easy and reverent to descend from your natural grief to the consideration of money . .? I do not. [*He finds* TRENCHARD *at his elbow.*] I hope you are getting some lunch, Trenchard.

EDWARD. This is business, and more than business, Booth. I choose now, because it is something I wish to say to the family, not write to each individually . . and it will be difficult to get us all together again.

BOOTH. [*Determined, at any rate, to give his sanction.*] Well, Trenchard, as Edward is in the position of trustee—executor . . I don't know your terms . . I suppose there's nothing more to be said.

TRENCHARD. I don't see what your objection is.

BOOTH. [*With some superiority.*] Don't you? I should not have called myself a sentimental man, but . .

EDWARD. You had better stay, Denis; you represent Ethel.

TREGONING. [*Who has not heard the beginning of this.*] Why? . .

HONOR *has obediently come down from her room. She is pale and thin, shaken with grief and worn out besides; for, needless to say, the brunt of her father's illness, the brunt of everything, has been on her. Six weeks' nursing, part of it hopeless, will exhaust anyone. Her handkerchief to her eyes, and every minute or two she cascades tears.* EDWARD *goes and affectionately puts his arm round her.*

EDWARD. My dear Honor, I am sorry to be so . . so merciless. There! . . there! [*He hands her into the room; then shuts the door; then turns and once more surveys the family, who this time mostly return the compliment. Then he says shortly.*] I think you might all sit down. [*But he goes close to his mother and speaks very distinctly, very kindly.*] Mother, we're all going to have a little necessary talk over matters . . now, because it's most convenient. I hope it won't . . I hope you don't mind. Will you come to the table?

> MRS. VOYSEY *looks up as if understanding more than he says.*

MRS. VOYSEY. Edward . .

EDWARD. Yes, mother?

BOOTH. [*Commandingly.*] You'll sit here, mother, of course.

> *He places her in her accustomed chair at the foot of the table. One by one the others sit down,* EDWARD *apparently last. But then he discovers that* HUGH *has lost himself in a corner of the room and is gazing into vacancy.*

EDWARD. Hugh, would you mind attending?

HUGH. What is it?

EDWARD. There's a chair.

> HUGH *takes it. Then for a minute—while* EDWARD *is trying to frame in coherent sentences what he must say to them—for a minute there is silence, broken only by* HONOR'S *sniffs, which culminate at last in a noisy little cascade of tears.*

BOOTH. Honor, control yourself.

> *And to emphasise his own perfect control he helps himself majestically to a glass of sherry. Then says . .*

BOOTH. Well, Edward?

EDWARD. I'll come straight to the point which concerns you. Our father's will gives certain sums to you all . . the gross amount something over a hundred thousand pounds. There will be no money.

> *He can get no further than the bare statement, which is received only with varying looks of be-*

wilderment, until MRS. VOYSEY, *discovering nothing from their faces, breaks this second silence.*

MRS. VOYSEY. I didn't hear.

HUGH. [*In his mother's ear.*] Edward says there's no money.

TRENCHARD. [*Precisely.*] I think you said . . 'will be.'

BOOTH. [*In a tone of mitigated thunder.*] Why will there be no money?

EDWARD. [*Letting himself go.*] Because every penny by right belongs to those clients whom our father spent his life in defrauding. When I say defrauding, I mean it in its worst sense . . swindling . . thieving. I have been in the swim of it, for the past year . . oh, you don't know the sink of iniquity . . and therefore I mean to collect every penny, any money that you can give me; put the firm into bankruptcy; pay back all these people what we can. I'll stand my trial . . it'll come to that with me . . and as soon as possible. [*He pauses, partly for breath, and glares at them all.*] Are none of you going to speak? Quite right, what is there to be said! [*Then with a gentle afterthought.*] I'm sorry to hurt you, mother.

The VOYSEY *family is simply buried deep by this avalanche of horror.* MRS. VOYSEY, *though, who has been watching* EDWARD *closely, says very calmly.*

MRS. VOYSEY. I can't hear quite all you say, but I guess what it is. You don't hurt me, Edward . . I have known of this for a long time.

EDWARD. [*With almost a cry.*] Oh, mother, did he know you knew?

MRS. VOYSEY. What do you say?

TRENCHARD. [*Collected and dry.*] I may as well tell you, Edward, I suspected everything wasn't right about the time of my last quarrel with my father. Of course, I took care not to pursue my suspicions. Was father aware that you knew, Mother?

MRS. VOYSEY. We never discussed it. There was once a great danger . . when you were all younger . . of his being found out. But we never discussed it.

EDWARD. [*Swallowing a fresh bitterness.*] I'm glad it isn't such a shock to all of you.

HUGH. [*Alive to a dramatic aspect of the matter.*] My God . . before the earth has settled on his grave!

EDWARD. I thought it wrong to postpone telling you.

> HONOR, *the word swindling having spelt itself out in her mind, at last gives way to a burst of piteous grief.*

HONOR. Oh, poor papa! . . poor papa!

EDWARD. [*Comforting her kindly.*] Honor, we shall want your help and advice.

> *The Major has recovered from the shock, to swell with importance. It being necessary to make an impression he instinctively turns first to his wife.*

BOOTH. I think, Emily, there was no need for you to have been present at this exposure, and that now you had better retire.

EMILY. Very well, Booth.

> *She gets up to go, conscious of her misdemeanour. But as she reaches the door, an awful thought strikes the Major.*

BOOTH. Good Heavens . . I hope the servants haven't been listening! See where they are, Emily . . and keep them away, distract them. Open the door suddenly. [*She does so, more or less, and there is no one behind it.*] That's all right.

> *Having watched his wife's departure, he turns with gravity to his brother.*

BOOTH. I have said nothing as yet, Edward. I am thinking.

TRENCHARD. [*A little impatient at this exhibition.*] That's the worst of these family practices . . a lot of money knocking around and no audit ever required. The wonder to me is to find an honest solicitor at all.

BOOTH. Really, Trenchard!

TRENCHARD. Well, the more able a man is the less the word Honesty bothers him . . and the Pater was an able man.

EDWARD. I thought that a year ago, Trenchard. I thought that at the worst he was a splendid criminal.

BOOTH. Really . . really, Edward!

EDWARD. And everything was to come right in the end . . we were all to be in reality as wealthy and as prosperous as we have seemed to be all these years. But when he fell ill . . towards the last he couldn't keep the facts from me any longer.

TRENCHARD. And these are?

EDWARD. Laughable. You wouldn't believe there were such fools in the world as some of these wretched clients have been. I tell you the firm's funds were just a lucky bag into which he dipped. Now sometimes their money doesn't even exist.

BOOTH. Where's it gone?

EDWARD. [*Very directly.*] You've been living on it.

BOOTH. Good God!

TRENCHARD. What can you pay in the pound?

EDWARD. Without help? . . six or seven shillings, I daresay. But we must do better than that.

To which there is no response.

BOOTH. All this is very dreadful. Does it mean beggary for the whole family?

EDWARD. Yes, it should.

TRENCHARD. [*Sharply.*] Nonsense!

EDWARD. [*Joining issue at once.*] What right have we to a thing we possess?

TRENCHARD. He didn't make you an allowance, Booth . . your capital's your own, isn't it?

BOOTH. [*Awkwardly placed between the two of them.*] Really . . I—I suppose so.

TRENCHARD. Then that's all right.

EDWARD. [*Vehemently.*] It's stolen money.

TRENCHARD. Booth took it in good faith.

BOOTH. I should hope so.

EDWARD. [*Dwelling on the words.*] It's stolen money.

BOOTH. [*Bubbling with distress.*] I say, what ought I to do?

TRENCHARD. Do . . my dear Booth? Nothing.

EDWARD. [*With great indignation.*] Trenchard, we owe reparation——

TRENCHARD. [*Readily.*] To whom? From which account was Booth's money taken?

EDWARD. [*Side tracked for the moment.*] I don't know . . I daresay from none directly.

TRENCHARD. Very well, then.

EDWARD. [*Grieved.*] Trenchard, you argue as he did——

TRENCHARD. Nonsense, my dear Edward. The law will take anything it has a right to, and all it can get; you needn't be afraid. There's no obligation, legal or moral, for us to throw our pounds into the wreck, that they may become pence.

EDWARD. I can hear him.

TRENCHARD. But what about your own position . . can we get you clear?

EDWARD. That doesn't matter.

> BOOTH's *head has been turning incessantly from one to the other, and by this he is just a bristle of alarm.*

BOOTH. But I say, you know, this is awful! Will this have to be made public?

TRENCHARD. No help for it.

> *The Major's jaw drops; he is speechless.* MRS. VOY-SEY's *dead voice steals in.*

MRS. VOYSEY. What is all this?

TRENCHARD. Edward wishes us to completely beggar ourselves in order to pay back to every client to whom father owed a pound perhaps ten shillings instead of seven.

MRS. VOYSEY. He will find that my estate has been kept quite separate.

EDWARD *hides his face in his hands.*

TRENCHARD. I'm very glad to hear it, Mother.

MRS. VOYSEY. When Mr. Barnes died, your father agreed to appointing another trustee.

TREGONING. [*Diffidently.*] I suppose, Edward, I'm involved.

EDWARD. [*Lifting his head quickly.*] Denis, I hope not. I didn't know that anything of yours——

TREGONING. Yes . . all that I got under my aunt's will.

EDWARD. You see how things are . . I've discovered no trace of that. We'll hope for the best.

TREGONING. [*Setting his teeth.*] It can't be helped.

MAJOR BOOTH *leans over the table and speaks in the loudest of whispers.*

BOOTH. Let me advise you to say nothing of this to Ethel at such a critical time.

TREGONING. Thank you, Booth, naturally I shall not.

HUGH, *by a series of contortions, has lately been giving evidence of a desire or intention to say something.*

EDWARD. Well, what is it, Hugh?

HUGH. I have been wondering . . if he can hear this conversation.

Up to now it has all been meaningless to HONOR, *in her nervous dilapidation, but this remark brings a fresh burst of tears.*

HONOR. Oh, poor papa . . poor papa!

MRS. VOYSEY. I think I'll go to my room. I can't hear what any of you are saying. Edward can tell me afterwards.

EDWARD. Would you like to go, too, Honor?

HONOR. [*Through her sobs.*] Yes, please, I would.

TREGONING. And I'll get out, Edward. Whatever you think fit to do . . Oh, well, I suppose there's only one thing to be done.

EDWARD. Only that.

TREGONING. I wish I were in a better position as to work, for Ethel's sake and—and the child's.

EDWARD. Shall I speak to Trenchard?

TREGONING. No . . he knows I exist in a wig and gown. If I can be useful to him, he'll be useful to me, I daresay. Good-bye, Hugh. Good-bye, Booth.

> *By this time* MRS. VOYSEY *and* HONOR *have been got out of the room;* TREGONING *follows them. So the four brothers are left together.* HUGH *is vacant,* EDWARD *does not speak,* BOOTH *looks at* TRENCHARD, *who settles himself to acquire information.*

TRENCHARD. How long have things been wrong?

EDWARD. He told me the trouble began in his father's time, and that he'd been battling with it ever since.

TRENCHARD. [*Smiling.*] Oh, come now .. that's impossible.

EDWARD. But I believed him! Now I look through his papers, I can find only one irregularity that's more than ten years old, and that's only to do with old George Booth's business.

BOOTH. But the Pater never touched his money . . why, he was a personal friend.

EDWARD. Did you hear what Denis said?

TRENCHARD.. Very curious his evolving that fiction about his father . . I wonder why. I remember the old man. He was as honest as the day.

EDWARD. To gain sympathy, I suppose.

TRENCHARD. I think one can trace the psychology of it deeper than that. It would add a fitness to the situation

. . his handing on to you an inheritance he had received.
You know every criminal has a touch of the artist in him.

HUGH. [*Suddenly roused.*] That's true.

TRENCHARD. What position did you take upon the matter when he told you?

EDWARD. [*Shrugging.*] You know what the Pater was
as well as I.

TRENCHARD. Well . . what did you attempt to do?

EDWARD. I urged him to start by making some of the
smaller accounts right. He said . . he said that would be
penny wise and pound foolish. So I did what I could
myself.

TRENCHARD. With your own money?

EDWARD. The little I had.

TRENCHARD. Can you prove that you did that?

EDWARD. I suppose I could.

TRENCHARD. It's a good point.

BOOTH. [*Not to be quite left out.*] Yes, I must say——

TRENCHARD. You ought to have written him a letter,
and left the firm the moment you found out. Even then,
legally . . ! But as he was your father. What was his
object in telling you? What did he expect you to do?

EDWARD. I've thought of every reason . . and now I
really believe it was that he might have someone to boast
to of his financial exploits.

TRENCHARD. [*Appreciatively.*] I daresay.

BOOTH. Scarcely matters to boast of.

TRENCHARD. Oh, you try playing the fool with other
people's money, and keeping your neck out of the noose
for twelve years. It's not so easy.

EDWARD. Then, of course, he always protested that
things would come right . . that he'd clear the firm and
have a fortune to the good. Or that if he were not spared
I might do it. But he must have known that was impossible.

TRENCHARD. But there's the gambler all over.

EDWARD. Why, he actually took the trouble to draw up this will!

TRENCHARD. That was childish.

EDWARD. I'm the sole executor.

TRENCHARD. So I should think . . Was I down for anything?

EDWARD. No.

TRENCHARD. [*Without resentment.*] How he did hate me!

EDWARD. You're safe from the results of his affection, anyway.

TRENCHARD. What on earth made you stay in the firm, once you knew?

EDWARD *does not answer for a moment.*

EDWARD. I thought I might prevent things from getting any worse. I think I did . . well, I should have done that if he'd lived.

TRENCHARD. You knew the risk you were running?

EDWARD. [*Bowing his head.*] Yes.

TRENCHARD, *the only one of the three who comprehends, looks at his brother for a moment with something that might almost be admiration. Then he stirs himself.*

TRENCHARD. I must be off. Business waiting . . end of term, you know.

BOOTH. Shall I walk to the station with you?

TRENCHARD. I'll spend a few minutes with Mother. [*He says, at the door, very respectfully.*] You'll count on my professional assistance, please, Edward.

EDWARD. [*Simply.*] Thank you, Trenchard.

So TRENCHARD *goes. And the Major, who has been endeavouring to fathom his final attitude, then comments——*

BOOTH. No heart, y'know! Great brain! If it hadn't

been for that distressing quarrel he might have saved our
poor father. Don't you think so, Edward?

EDWARD. Perhaps.

HUGH. [*Giving vent to his thoughts at last with something of a relish.*] The more I think this out, the more
devilishly humorous it gets. Old Booth breaking down by
the grave . . Colpus reading the service . .

EDWARD. Yes, the Vicar's badly hit.

HUGH. Oh, the Pater had managed his business for
years.

BOOTH. Good God . . how shall we ever look old Booth
in the face again?

EDWARD. I don't worry about him; he can die quite
comfortably enough on six shillings in the pound. It's
one or two of the smaller fry who will suffer.

BOOTH. Now, just explain to me . . I didn't interrupt
while Trenchard was talking . . of what exactly did this
defrauding consist?

EDWARD. Speculating with a client's capital . . pocket-
ing the gains, cutting the losses; meanwhile paying the
client his ordinary income.

BOOTH. So that he didn't find it out?

EDWARD. Quite so.

BOOTH. In point of fact, he doesn't suffer?

EDWARD. He doesn't suffer till he finds it out.

BOOTH. And all that's wrong now is that some of their
capital is missing.

EDWARD. [*Half amused, half amazed at this process of
reasoning.*] Yes, that's all that's wrong.

BOOTH. What is the ah—deficit? [*The word rolls from
his tongue.*]

EDWARD. Anything between two and three hundred
thousand pounds.

BOOTH. [*Very impressed, and not unfavourably.*] Dear
me . . this is a big affair!

HUGH. [*Following his own line of thought.*] Quite apart from the rights and wrongs of this, only a very able man could have kept a straight face to the world all these years, as Pater did.

BOOTH. I suppose he sometimes made money by these speculations.

EDWARD. Very often. His own expenditure was heavy, as you know.

BOOTH. [*With gratitude for favors received.*] He was a very generous man.

HUGH. Did nobody ever suspect him?

EDWARD. You see, Hugh, when there was any danger . . when a trust had to be wound up . . he'd make a great effort, and put the accounts straight.

BOOTH. Then he did put some accounts straight?

EDWARD. Yes, when he couldn't help himself.

> BOOTH *looks very enquiring, and then squares him-
> self up to the subject.*

BOOTH. Now look here, Edward. You told us that he told you that it was the object of his life to put these accounts straight. Then you laughed at that. Now you tell me that he did put some accounts straight.

EDWARD. [*Wearily.*] My dear Booth, you don't understand.

BOOTH. Well, let me understand . . I am anxious to understand.

EDWARD. We can't pay ten shillings in the pound.

BOOTH. That's very dreadful. But do you know that there wasn't a time when we couldn't have paid five?

EDWARD. [*Acquiescent.*] I don't know.

BOOTH. Very well, then! If what he said was true about his father and all that . . and why shouldn't we believe him if we can? . . and he did effect an improvement, that's all to his credit. Let us at least be just, Edward.

EDWARD. [*Patiently polite.*] I am very sorry to appear unjust. He has left me in a rather unfortunate position.

BOOTH. Yes, his death was a tragedy. It seems to me that if he had been spared he might have succeeded at length in this tremendous task, and restored to us our family honour.

EDWARD. Yes, Booth, he spoke very feelingly of that.

BOOTH. [*Irony lost upon him.*] I can well believe it. And I can tell you that now . . I may be right or I may be wrong . . I am feeling far less concerned about the clients' money than I am at the terrible blow to the Family which this exposure will strike. Money, after all, can to a certain extent be done without . . but Honour——

This is too much for EDWARD.

EDWARD. Our honour! Does one of you mean to give me a single penny towards undoing all the wrong that has been done?

BOOTH. I take Trenchard's word for it that that would be illegal.

EDWARD. Well . . don't talk to me of honour.

BOOTH. [*Somewhat nettled at this outburst.*] I am speaking of the public exposure. Edward, can't that be prevented?

EDWARD. [*With quick suspicion.*] How?

BOOTH. Well . . how was. it being prevented before he died—before we knew anything about it?

EDWARD. [*Appealing to the spirits that watch over him.*] Oh, listen to this! First Trenchard . . and now you! You've the poison in your blood, every one of you. Who am I to talk? I daresay so have I.

BOOTH. [*Reprovingly.*] I am beginning to think that you have worked yourself into rather an hysterical state over this unhappy business.

EDWARD. [*Rating him.*] Perhaps you'd have been glad . . glad if I'd held my tongue and gone on lying and cheating . . and married and begotten a son to go on lying and cheating after me . . and to pay you your interest . . your interest in the lie and the cheat.

BOOTH. [*With statesmanlike calm.*] Look here, Edward, this rhetoric is exceedingly out of place. The simple question before us is . . What is the best course to pursue?

EDWARD. There is no question before us. There's only one course to pursue.

BOOTH. [*Crushingly.*] You will let me speak, please. In so far as our poor father was dishonest to his clients, I pray that he may be forgiven. In so far as he spent his life honestly endeavouring to right a wrong which he had found already committed . . I forgive him. I admire him, Edward. And I feel it my duty to—er—reprobate most strongly the—er—gusto with which you have been holding him up in memory to us . . ten minutes after we have stood round his grave . . as a monster of wickedness. I think I may say I knew him as well as you . . better. And . . thank God! . . there was not between him and me this —this unhappy business to warp my judgment of him. [*He warms to his subject.*] Did you ever know a more charitable man . . a larger-hearted? He was a faithful husband . . and what a father to all of us, putting us out into the world and fully intending to leave us comfortably settled there. Further . . as I see this matter, Edward . . when as a young man he was told this terrible secret, and entrusted with such a frightful task . . did he turn his back on it like a coward? No. He went through it heroically to the end of his life. And as he died I imagine there was no more torturing thought than that he had left his work unfinished. [*He is very satisfied with this peroration.*] And now if all these clients can be kept receiving their natural income, and if Father's plan could be carried out of gradually replacing the capital——

EDWARD *at this raises his head and stares with horror,*

EDWARD. You're appealing to me to carry on this . . Oh, you don't know what you're talking about!

> *The Major, having talked himself back to a proper eminence, remains good-tempered.*

BOOTH. Well, I'm not a conceited man . . but I do think that I can understand a simple financial problem when it has been explained to me.

EDWARD. You don't know the nerve . . the unscrupulous daring it requires to——

BOOTH. Of course, if you're going to argue round your own incompetence——

EDWARD. [*Very straight.*] D'you want your legacy?

BOOTH. [*With dignity.*] In one moment I shall get very angry. Here am I doing my best to help you and your clients . . and there you sit imputing to me the most sordid motives. Do you suppose I should touch or allow to be touched the money which father has left us till every client's claim was satisfied?

EDWARD. My dear Booth, I'm sure you mean well——

BOOTH. I'll come down to your office and work with you.

> *At this cheerful prospect even poor* EDWARD *can't help smiling.*

EDWARD. Why, you'd be found out at once.

BOOTH. [*Feeling that it is a chance lost.*] Well, of course the Pater never consulted me. I only know what I feel ought to be possible. I can but make the suggestion.

> *At this point* TRENCHARD *looks round the door to say* . .

TRENCHARD. Are you coming, Booth?

BOOTH. Yes, certainly. I'll talk this over with Trenchard. [*As he gets up and automatically stiffens, he is reminded of the occasion, and his voice drops.*] I say . . we've been speaking very loud. You must do nothing rash. I've no doubt I can devise something which will obviate . . and then I'm sure I shall convince you . . [*Glancing into*

the hall, he apparently catches TRENCHARD'S *impatient eye,
for he departs abruptly, saying* . .] All right, Trenchard,
you've eight minutes.

> BOOTH'S *departure leaves* HUGH, *at any rate, really
> at his ease.*

HUGH.   What an experience for you, Edward!

EDWARD.   [*Bitterly.*]   And I feared what the shock
might be to you all! Booth has made a good recovery.

HUGH.   You wouldn't have him miss such a chance of
booming at us all?

EDWARD.   It's strange the number of people who believe
you can do right by means which they know to be wrong.

HUGH.   [*Taking great interest in this.*] Come, what do
we know about right and wrong? Let's say legal and
illegal. You're so down on the Governor because he has
trespassed against the etiquette of your own profession.
But now he's dead . . and if there weren't the disgrace to
think of . . it's no use the rest of us pretending to feel
him a criminal, because we don't. Which just shows that
money . . and property——

> *At this point he becomes conscious that* ALICE MAIT-
> LAND *is standing behind him, her eyes fixed on his
> brother. So he interrupts himself to ask* . .

HUGH.   D'you want to speak to Edward?

ALICE.   Please, Hugh.

HUGH.   I'll go.

> *He goes, a little martyrlike, to conclude the evolu-
> tion of his theory in soliloquy; his usual fate.* ALICE
> *still looks at* EDWARD *with soft eyes, and he at her
> rather appealingly.*

ALICE.   Auntie has told me.

EDWARD.   He was fond of you. Don't think worse of
him than you can help.

ALICE.   I'm thinking of you.

EDWARD.   I may just escape.

ALICE. So Trenchard says.

EDWARD. My hands are clean, Alice.

ALICE. [*Her voice falling lovingly.*] I know that.

EDWARD. Mother's not very upset.

ALICE. She had expected a smash in his life time.

EDWARD. I'm glad that didn't happen.

ALICE. Yes . . as the fault was his it won't hurt you so much to stand up to the blame.

> EDWARD *looks puzzled at this for a moment, then gives it up.*

EDWARD. I'm hurt enough now.

ALICE. Why, what have the boys done? It was a mercy to tell Honor just at this time. She can grieve for his death and his disgrace at the same time . . and the one grief lessens the other perhaps.

EDWARD. Oh, they're all shocked enough at the disgrace . . but will they open their purses to lessen the disgrace?

ALICE. Will it seem less disgraceful to have stolen ten thousand pounds than twenty?

EDWARD. I should think so.

ALICE. I should think so, but I wonder if that's the Law. If it isn't, Trenchard wouldn't consider the point. I'm sure Public Opinion doesn't say so . . and that's what Booth is considering.

EDWARD. [*With contempt.*] Yes.

ALICE. [*Ever so gently ironical.*] Well, he's in the Army . . he's almost in Society . . and he has to get on in both; one mustn't blame him. Of course, if the money could have been given up with a flourish of trumpets . . ! But even then I doubt whether the advertisement would bring in what it cost.

EDWARD. [*Very serious.*] But when one thinks how the money was obtained!

ALICE. When one thinks how most money is obtained!

EDWARD. They've not earned it.

ALICE. [*Her eyes humorous.*] If they had, they might have given it you and earned more. Did I ever tell you what my guardian said to me when I came of age?

EDWARD. I'm thankful your money's not been in danger.

ALICE. It might have been, but I was made to look after it myself . . much against my will. My guardian was a person of great character and no principles, the best and most lovable man I've ever met . . I'm sorry you never knew him, Edward . . and he said once to me . . You've no right to your money. You've not earned it or deserved it in any way. Therefore, don't be surprised or annoyed if any enterprising person tries to get it from you. He has at least as much right to it as you have . . if he can use it better, he has more right. Shocking sentiments, aren't they? No respectable man of business could own to them. But I'm not so sorry for some of these clients as you are, Edward.

> EDWARD *shakes his head, treating these paradoxes as they deserve.*

EDWARD. Alice . . one or two of them will be beggared.

ALICE. [*Sincerely.*] Yes, that is serious. What's to be done?

EDWARD. There's old nurse . . with her poor little savings gone!

ALICE. Surely those can be spared her?

EDWARD. The Law's no respecter of persons . . that's its boast. Old Booth, with more than he wants, will keep enough. My old nurse, with just enough, may starve. But it'll be a relief to clear out this nest of lies, even though one suffers one's self. I've been ashamed to walk into that office, Alice . . I'll hold my head high in prison, though.

> *He shakes himself stiffly erect, his chin high.* ALICE *quizzes him.*

ALICE. Edward, I'm afraid you're feeling heroic.

EDWARD. I!

ALICE. Don't be so proud of your misfortune. You looked quite like Booth for the moment. [*This effectually removes the starch.*] It will be very stupid to send you to prison, and you must do your best to keep out. [*She goes on very practically.*] We were discussing if anything could be done for these one or two people who'll be beggared.

EDWARD. Yes, Alice. I'm sorry nothing can be done for them.

ALICE. It's a pity.

EDWARD. I suppose I was feeling heroic. I didn't mean to.

He has become a little like a child with her.

ALICE. That's the worst of acting on principle . . one begins thinking of one's attitude instead of the use of what one is doing.

EDWARD. I'm exposing this fraud on principle.

ALICE. Perhaps that's what's wrong.

EDWARD. Wrong!

ALICE. My dear Edward, if people are to be ruined . . !

EDWARD. What else is there to be done?

ALICE. Well . . have you thought?

EDWARD. There's nothing else to be done.

ALICE. On principle.

He looks at her; she is smiling, it is true, but smiling quite gravely. EDWARD *is puzzled. Then the yeast of her suggestion begins to work in his mind slowly, perversely at first.*

EDWARD. It had occurred to Booth . . .

ALICE. Oh, anything may occur to Booth.

EDWARD. . . In his grave concern for the family honour that I might quietly cheat the firm back into credit again.

ALICE. How stupid of Booth!

EDWARD. Well . . like my father . . Booth believes in himself.

ALICE.   Yes, he's rather a credulous man.

EDWARD.   [*Ignoring her little joke.*]   He might have
been lucky, and have done some good.   I'm a weak sort of
creature—just a collection of principles, as you say.   Look,
all I've been able to do in this business . . at the cost of
my whole life perhaps . . has been to sit senselessly by my
father's side and prevent things going from bad to worse.

ALICE.   That was worth doing.   The cost is your own
affair.

> *She is watching him, stilly and closely.   Suddenly*
> *his face lights a little, and he turns to her.*

EDWARD.   Alice . . there's something else I could do.

ALICE.   What?

EDWARD.   It's illegal.

ALICE.   So much the better, perhaps.   Oh, I'm lawless
by birthright, being a woman.

EDWARD.   I could take the money that's in my father's
name, and use it only to put right the smaller accounts.
It'd take a few months to do it well . . and cover the
tracks.   That'd be necessary.

ALICE.   Then you'd give yourself up as you'd meant to
do now?

EDWARD.   Yes . . practically.

ALICE.   It'd be worse for you then at the trial?

EDWARD.   [*With a touch of another sort of pride.*]   You
said that was my affair.

ALICE.   [*Pain in her voice and eyes.*]   Oh, Edward!

EDWARD.   Shall I do this?

ALICE.   [*Turning away.*]   Why must you ask me?

EDWARD.   You mocked at my principles, didn't you?
You've taken them from me.   The least you can do
is to give me advice in exchange.

ALICE.   [*After a moment.*]   No . . decide for yourself.

> *He jumps up, and begins to pace about, doubtful,*
> *distressed.*

EDWARD. Good Lord . . it means lying and shuffling!

ALICE. [*A little trembling.*] In a good cause.

EDWARD. Ah . . but lying and shuffling takes the fine edge off one's soul.

ALICE. [*Laughing at the quaintness of her own little epigram.*] Edward, are you one of God's dandies?

EDWARD. And . . Alice, it wouldn't be easy work. It wants qualities I haven't got. I should fail.

ALICE. Would you?

He catches a look from her.

EDWARD. Well, I might not.

ALICE. And you don't need success for a lure. That's like a common man.

EDWARD. You want me to try to do this?

For answer she dares only put out her hand, and he takes it.

ALICE. Oh, my dear . . cousin!

EDWARD. [*Excitedly.*] My people will have to hold their tongues. I needn't have told them all this to-day.

ALICE. Don't tell them the rest . . they won't understand. I shall be jealous if you tell them.

EDWARD. [*Looking at her as she at him.*] Well, you've the right to be. This deed . . it's not done yet . . is your property.

ALICE. Thank you. I've always wanted to have something useful to my credit . . and I'd almost given up hoping.

Then suddenly his face changes, his voice changes, and he grips the hand he is holding so tightly as to hurt her.

EDWARD. Alice, if my father's story were true . . he must have begun like this. Trying to do the right thing in the wrong way . . then doing the wrong thing . . then bringing himself to what he was . . and so me to this. [*He flings away from her.*] No, Alice, I won't do it. I daren't take that first step down. It's a worse risk than any failure. Think . . I might succeed.

ALICE stands very still, looking at him.

ALICE. It's a big risk. Well . . I'll take it.

He turns to her in wonder.

EDWARD. You?

ALICE. I'll risk your becoming a bad man. That's a big risk for me.

He understands, and is calmed and made happy.

EDWARD. Then there is no more to be said, is there?

ALICE. Not now. [*As she drops this gentle hint she hears something—the hall door opening.*] Here's Booth back again.

EDWARD. [*With a really mischievous grin.*] He'll be so glad he's convinced me.

ALICE. I must go back to Honor, poor girl. I wonder she has a tear left.

She leaves him briskly, brightly; leaves her cousin with his mouth set and a light in his eyes.

THE FOURTH ACT

MR. VOYSEY'S *room at the office is* EDWARD'S *now. It has somehow lost that brilliancy which the old man's occupation seemed to give it. Perhaps it is only because this December morning is dull and depressing, but the fire isn't bright, and the panels and windows don't shine as they did. There are no roses on the table, either.* EDWARD, *walking in as his father did, hanging his hat and coat where his father's used to hang, is certainly the palest shadow of that other masterful presence. A depressed, drooping shadow, too. This may be what* PEACEY *feels, if no more, for he looks very surly as he obeys the old routine of following his chief to this room on his arrival. Nor has* EDWARD *so much as a glance for his clerk. They exchange the formalest of greetings.* EDWARD *sits joylessly to his desk, on which the morning's pile of letters lies, unopened now.*

PEACEY. Good morning, sir.

EDWARD. Good morning, Peacey. Have you any notes for me?

PEACEY. Well, I've hardly been through the letters yet, sir.

EDWARD. [*His eyebrows meeting.*] Oh . . and I'm half an hour late myself this morning.

PEACEY. I'm very sorry, sir.

EDWARD. If Mr. Bullen calls, you had better show him all those papers I gave you. Write to Metcalfe as soon as possible; say I interviewed Mr. Vickery myself this morning, and the houses will not be proceeded with. Better let me see the letter.

PEACEY. Very good, sir.

EDWARD. That's all, thank you.

> PEACEY *gets to the door, where he stops, looking not only surly but nervous now.*

PEACEY. May I speak to you a moment, sir?

EDWARD. Certainly.

> PEACEY, *after a moment, makes an effort, purses his mouth, and begins.*

PEACEY. Bills are beginning to come in upon me as is usual at this season, sir. My son's allowance at Cambridge is now rather a heavy item of my expenditure. I hope that the custom of the firm isn't to be neglected now that you are the head of it, Mr. Edward. Two hundred your father always made it at Christmas . . in notes, if you please.

> *Towards the end of this* EDWARD *begins to pay great attention. When he answers his voice is harsh.*

EDWARD. Oh, to be sure . . your hush money.

PEACEY. [*Bridling.*] That's not a very pleasant word.

EDWARD. This is a very unpleasant subject.

PEACEY. I'm sure it isn't my wish to bring out in cold conversation what I know of the firm's position. Your father always gave me the notes in an envelope when he shook hands with me at Christmas.

EDWARD. [*Blandly.*] And I've been waiting for you to ask me.

PEACEY. Well, we'll say no more about it. There's always a bit of friction in coming to an understanding about anything, isn't there, sir?

> *He is going, when* EDWARD'S *question stops him.*

EDWARD. Why didn't you speak to me about this last Christmas?

PEACEY. I knew you were upset at your father's death.

EDWARD. No, no. My father died the August before that.

PEACEY. Well . . truthfully, Mr. Edward?

EDWARD. As truthfully as you think suitable.

The irony of this is wasted on PEACEY, *who becomes pleasantly candid.*

PEACEY. Well, I couldn't make you out last Christmas. I'd always thought there must be a smash when your father died . . but it didn't come. But then again at Christmas you seemed all on edge, and I didn't know what might happen. So I thought I'd better keep quiet and say nothing.

EDWARD. I see. This little pull of yours over the firm is an inheritance from your father, isn't it?

PEACEY. [*Discreetly.*] When he retired, sir, he said to me . . I've told the Governor you know what I know. And Mr. Voysey said to me . . 'I treat you as I did your father, Peacey.' I never had another word on the subject with him.

EDWARD. A very decent arrangement. Your son's at Cambridge, you say, Peacey?

PEACEY. Yes.

EDWARD. I wonder you didn't bring him into the firm.

PEACEY. [*Taking this very kind.*] Thank you, sir . . I thought of it. But then I thought that two generations going in for this sort of thing was enough.

EDWARD. That's a matter of taste.

PEACEY. And then, sir . . I don't want to hurt your feelings, but things simply cannot go on for ever. The marvel to me is that the game has been kept up as it has. So now, if he does well at Cambridge, I hope he'll go to the bar. He has a distinct talent for patiently applying himself to the details of a thing.

EDWARD. I hope he'll do well. I'm glad to have had

this talk with you, Peacey. I'm sorry you can't have the money you want.

> *He returns to his letters, a little steely-eyed.* PEACEY, *quite at his ease, makes for the door yet again, saying . .*

PEACEY. Oh, any time will do, sir.

EDWARD. You can't have the money at all.

PEACEY. [*Brought up short.*] Can't I?

EDWARD. [*Very decidedly indeed.*] No . . I made up my mind about that eighteen months ago. Since my father's death the trust business of the firm has not been conducted as it was formerly. We no longer make illicit profits out of our clients. There are none for you to share.

> *Having thus given the explanation he considers due, he goes on with his work. But* PEACEY *has flushed up.*

PEACEY. Look here, Mr. Edward, I'm sorry I began this discussion. You'll give me my two hundred as usual, please, and we'll drop the subject.

EDWARD. By all means drop the subject.

PEACEY. [*His voice rising sharply.*] I want the money. I think it is not gentlemanly in you, Mr. Edward, to make these excuses to try to get out of paying it me. Your father would never have made such an excuse.

EDWARD. [*Flabbergasted.*] Do you think I'm lying to you?

PEACEY. [*With a deprecating swallow.*] I don't wish to criticise your statements or your actions at all, sir. It was no concern of mine how your father treated his clients.

EDWARD. I understand. And now it's no concern of yours how honest I am. You want your money just the same.

PEACEY. Well, don't be sarcastic . . a man does get used to a state of affairs whatever it may be.

EDWARD. [*With considerable force.*] My friend, if I drop sarcasm I shall have to tell you very candidly what I think of you.

PEACEY. That I'm a thief because I've taken money from a thief!

EDWARD. Worse than a thief. You're content that others should steal for you.

PEACEY. And who isn't?

> EDWARD *is really pleased with the aptness of this. He at once changes his tone, which indeed had become rather bullying.*

EDWARD. Ah, Peacey, I perceive that you study sociology. Well, that's too big a question to enter into now. The application of the present portion of it is that I have for the moment, at some inconvenience to myself, ceased to receive stolen goods and therefore am in a position to throw a stone at you. I have thrown it.

> PEACEY, *who would far sooner be bullied than talked to like this, turns very sulky.*

PEACEY. And now I'm to leave the firm, I suppose?

EDWARD. Not unless you wish.

PEACEY. I happen to think the secret's worth its price.

EDWARD. Perhaps someone will pay it you.

PEACEY. [*Feebly threatening.*] You're presuming upon its not being worth my while to make use of what I know.

EDWARD. [*Not unkindly.*] My good Peacey, it happens to be the truth I told you just now. Well, how on earth do you suppose you can successfully blackmail a man, who has so much to gain by exposure and so little to lose as I?

PEACEY. [*Peeving.*] I don't want to ruin you, sir, and I have a great regard for the firm . . but you must see that I can't have my income reduced in this way without a struggle.

EDWARD. [*With great cheerfulness.*] Very well, my friend, struggle away.

PEACEY. [*His voice rising high and thin.*] For one
thing, sir, I don't think it fair dealing on your part to dock
the money suddenly. I have been counting on it most of
the year, and I have been led into heavy expenses. Why
couldn't you have warned me?

EDWARD. That's true, Peacey, it was stupid of me. I
apologise for the mistake.

PEACEY *is a little comforted by this quite candid
    acknowledgment.*

PEACEY. Perhaps things may be easier for you by next
Christmas.

EDWARD. I hope so.

PEACEY. Then . . perhaps you won't be so particular.
At this gentle insinuation EDWARD *looks up exasper-
    ated.*

EDWARD. So you don't believe what I told you?

PEACEY. Yes, I do.

EDWARD. Then you think that the fascination of swindling one's clients will ultimately prove irresistible?

PEACEY. It's what happened to your father, I suppose
you know.

This gives EDWARD *such pause that he drops his
    masterful tone.*

EDWARD. I didn't.

PEACEY. He got things as right as rain once.

EDWARD. Did he?

PEACEY. . . My father told me. Then he started again.

EDWARD. But how did you find that out?

PEACEY. [*Expanding pleasantly.*] Well, being so long
in his service, I grew to understand your father. But
when I first came into the firm, I simply hated him. He
was that sour; so snappy with everyone . . as if he had a
grievance against the whole world.

EDWARD. [*Pensively.*] It seems he had in those days.

PEACEY. Well, as I said, his dealings with his clients

were no business of mine. And I speak as I find. He was very kind to me . . always thoughtful and considerate. He grew to be so pleasant and generous to everyone——

EDWARD. That you have great hopes of me yet?

PEACEY. [*Who has a simple mind.*] No, Mr. Edward, no. You're different from your father . . one must make up one's mind to that. And you may believe me or not but I should be very glad to know that the firm was solvent and going straight. There have been times when I have sincerely regretted my connection with it. If you'll let me say so, I think it's very noble of you to have undertaken the work you have. [*Then, as everything seems smooth again.*] And Mr. Edward, if you'll give me enough to cover this year's extra expense I think I may promise you that I shan't expect money again.

EDWARD. [*Good-tempered, as he would speak to an importunate child.*] No, Peacey, no!

PEACEY. [*Fretful again.*] Well, sir, you make things very difficult for me.

EDWARD. Here's a letter from Mr. Cartwright which you might attend to. If he wants an appointment with me, don't make one till the New Year. His case can't come on before February.

PEACEY. [*Taking the letter.*] I am anxious to meet you in every way——[*He is handed another.*]

EDWARD. "Perceval Building Estate" . . that's yours, too.

PEACEY. [*Putting them both down resolutely.*] But I refuse to be ignored. I must consider my whole position. I hope I may not be tempted to make use of the power I possess. But if I am driven to proceed to extremities . .

EDWARD. [*Breaking in upon this bunch of tags.*] My dear Peacey, don't talk nonsense . . you couldn't proceed to an extremity to save your life. You've taken this money irresponsibly for all these years. You'll find you're no

longer capable even of such a responsible act as tripping
up your neighbour.

> *This does completely upset the gentle blackmailer.*
> *He loses one grievance in another.*

PEACEY.   Really, Mr. Edward, I am a considerably older
man than you, and I think that whatever our positions——

EDWARD.   Don't let us argue, Peacey.   You're quite
at liberty to do whatever you think worth while.

PEACEY.   It isn't that, sir.   But these personalities——

EDWARD.   Oh . . I apologise.   Don't forget the letters.

PEACEY.   I will not, sir.

> *He takes them with great dignity, and is leaving the*
> *room.*

PEACEY.   Here's Mr. Hugh, waiting.

EDWARD.   To see me?   Ask him in.

PEACEY.   Come in, Mr. Hugh, please.

> HUGH *comes in,* PEACEY *holding the door for him*
> *with a frigid politeness of which he is quite oblivi-*
> *ous. At this final slight* PEACEY *goes out in dudgeon.*

EDWARD.   How are you, Hugh?

HUGH.   Good Lord!

> *And he throws himself into the chair by the fire.*
> EDWARD, *quite used to this sort of thing, goes quietly*
> *on with his work, adding, encouragingly, after a*
> *moment . .*

EDWARD.   How's Beatrice?

HUGH.   She's very busy.

> *He studies his boots with the gloomiest expression.*
> *And indeed, they are very dirty, and his turned-up*
> *trousers are muddy at the edge.   They are dark*
> *trousers, and well cut, but he wears with them a loose*
> *coat and waistcoat of a peculiar light brown check.*
> *Add to this the roughest of overcoats and a very soft*
> *hat.   Add also the fact that he doesn't shave well or*
> *regularly, and that his hair wants cutting, and*

HUGH'S *appearance this morning is described. As he is quite capable of sitting silently by the fire for a whole morning,* EDWARD *asks him at last . .*

EDWARD. What d'you want?

HUGH. [*With vehemence.*] I want a machine gun planted in Regent Street . . and one in the Haymarket . . and one in Leicester Square and one in the Strand . . and a dozen in the City. An earthquake would be simpler. Or why not a nice clean tidal wave? It's no good preaching and patching up any longer, Edward. We must begin afresh. Don't you feel, even in your calmer moments, that this whole country is simply hideous? The other nations must look after themselves. I'm patriotic . . I only ask that we should be destroyed.

EDWARD. It has been promised.

HUGH. I'm sick of waiting. [*Then as* EDWARD *says nothing.*] You say this is the cry just of the weak man in despair! I wouldn't be anything but a weak man in this world. I wouldn't be a king, I wouldn't be rich . . I wouldn't be a Borough Councillor . . I should be so a s h a m e d. I've walked here this morning from Hampstead. I started to curse because the streets were dirty. You'd think that an Empire could keep its streets clean! But then I saw that the children were dirty, too.

EDWARD. That's because of the streets.

HUGH. Yes, it's holiday time. Those that can cross a road safely are doing some work now . . earning some money. You'd think a governing race, grabbing responsibilities, might care for its children.

EDWARD. Come, we educate them now. And I don't think many work in holiday time.

HUGH. [*Encouraged by contradiction.*] We teach them all that we're not ashamed of . . and much that we ought to be . . and the rest they find out for themselves. Oh, every man and woman I met was muddy-eyed! They'd joined the great conspiracy which we call our civilization. They've been educated! They believe in the Laws and the Money-market and Respectability. Well, at least they suffer for their beliefs. But I'm glad I don't make the laws . . and that I haven't any money . . and that I hate respectability . . or I should be so ashamed. By the bye, that's what I've come for.

EDWARD. [*Pleasantly.*] What? I thought you'd only come to talk.

HUGH. You must take that money of mine for your clients. Of course you ought to have had it when you asked for it. It has never belonged to me. Well . . it has never done me any good. I have never made any use of it, and so it has been just a clog to my life.

EDWARD. [*Surprised.*] My dear Hugh . . this is very generous of you.

HUGH. Not a bit. I only want to start fresh and free.

EDWARD. [*Sitting back from his work.*] Hugh, do you really think that money has carried a curse with it?

HUGH. [*With great violence.*] Think! I'm the proof of it, and look at me. When I said I'd be an artist the Governor gave me a hundred and fifty a year . . the rent of a studio and the price of a velvet coat he thought it; that was all he knew about Art. Then my respectable training got me engaged and married. Marriage in a studio puzzled the Governor, so he guessed it at *two* hundred and fifty a year . . and looked for lay figure-babies, I suppose. What had I to do with Art? Nothing I've done yet but reflects our drawing-room at Chislehurst.

EDWARD. [*Considering.*] Yes . . What do you earn in a year? I doubt if you can afford to give this up.

HUGH. Oh, Edward . . you clank the chain with the best of them. That word Afford! I want to be free from my advantages. Don't you see I must find out what I'm worth in m y s e l f . . whether I even exist or not? Perhaps I'm only a pretence of a man animated by an income.

EDWARD. But you can't return to nature on the London pavements.

HUGH. No. Nor in England at all . . it's nothing but a big back garden. [*Now he collects himself for a final outburst.*] But if there's no place on this earth where a man can prove his right to live by some other means than robbing his neighbour . . I'd better go and request the next horse I meet to ride me . . to the nearest lunatic asylum.

EDWARD *waits till the effects of this explosion are over.*

EDWARD. And what does Beatrice say to your emigrating to the backwoods . . if that is exactly what you mean?

HUGH. Now that we're separating——

EDWARD. [*Taken aback.*] What?

HUGH. We mean to separate.

EDWARD. This is the first I've heard of it.

HUGH. Beatrice is making some money by her books, so it has become possible.

EDWARD. [*Humorously.*] Have you told anyone yet?

HUGH. We mean to now. I think a thing comes to pass quicker in public.

EDWARD. Say nothing at home until after Christmas.

HUGH. Oh, Lord, I forgot! They'll discuss it solemnly. [*Then he whistles.*] Emily knows!

EDWARD. [*Having considered.*] I shan't accept this money from you . . there's no need. All the good has been done that I wanted to do. No one will be beggared now. So why should you be?

HUGH. [*With clumsy affection.*] We've taken a fine lot of interest in your labours, haven't we, Hercules?

EDWARD. You hold your tongue about the office affairs, don't you? It's not safe.

HUGH. When will you be quit of the beastly business?

EDWARD. [*Becoming reserved and cold at once.*] I'm in no hurry.

HUGH. What do you gain by hanging on now?

EDWARD. Occupation.

HUGH. But, Edward, it must be an awfully wearying state of things. I suppose any moment a policeman may knock at the door . . so to speak?

EDWARD. [*Appreciating the figure of speech.*] Any moment. I take no precautions. I suppose that's why he doesn't come. At first I listened for him, day by day. Then I said to myself . . next week. But a year has gone by and more. I've ceased expecting to hear the knock at all.

HUGH. But look here . . is all this worth while?

EDWARD. [*Supremely ironical.*] My dear Hugh, what a silly question!

HUGH. [*Very seriously.*] But have you the right to make a mean thing of your life like this?

EDWARD. Does my life matter?

HUGH. Well . . of course!

EDWARD. I find no evidence to convince me of it. The World that you talk about so finely is using me up. A little wantonly . . a little needlessly, I do think. But she knows her own damn business . . or so she says, if you try to teach it her. And why should I trouble to fit myself for better work than she has given me to do . . nursing fools' money?

HUGH. [*Responding at once to this vein.*] Edward, we must turn this world upside down. It's her stupidity that drives me mad. We all want a lesson in values. We're never taught what is worth having and what isn't. Why should your r e a l happiness be sacrificed to the s h a m happiness which people have invested in the firm?

EDWARD. I suppose their money means such happiness to them as they understand.

HUGH. Then we want another currency. We must learn to express ourselves in terms of vitality. There can be no other standard of worth in life, can there? I never believed that money was valuable. I remember once giving a crossing sweeper a sovereign. The sovereign was nothing. But the sensation I gave him was an intrinsically valuable thing.

He is fearfully pleased with his essay in philosophy.

EDWARD. He could buy other sensations with the sovereign.

HUGH. But none like the first. [*Then the realities of life overwhelm him again.*] And yet . . we're slaves! Beatrice won't let me go until we're each certain of two hundred a year. And she's quite right . . I should only get into debt. You know that two fifty a year of mine is a hundred and eighty now.

EDWARD. [*Mischievous.*] Why would you invest sensationally?

HUGH. [*With great seriousness.*] I put money into things which I know ought to succeed . .

The telephone rings. EDWARD *speaks through it.*

EDWARD. Certainly . . bring him in. [*Then to his brother, who sits on the table idly disarranging everything.*] You'll have to go now, Hugh.

HUGH. [*Shaking his head gloomily.*] You're one of the few people I can talk to, Edward.

EDWARD. I like listening.

HUGH. [*As much cheered as surprised.*] Do you! I suppose I talk a lot of rot . . but . .

In comes old MR. GEORGE BOOTH, *older too in looks than he was eighteen months back. Very dandyishly dressed, he still seems by no means so happy as his clothes might be making him.*

MR. BOOTH. 'Ullo, Hugh! I thought I should find you, Edward.

EDWARD. [*Formally.*] Good morning, Mr. Booth.

HUGH. [*As he collects his hat, his coat, his various properties.*] Well . . Beatrice and I go down to Chislehurst to-morrow. I say . . d'you know that old Nursie is furious with you about something?

EDWARD. [*Shortly.*] Yes, I know. Good-bye.

HUGH. How are you?

> *He launches this enquiry at* MR. BOOTH *with great suddenness just as he leaves the room. The old gentleman jumps; then jumps again at the slam of the door. And then he frowns at* EDWARD *in a frightened sort of way.*

EDWARD. Will you come here . . or will you sit by the fire?

MR. BOOTH. This'll do. I shan't detain you long.

> *He take the chair by the table and occupies the next minute or two carefully disposing of his hat and gloves.*

EDWARD. Are you feeling all right again?

MR. BOOTH. A bit dyspeptic. How are you?

EDWARD. Quite well, thanks.

MR. BOOTH. I'm glad . . I'm glad. [*He now proceeds to cough a little, hesitating painfully.*] I'm afraid this isn't very pleasant business I've come upon.

EDWARD. D'you want to go to Law with anyone?

MR. BOOTH. No . . oh, no. I'm getting too old to quarrel.

EDWARD. A pleasant symptom.

MR. BOOTH. [*With a final effort.*] I mean to withdraw my securities from the custody of your firm . . [*and he adds apologetically*] with the usual notice, of course.

> *It would be difficult to describe what* EDWARD *feels at this moment. Perhaps something of the shock that the relief of death may be as an end to pain so*

long endured that it has been half forgotten. He
answers very quietly, without a sign of emotion.

EDWARD. Thank you . . May one ask why?

MR. BOOTH. [*Relieved that the worst is over.*] Certainly . . certainly. My reason is straightforward and simple
and well considered. I think you must know, Edward, I
have never been able to feel that implicit confidence in
your ability which I had in your father's. Well, it is
hardly to be expected, is it?

EDWARD. [*With a grim smile.*] No.

MR. BOOTH. I can say that without unduly depreciating
you. Men like your father are few and far between. As
far as I know, things proceed at this office as they have
always done, but . . since his death I have not been happy
about my affairs.

EDWARD. [*Speaking as it is his duty to.*] I think you
need be under no apprehension . .

MR. BOOTH. I daresay not. But that isn't the point.
Now, for the first time in my long life, I am worried about
money affairs; and I don't like the feeling. The possession of money has always been a pleasure to me . . and
for what are perhaps my last years I don't wish that to be
otherwise. You must remember you have practically my
entire property unreservedly in your control.

EDWARD. Perhaps we can arrange to hand you over the
reins to an extent which will ease your mind, and at the
same time not . .

MR. BOOTH. I thought of that. Believe me, I have every
wish not to slight unduly your father's son. I have not
moved in the matter for eighteen months. I have not been
able to make up my mind to. Really, one feels a little helpless . . and the transaction of business requires more energy than . . But I saw my doctor yesterday, Edward, and
he told me . . well, it was a warning. And so I felt it my
duty at once to . . especially as I made up my mind to it

some time ago. [*He comes to the end of this havering at last, and adds.*] In point of fact, Edward, more than a year before your father died I had quite decided that my affairs could never be with you as they were with him.

> EDWARD *starts almost out of his chair, his face pale, his eyes black.*

EDWARD. Did h e know that?

MR. BOOTH. [*Resenting this new attitude.*] I think I never said it in so many words. But he may easily have guessed.

EDWARD. [*As he relaxes, and turns, almost shuddering, from the possibility of dreadful knowledge.*] No . . no . . he never guessed. [*Then with a sudden fresh impulse.*] I hope you won't do this, Mr. Booth.

MR. BOOTH. I have quite made up my mind.

EDWARD. You must let me persuade you——

MR. BOOTH. [*Conciliatory.*] I shall make a point of informing your family that you are in no way to blame in the matter. And in the event of any personal legal difficulties I shall always be delighted to come to you. My idea is for the future to employ merely a financial agent——

EDWARD. [*Still quite unstrung really, and his nerves betraying him.*] If you had made up your mind before my father died to do this, you ought to have told h i m.

MR. BOOTH. Please allow me to know my own business best. I did not choose to distress him by——

EDWARD. [*Pulling himself together: speaking half to himself.*] Well . . well . . this is one way out. And it's not my fault.

MR. BOOTH. You're making a fearful fuss about a very simple matter, Edward. The loss of one client, however important he may be . . Why, this is one of the best family practices in London. I am surprised at your lack of dignity.

> EDWARD *yields smilingly to this assertiveness.*

EDWARD. True . . I have no dignity. Will you walk off with your papers now?

MR. BOOTH. What notice is usual?

EDWARD. To a good solicitor, five minutes. Ten to a poor one.

MR. BOOTH. You'll have to explain matters a bit to me. *Now* EDWARD *settles to his desk again; really with a certain grim enjoyment of the prospect.*

EDWARD. Yes, I had better. Well, Mr. Booth, how much do you think you're worth?

MR. BOOTH. [*Easily.*] I couldn't say off hand.

EDWARD. But you've a rough idea?

MR. BOOTH. To be sure.

EDWARD. You'll get not quite half that out of us.

MR. BOOTH. [*Precisely.*] I think I said I had made up my mind to withdraw the whole amount.

EDWARD. You should have made up your mind sooner.

MR. BOOTH. I don't in the least understand you, Edward.

EDWARD. A great part of your capital doesn't exist.

MR. BOOTH. [*With some irritation.*] Nonsense! It must exist. [*He scans* EDWARD'S *set face in vain.*] You mean that it won't be prudent to realise? You can hand over the securities. I don't want to reinvest simply because——

EDWARD. I can't hand over what I haven't got.

This sentence falls on the old man's ears like a knell.

MR. BOOTH. Is anything . . w r o n g?

EDWARD. [*Grim and patient.*] How many more times am I to say that we have robbed you of nearly half your property?

MR. BOOTH. [*His senses failing him.*] Say that again.

EDWARD. It's quite true.

MR. BOOTH. My money . . g o n e?

EDWARD. Yes.

MR. BOOTH. [*Clutching at a straw of anger.*] You've been the thief . . you . . you . . ?

EDWARD.   I wouldn't tell you if I could help it . . my father.

> *That actually calls the old man back to something like dignity and self-possession. He thumps on* EDWARD'S *table furiously.*

MR. BOOTH.   I'll make you prove that.

> *And now* EDWARD *buries his face in his arms and just goes off into hysterics.*

EDWARD.   Oh, you've fired a mine!

MR. BOOTH.   [*Scolding him well.*] Slandering your dead father . . and lying to me, revenging yourself by frightening me . . because I detest you.

EDWARD.   Why . . haven't I thanked you for putting an end to all my troubles? I do . . I promise you I do.

MR. BOOTH.   [*Shouting, and his sudden courage failing as he shouts.*] Prove this . . prove it to me! I'm not to be frightened so easily. One can't lose half of all one has and then be told of it in two minutes . . sitting at a table. [*His voice falls off to a piteous whimper.*]

EDWARD.   [*Quietly now, and kindly.*] If my father had told you this in plain words you'd have believed him.

MR. BOOTH.   [*Bowing his head.*] Yes.

> EDWARD *looks at the poor old thing with great pity.*

EDWARD.   What on earth did you want to withdraw your account for? You need never have known . . you could have died happy. Settling with all those charities in your will would certainly have smashed us up. But proving your will is many years off yet, we'll hope.

MR. BOOTH.   [*Pathetic and bewildered.*] I don't understand. No, I don't understand . . because your father . . But I m u s t understand, Edward.

EDWARD.   Don't shock yourself trying to understand my father, for you never will. Pull yourself together, Mr. Booth. After all, this isn't a vital matter to you. It's

not even as if you had a family to consider . . like some
of the others.

MR. BOOTH. [*Vaguely.*] What others?

EDWARD. Don't imagine your money has been specially
selected for pilfering.

MR. BOOTH. [*With solemn incredulity.*] One has read
of this sort of thing, but . . I thought people always got
found out.

EDWARD. [*Brutally humorous.*] Well . . we are found
out. You've found us out.

MR. BOOTH. [*Rising to the full appreciation of his
wrongs.*] Oh . . I've been foully cheated!

EDWARD. [*Patiently.*] I've told you so.

MR. BOOTH. [*His voice breaks, he appeals pitifully.*]
But by you, Edward . . say it's by you.

EDWARD. [*Unable to resist his quiet revenge.*] I've not
the ability or the personality for such work, Mr. Booth . .
nothing but principles, which forbid me even to lie to you.

*The old gentleman draws a long breath, and then
speaks with great awe, blending into grief.*

MR. BOOTH. I think your father is in Hell . . I'd have
gone there myself to save him from it. I loved him very
truly. How he could have had the heart! We were
friends for nearly fifty years. Am I to think now he only
cared for me to cheat me?

EDWARD. [*Venturing the comfort of an explanation.*]
No . . he didn't value money as you do.

MR. BOOTH. [*With sudden shrill logic.*] But he took it.
What d'you mean by that?

*EDWARD leans back in his chair and changes the
tenor of their talk.*

EDWARD. Well, you're master of the situation now.
What are you going to do?

MR. BOOTH. To get my money back.

EDWARD. No, that's gone.

MR. BOOTH. Then give me what's left, and——

EDWARD. Are you going to prosecute?

MR. BOOTH. [*Shifting uneasily in his chair.*] Oh, dear
. . is that necessary? Can't somebody else do that? I
thought the Law——

EDWARD. You need not prosecute, you know.

MR. BOOTH. What'll happen if I don't?

EDWARD. What do you suppose I'm doing here now?

MR. BOOTH. [*As if he were being asked a riddle.*] I
don't know.

EDWARD. [*Earnestly.*] I'm trying to straighten things
a little. I'm trying to undo what my father did . . to do
again what he undid. It's a poor, dull sort of work now . .
throwing penny after penny, hardly earned, into the pit of
our deficit. But I've been doing that for what it's worth,
in the time that was left to me . . till this should happen.
I never thought you'd bring it to pass. I can continue to
do that, if you choose . . until the next smash comes. I'm
pleased to call this my duty. [*He searches* MR. BOOTH'S
*face, and finds there only disbelief and fear. He bursts
out.*] Oh, why won't you believe me? It can't hurt you
to believe it.

MR. BOOTH. You must admit, Edward, it isn't easy to
believe anything in this office . . just for the moment.

EDWARD. [*Bowing to the extreme reasonableness of
this.*] I suppose not. I can prove it to you. I'll take you
through the books . . you won't understand them . . but
I could prove it.

MR. BOOTH. I think I'd rather not. D'you think I ought
to hold any further communication with you at all? [*And
at this he takes his hat.*]

EDWARD. [*With a little explosion of contemptuous anger.*] Certainly not. Prosecute . . prosecute!

MR. BOOTH. [*With dignity.*] Don't lose your temper.
You know it's my place to be angry with you.

EDWARD. I beg your pardon. [*Then he is elaborately explanatory.*] I shall be g r a t e f u l if you'll prosecute.

MR. BOOTH. [*More puzzled than ever.*] There's something in this which I don't understand.

EDWARD. [*With deliberate unconcern.*] Think it over.

MR. BOOTH. [*Hesitating, fidgetting.*] But surely I oughtn't to have to make up my mind! There must be a right or wrong thing to do. Edward, can't y o u tell me?

EDWARD. I'm prejudiced.

MR. BOOTH. [*Angrily.*] What do you mean by placing me in a dilemma? I believe you're simply trying to practise upon my goodness of heart. Certainly I ought to prosecute at once . . Oughtn't I? [*Then at the nadir of helplessness.*] Can't I consult another solicitor?

EDWARD. [*His chin in the air.*] Write to the Times about it!

MR. BOOTH. [*Shocked and grieved at his attitude.*] Edward, how can you be so cool and heartless?

EDWARD. [*Changing his tone.*] D'you think I shan't be glad to sleep at nights?

MR. BOOTH. Perhaps you'll be put in prison?

EDWARD. I a m in prison . . a less pleasant one than Wormwood Scrubbs. But we're all prisoners, Mr. Booth.

MR. BOOTH. [*Wagging his head.*] Yes, this is what comes of your philosophy. Why aren't you on your knees?

EDWARD. To you?

This was not what MR. BOOTH *meant, but as he gets up from his chair he feels all but mighty.*

MR. BOOTH. And why should you expect me to shrink from vindicating the law?

EDWARD. [*Shortly.*] I don't. I've explained you'll be doing me a kindness. When I'm wanted you'll find me here at my desk. [*Then as an afterthought.*] If you take long to decide . . don't alter your behaviour to my family

in the meantime. They know the main points of the business, and——

MR. BOOTH. [*Knocked right off his balance.*] Do they?
Good God! . . I'm invited to dinner the day after to-
morrow . . that's Christmas Eve. The hypocrites!

EDWARD. [*Unmoved.*] I shall be there . . that will
have given you two days. Will you tell me then?

MR. BOOTH. [*Protesting violently.*] I can't go to dinner
. . I can't eat with them! I must be ill!

EDWARD. [*With a half smile.*] I remember I went to
dinner at Chislehurst to tell my father of my decision.

MR. BOOTH. [*Testily.*] What decision?

EDWARD. To remain in the firm when I first knew of
the difficulties.

MR. BOOTH. [*Interested.*] Was I present?

EDWARD. I daresay.

> MR. BOOTH *stands there, hat, stick and gloves in
> hand, shaken by his experience, helpless, at his wits'
> end. He falls into a sort of fretful reverie, speak-
> ing half to himself, but yet as if he hoped that* ED-
> WARD, *who is wrapped in his own thoughts, would
> have the decency to answer, or at least listen, to
> what he is saying.*

MR. BOOTH. Yes, how often I dined with him! Oh, it
was monstrous! [*His eyes fall on the clock.*] It's nearly
lunch time now. Do you know, I still can hardly believe
all this? I wish I hadn't found it out. If he hadn't died I
should never have found it out. I hate to have to be vindictive . . it's not my nature. Indeed, I'm sure I'm more
grieved than angry. But it isn't as if it were a small sum.
And I don't see that one is called upon to forgive crimes
. . or why does the Law exist? I feel that this will go
near to killing me. I'm too old to have such troubles . .
it isn't right. And now if I have to prosecute——

EDWARD. [*At last throwing in a word.*] You need not.

MR. BOOTH. [*Thankful for the provocation.*] Don't you attempt to influence me, sir!

> *He turns to go.*

EDWARD. With the money you have left . . .

> EDWARD *follows him politely.* MR. BOOTH *flings the door open.*

MR. BOOTH. Make out a cheque for that at once and send it me.

EDWARD. You could . . .

MR. BOOTH. [*Clapping his hat on, stamping his stick.*] I shall do the right thing, sir, never fear.

> *So he marches off in fine style, having, he thinks, had the last word and all. But* EDWARD, *closing the door after him, mutters . .*

EDWARD. . . Save your soul! . . I'm afraid I was going to say.

THE FIFTH ACT

Naturally, it is the dining-room—consecrated as it is to the distinguishing orgie of the season—which bears the brunt of what an English household knows as Christmas decorations. They consist chiefly of the branches of holly (that unyielding tree), stuck cockeyed behind the top edges of the pictures. The one picture conspicuously not decorated is that which now hangs over the fireplace, a portrait of MR. VOYSEY, with its new gilt frame and its brass plate marking it also as a presentation. HONOR, hastily, and at some hodily peril, pulled down the large bunch of mistletoe which a callous housemaid had suspended above it, in time to obviate the shock to family feelings which such impropriety would cause. Otherwise the only difference between the dining-room's appearance at half past nine on Christmas eve and on any other evening in the year is that little piles of queer-shaped envelopes seem to be lying about, while there is quite a lot of tissue paper and string to be seen peeping from odd corners. The electric light is reduced to one bulb, but when the maid opens the door, showing in MR. GEORGE BOOTH, she switches on the rest.

PHŒBE.   This room is empty, sir.   I'll tell Mr. Edward. *She leaves him to fidget towards the fireplace and back, not removing his comforter or his coat, scarcely turning down the collar, screwing his cap in his*

> *hands. In a very short time* EDWARD *comes in, shutting the door, and taking stock of the visitor before he speaks.*

EDWARD. Well?

MR. GEORGE BOOTH. [*Feebly.*] I hope my excuse for not coming to dinner was acceptable. I did have . . I have a very bad headache.

EDWARD. I daresay they believed it.

MR. GEORGE BOOTH. I have come immediately to tell you of my decision . . perhaps this trouble will then be a little more off my mind.

EDWARD. What is it?

MR. GEORGE BOOTH. I couldn't think the matter out alone. I went this afternoon to talk it all over with my old friend Colpus. [*At this news* EDWARD'S *eyebrows contract and then rise.*] What a terrible shock to him!

EDWARD. Oh, nearly three of his four thousand pounds are quite safe.

MR. GEORGE BOOTH. That you and your father . . you, whom he baptised . . should have robbed him! I never saw a man so utterly prostrate with grief. That it should have been your father! And his poor wife! . . though she never got on with your father.

EDWARD. [*With cheerful irony.*] Oh, Mrs. Colpus knows, too, does she?

MR. GEORGE BOOTH. Of course he told Mrs. Colpus. This is an unfortunate time for the storm to break on him. What with Christmas Day and Sunday following so close, they're as busy as can be. He has resolved that during this season of peace and goodwill he must put the matter from him if he can. But once Christmas is over . . ! [*He envisages the Christian old Vicar giving* EDWARD *a hell of a time then.*]

EDWARD. [*Coolly.*] So I conclude you mean to prosecute. For if you don't, you've given the Colpuses a lot of

unnecessary pain . . and inflicted a certain amount of loss
by telling them.

MR. GEORGE BOOTH. [*Naïvely.*] I never thought of that.
No, Edward, I have decided not to prosecute.

EDWARD *hides his face for a moment.*

EDWARD. And I've been hoping to escape! Well . . it
can't be helped. [*And he sets his teeth.*]

MR. GEORGE BOOTH. [*With touching solemnity.*] I think
I could not bear to see the family I have loved brought
to such disgrace.

EDWARD. So you'll compound my felony?

MR. GEORGE BOOTH. [*A little nervous.*] That's only your
joke!

EDWARD. You'll come to no harm.

MR. GEORGE BOOTH. On the contrary. And I want to
ask your pardon, Edward, for some of the hard thoughts I
have had of you. I consider this effort of yours to restore
to the firm the credit which your father lost a very strik-
ing one. What improvements have you effected so far?

EDWARD. [*Wondering what is coming now.*] I took the
money that my father left . .

MR. GEORGE BOOTH. And I suppose you take the ordinary
profits of the firm?

EDWARD. Yes. It costs me very little to live.

MR. GEORGE BOOTH. Do you restore to the clients all
round, in proportion to the amount they have lost?

EDWARD. [*Cautiously.*] That's the law.

MR. GEORGE BOOTH. D'you think that's quite fair?

EDWARD. No, I don't.

MR. GEORGE BOOTH. No, I consider the treachery to have
been blacker in some cases than in others.

EDWARD. [*His face brightening a little.*] Are you going
to help me in this work of mine?

MR. GEORGE BOOTH. Surely, by consenting not to prosecute I am doing so.

EDWARD. Will you do no more?

MR. GEORGE BOOTH. Well, as far as my own money is concerned, this is my proposal. [*He coughs, and proceeds very formally.*] Considering how absolutely I trusted your father, and believed in him, I think you should at once return me the balance of my capital that there is left.

EDWARD. [*Cold again.*] That is being done.

MR. GEORGE BOOTH. Good. That you should continue to pay me a fair interest upon the rest of that capital, which ought to exist and does not. And that you should, year by year, pay me back by degrees out of the earnings of the firm as much of that capital as you can afford. We will agree upon the sum . . say a thousand a year. I doubt if you can ever restore me all that I have lost, but do your best, and I shan't complain. There . . I think that is fair dealing !

> EDWARD *does not take his eyes off* MR. BOOTH *until the whole meaning of this proposition has settled in his brain. Then, without warning, he goes off into peals of laughter, much to the alarm of* MR. BOOTH, *who has never thought him over-sane.*

EDWARD. How funny ! How very funny !

MR. GEORGE BOOTH. Edward, don't laugh.

EDWARD. I never heard anything quite so funny !

MR. GEORGE BOOTH. Edward, stop laughing !

EDWARD. What will Colpus . . what will all the other Christian gentlemen demand? Pounds of flesh! Pounds of flesh !

MR. GEORGE BOOTH. Don't be hysterical. I demand what is mine . . in such quantities as you can afford.

> EDWARD'S *laughter gives way to the deepest anger of which he is capable.*

EDWARD. I'm giving my soul and body to restoring you and the rest of you to your precious money bags . . and you'll wring me dry. Won't you? Won't you?

MR. GEORGE BOOTH.   Now be reasonable. Argue the point quietly.

EDWARD.   Go to the devil, sir!

And with that he turns away from the flabbergasted old gentleman.

MR. GEORGE BOOTH.   Don't be rude.

EDWARD.   [*His anger vanishing.*] I beg your pardon.

MR. GEORGE BOOTH.   You're excited. Take time to think of it. I'm reasonable.

EDWARD.   [*His sense of humour returning.*]   Most! Most! [*There is a knock at the door.*] Come in! Come in!

HONOR *intrudes an apologetic head.*

HONOR.   Am I interrupting business? I'm so sorry.

EDWARD.   [*Crowing in a mirthless enjoyment of his joke.*] No! Business is over . . quite over. Come in, Honor.

HONOR *puts on the table a market basket bulging with little paper parcels, and, oblivious to* MR. BOOTH'S *distracted face, tries to fix his attention.*

HONOR.   I thought, dear Mr. Booth, perhaps you wouldn't mind carrying round this basket of things yourself. It's so very damp underfoot that I don't want to send one of the maids out to-night if I can possibly avoid it . . and if one doesn't get Christmas presents the very first thing on Christmas morning quite half the pleasure in them is lost, don't you think?

MR. GEORGE BOOTH.   Yes . . yes.

HONOR.   [*Fishing out the parcels one by one.*] This is a bell for Mrs. Williams . . something she said she wanted so that you can ring that for her, which saves the maids. Cap and apron for Mary. Cap and apron for Ellen. Shawl for Davis, when she goes out to the larder. All useful presents. And that's something for you, but you're not to look at it till the morning.

Having shaken each of these at the old gentleman, she proceeds to re-pack them. He is now trembling with anxiety to escape before any more of the family find him there.

MR. GEORGE BOOTH. Thank you . . thank you! I hope my lot has arrived. I left instructions . .

HONOR. Quite safely . . and I have hidden them. Presents are put on the breakfast table to-morrow.

EDWARD. [*With an inconsequence that still further alarms* MR. BOOTH.] When we were all children our Christmas breakfast was mostly made off chocolates.

Before the basket is packed, MRS. VOYSEY *sails slowly into the room, as smiling and as deaf as ever.* MR. BOOTH *does his best not to scowl at her.*

MRS. VOYSEY. Are you feeling better, George Booth?

MR. GEORGE BOOTH. No. [*Then he elevates his voice, with a show of politeness.*] No, thank you . . I can't say I am.

MRS. VOYSEY. You don't look better.

MR. GEORGE BOOTH. I still have my headache. [*With a distracted shout.*] Headache.

MRS. VOYSEY. Bilious, perhaps! I quite understand you didn't care to dine. But why not have taken your coat off? How foolish, in this warm room!

MR. GEORGE BOOTH. Thank you. I'm just going.

He seizes the market basket. At that moment MRS. HUGH *appears.*

BEATRICE. Your shawl, mother. [*And she clasps it round* MRS. VOYSEY's *shoulders.*]

MRS. VOYSEY. Thank you, Beatrice. I thought I had it on. [*Then to* MR. BOOTH, *who is now entangled in his comforter.*] A merry Christmas to you.

BEATRICE. Good evening, Mr. Booth.

MR. GEORGE BOOTH. I beg your pardon. Good evening, Mrs. Hugh.

HONOR. [*With sudden inspiration, to the company in*

general.]   Why shouldn't I write in here . . now the table's cleared!

MR. GEORGE BOOTH.   [*Sternly, now he is safe by the door.*]   Will you see me out, Edward?

EDWARD.   Yes.

> *He follows the old man and his basket, leaving the others to distribute themselves about the room. It is a custom of the female members of the* VOYSEY *family, especially about Christmas time, to return to the dining-room, when the table has been cleared, and occupy themselves in various ways which require space and untidiness. Sometimes, as the evening wears on, they partake of cocoa, sometimes they abstain.* BEATRICE *has a little work-basket, containing a buttonless glove and such things, which she is rectifying.* HONOR'S *writing is done with the aid of an enormous blotting book, which bulges with apparently a year's correspondence. She sheds its contents upon the end of the dining table and spreads them abroad.* MRS. VOYSEY *settles to the fire, opens the Nineteenth Century, and is instantly absorbed in it.*

BEATRICE.   Where's Emily?

HONOR.   [*Mysteriously.*]   Well, Beatrice, she's in the library, talking to Booth.

BEATRICE.   Talking to her husband; good Heavens! I know she has taken my scissors.

HONOR.   I think she's telling him about you.

BEATRICE.   What about me?

HONOR.   You and Hugh.

BEATRICE.   [*With a little movement of annoyance.*]   I suppose this is Hugh's fault. It was carefully arranged no one was to be told till after Christmas.

HONOR.   Emily told me . . and Edward knows . . and Mother knows . .

BEATRICE. I warned Mother a year ago.

HONOR. Everyone seems to know but Booth . . so I thought he'd better be told. I suggested one night so that he might have time to think over it . . but Emily said that'd wake Alfred. Besides, she's nearly always asleep herself when he comes to bed.

BEATRICE. Why do they still have that baby in their room?

HONOR. Emily considers it her duty.

At this moment EMILY *comes in, looking rather trodden upon.* HONOR *concludes in the most audible of whispers . .*

HONOR. Don't say anything . . it's my fault.

BEATRICE. [*Fixing her with a severe forefinger.*] Emily . . have you taken my best scissors?

EMILY. [*Timidly.*] No, Beatrice.

HONOR. [*Who is diving into the recesses of the blotting book.*] Oh, here they are! I must have taken them. I do apologise!

EMILY. [*More timidly still.*] I'm afraid Booth's rather cross . . he's gone to look for Hugh.

BEATRICE. [*With a shake of her head.*] Honor . . I've a good mind to make you sew on these buttons for me.

In comes the Major, strepitant. He takes, so to speak, just time enough to train himself on BEATRICE, *and then fires.*

BOOTH. Beatrice, what on earth is this Emily has been telling me?

BEATRICE. [*With elaborate calm.*] Emily, what have you been telling Booth?

BOOTH. Please . . please do not prevaricate. Where is Hugh?

MRS. VOYSEY. [*Looking over her spectacles.*] What did you say, Booth?

BOOTH. I want Hugh, Mother.

MRS. VOYSEY. I thought you were playing billiards together.

> EDWARD *strolls back from despatching* MR. BOOTH, *his face thoughtful.*

BOOTH. [*Insistently.*] Edward, where is Hugh?

EDWARD. [*With complete indifference.*] I don't know.

BOOTH. [*In trumpet tones.*] Honor, will you oblige me by finding Hugh, and saying I wish to speak to him, here, immediately?

> HONOR, *who has leapt at the sound of her name, flies from the room without a word.*

BEATRICE. I know quite well what you want to talk about, Booth. Discuss the matter by all means, if it amuses you . . but don't shout.

BOOTH. I use the voice Nature has gifted me with, Beatrice.

BEATRICE. [*As she searches for a glove button.*] Certainly Nature did let herself go over your lungs.

BOOTH. [*Glaring round with indignation.*] This is a family matter, otherwise I should not feel it my duty to interfere . . as I do. Any member of the family has a right to express an opinion. I want Mother's. Mother, what do you think?

MRS. VOYSEY. [*Amicably.*] What about?

BOOTH. Hugh and Beatrice separating.

MRS. VOYSEY. They haven't separated.

BOOTH. But they mean to.

MRS. VOYSEY. Fiddle-de-dee!

BOOTH. I quite agree with you.

BEATRICE. [*With a charming smile.*] This reasoning would convert a stone.

BOOTH. Why have I not been told?

BEATRICE. You have just been told.

BOOTH. [*Thunderously.*] Before.

BEATRICE. The truth is, dear Booth, we're all so afraid of you.

BOOTH. [*A little mollified.*] Ha . . I should be glad to think that.

BEATRICE. [*Sweetly.*] Don't you?

BOOTH. [*Intensely serious.*] Beatrice, your callousness shocks me! That you can dream of deserting Hugh . . a man of all others who requires constant care and attention.

BEATRICE. May I remark that the separation is as much Hugh's wish as mine?

BOOTH. I don't believe that.

BEATRICE. [*Her eyebrows up.*] Really!

BOOTH. I don't imply that you're lying. But you must know that it's Hugh's nature to wish to do anything that he thinks anybody wishes him to do. All my life I've had to stand up for him . . and, by Jove, I'll continue to do so.

EDWARD. [*From the depths of his armchair.*] If you'd taught him to stand up for himself——

The door is flung almost off its hinges by HUGH, *who then stands stamping, and pale green with rage.*

HUGH. Look here, Booth . . I will not have you interfering with my private affairs. Is one never to be free from your bullying?

BOOTH. You ought to be grateful.

HUGH. Well, I'm not.

BOOTH. This is a family affair.

HUGH. It is not!

BOOTH. [*At the top of his voice.*] If all you can do is to contradict me, you'd better listen to what I've got to say . . quietly.

HUGH, *quite shouted down, flings himself petulantly into a chair. A hush falls.*

EMILY. [*In a still small voice.*] Would you like me to go, Booth?

BOOTH. [*Severely.*] No, Emily. Unless anything has

been going on which cannot be discussed before you . .
[*Then more severely still.*]   And I hope that is not so.

HUGH. [*Muttering rebelliously.*]   Oh, you have the
mind of a . . cheap schoolmaster!

BOOTH.   Why do you wish to separate?

HUGH.   What's the use of telling you? You won't understand.

BEATRICE. [*Who sews on, undisturbed.*]   We don't get
on well together.

BOOTH. [*Amazedly.*]   Is that all?

HUGH. [*Snapping at him.*]   Yes, that's all. Can you
find a better reason?

BOOTH. [*With brotherly contempt.*]   I have given up
expecting common sense from you. But Beatrice—! [*His
tone implores her to be reasonable.*]

BEATRICE.   It doesn't seem to me any sort of sense that
people should live together for purposes of mutual irritation.

BOOTH. [*Protesting.*]   My dear girl! . . that sounds
like a quotation from your last book.

BEATRICE.   It isn't. I do think, Booth, you might read
that book . . for the honour of the Family.

BOOTH. [*Successfully side-tracked* . .]   I have bought
it, Beatrice, and——

BEATRICE.   That's the principal thing, of course——

BOOTH. [. . *and discovering it.*]   But do let us keep to
the subject.

BEATRICE. [*With flattering sincerity.*]   Certainly, Booth.
And there is hardly any subject that I wouldn't ask your
advice about. But upon this . . do let me know better.
Hugh and I will be happier apart.

BOOTH. [*Obstinately.*]   Why?

BEATRICE. [*With resolute patience, having vented a little sigh.*]   Hugh finds that my opinions distress him. And
I have at last lost patience with Hugh.

MRS. VOYSEY. [*Who has been trying to follow this through her spectacles.*] What does Beatrice say?

BOOTH. [*Translating into a loud sing-song.*] That she wishes to leave her husband because she has lost patience!

MRS. VOYSEY. [*With considerable acrimony.*] Then you must be a very ill-tempered woman. Hugh has a sweet nature.

HUGH. [*Shouting self-consciously.*] Nonsense, mother!

BEATRICE. [*Shouting good-humouredly.*] I quite agree with you, mother. [*She continues to her husband in an even just tone.*] You have a sweet nature, Hugh, and it is most difficult to get angry with you. I have been seven years working up to it. But now that I am angry, I shall never get pleased again.

> *The Major returns to his subject, refreshed by a moment's repose.*

BOOTH. How has he failed in his duty? Tell us. I'm not bigoted in his favour. I know your faults, Hugh.

> *He wags his head at* HUGH, *who writhes with irritation.*

HUGH. Why can't you leave them alone . . leave us alone?

BEATRICE. I'd state my case against Hugh, if I thought he'd retaliate.

HUGH. [*Desperately rounding on his brother.*] If I tell you, you won't understand. You understand nothing! Beatrice is angry with me because I won't prostitute my art to make money.

BOOTH. [*Glancing at his wife.*] Please don't use metaphors of that sort.

BEATRICE. [*Reasonably.*] Yes, I think Hugh ought to earn more money.

BOOTH. [*Quite pleased to be getting along at last.*] Well, why doesn't he?

HUGH. I don't want money.

BOOTH.   You can't say you don't want money any more than you can say you don't want bread.

BEATRICE.   [*As she breaks off her cotton.*]   It's when one has known what it is to be a little short of both . .

> *Now the Major spreads himself, and begins to be very wise, while* HUGH, *to whom this is more intolerable than all, can only clutch his hair.*

BOOTH.   You know I never considered Art a very good profession for you, Hugh.   And you won't even stick to one department of it.   It's a profession that gets people into very bad habits, I consider.   Couldn't you take up something else?   You could still do those wood-cuts in your spare time to amuse yourself.

HUGH.   [*Commenting on this with two deliberate shouts of simulated mirth.*]   Ha! Ha!

BOOTH.   [*Sublimely superior.*]   Well, it wouldn't much matter if you didn't do them at all!

BEATRICE.   [*Subtly.*]   Booth, there speaks the true critic.

BOOTH.   [*Deprecating any title to omniscience.*]   Well, I don't pretend to know much about Art, but——

HUGH.   It would matter to me.   There speaks the artist.

BEATRICE.   The arrogance of the artist.

HUGH.   We have a right to be arrogant.

BEATRICE.   Good workmen are humble.

HUGH.   And look to their wages.

BEATRICE.   Well, I'm only a workman.

> *With that she breaks the contact of this quiet, deadly, hopeless little quarrel by turning her head away. The Major, who has given it most friendly attention, comments . .*

BOOTH.   Of course! Quite so! I'm sure all that is a very interesting difference of opinion.

> MRS. VOYSEY *leaves her armchair for her favourite station at the dining table.*

MRS. VOYSEY.   Booth is the only one of you that I can

hear at all distinctly. But if you two foolish young people
think you want to separate . . try it. You'll soon come
back to each other and be glad to. People can't fight
against Nature for long. And marriage is a natural state
. . once you're married.

BOOTH. [*With intense approval.*] Quite right, Mother.

MRS. VOYSEY. I know.

> *She resumes the Nineteenth Century. The Major,
> to the despair of everybody, makes yet another start,
> trying oratory this time.*

BOOTH. My own opinion is, Beatrice and Hugh, that
you don't realise the meaning of the word marriage. I
don't call myself a religious man . . but dash it all, you
were married in church! . . And you then entered upon
an awful compact! . . Surely . . as a woman, Beatrice . .
the religious point of it ought to appeal to you. Good
Lord, suppose everybody were to carry on like this! And
have you considered, Beatrice, that . . whether you're
right or whether you're wrong . . if you desert Hugh, you
cut yourself off from the Family?

BEATRICE. [*With the sweetest of smiles.*] That will
distress me terribly.

BOOTH. [*Not doubting her for a moment.*] Of course.

> HUGH *flings up his head and finds relief at last in
> many words.*

HUGH. I wish to Heaven I'd ever been able to cut myself off from the family! Look at Trenchard.

BOOTH. [*Gobbling a little at this unexpected attack.*] I
do not forgive Trenchard for quarreling with and deserting our Father.

HUGH. Trenchard quarreled because that was his only
way of escape.

BOOTH. Escape from what?

HUGH. From tyranny! . . from hypocrisy! . . from
boredom! . . from his Happy English Home!

BEATRICE. [*Kindly.*] Hugh . . Hugh . . It's no use.

BOOTH. [*Attempting sarcasm.*] Speak so that Mother can hear you!

But HUGH *isn't to be stopped now.*

HUGH. Why are we all dull, cubbish, uneducated, hopelessly middle-class . . that is, hopelessly out of date?

BOOTH. [*Taking this as very personal.*] Cubbish!

HUGH. . . Because it's the middle-class ideal that you should respect your parents . . live with them . . think with them . . grow like them. Natural affection and gratitude! That's what's expected, isn't it?

BOOTH. [*Not to be obliterated.*] Certainly.

HUGH. Keep your children ignorant of all that you don't know, penniless except for your good pleasure, dependent on you for permission to breathe freely . . and be sure that their gratitude will be most disinterested, and affection very natural. If your father's a drunkard, or poor, then perhaps you get free, and can form an opinion or two of your own . . and can love him or hate him as he deserves. But our Father and Mother were models. They did their duty by us . . and taught us ours. Trenchard escaped, as I say. You took to the Army . . so of course you've never discovered how behind the times you are. [*The Major is stupent.*] I tried to express myself in art . . and found there was nothing to express . . I'd been so well brought up. D'you blame me if I wander about in search of a soul of some sort? And Honor——

BOOTH. [*Disputing savagely.*] Honor is very happy at home. Everyone loves her.

HUGH. [*With fierce sarcasm.*] Yes . . what do we call her? Mother's right hand! I wonder they bothered to give her a name. By the time little Ethel came they were tired of training children. . [*His voice loses its sting; he doesn't complete this sentence.*]

BEATRICE. Poor little Ethel . .

BOOTH. Poor Ethel!

They speak as one speaks of the dead, and so the wrangling stops. Then EDWARD *interposes quietly.*

EDWARD. Yes, Hugh, if we'd been poor . .

HUGH. I haven't spoken of your fate, Edward. That's too shameful.

EDWARD. . . We should at least have learnt how to spend money.

BOOTH. [*Pathetically.*] Really, Edward, need you attack me?

HUGH. Well . . you're so proud of representing the family!

BOOTH. And may I ask what we're discussing now?

BEATRICE. Yes, Edward. I knew how to get the greatest possible happiness out of a five-pound note years before I had one.

EDWARD. The first man who saved a sovereign has made a prisoner of me.

BOOTH. [*Determined to capture the conversation again.*] Has made a . . ?

EDWARD. Will make . . if you understand that better, Booth.

BOOTH. I don't understand it at all. [*They leave him the field.*] And why, for no earthly reason, we must suddenly open up a—a street, which is very painful . . I really cannot see. One never knows who may be listening. [*He glances most uneasily towards the door and drops his voice.*] In that unhappy business, Edward, you very wisely did what we all felt to be your duty. I'm sure we all hope you have succeeded in your endeavours. But the least we can do now in respect to our poor Father's memory is to bury the matter in—in decent oblivion. And please . . please don't talk of prison. I thought you'd given up that idea long ago. [*Having dismissed that subject unopposed, he takes a long breath.*] Now we will return to the original subject of discussion. Hugh, this question of a separation——

> *Past all patience,* HUGH *jumps up and flings his chair back to its place.*

HUGH. Beatrice and I mean to separate. And nothing you may say will prevent us. The only difficulty in the way is money. Can we command enough to live apart comfortably?

BOOTH. Well?

HUGH. Well . . we can't.

BOOTH. Well?

HUGH. So we can't separate.

BOOTH. [*Speaking with bewilderment.*] Then what in Heaven's name have we been discussing it for?

HUGH. I haven't discussed it! I don't want to discuss it! Why can't you mind your own business? Now I'll go back to the billiard room and my book.

> *He is gone before the poor Major can recover his lost breath.*

BOOTH. [*As he does recover it.*] I am not an impatient man . . but really . . [*And then words fail him.*]

BEATRICE. [*Commenting calmly.*] Of course, Hugh was a spoilt child. They grow to hate their parents sooner than others. He still cries for what he wants. That makes him a wearisome companion.

BOOTH. [*Very sulky now.*] You married him with your eyes open, I suppose?

BEATRICE. How few women marry with their eyes open!

BOOTH. You have never made the best of Hugh.

BEATRICE. I have spared him that indignity.

BOOTH. [*Vindictively.*] I am very glad that you can't separate.

BEATRICE. As soon as I'm reasonably sure of earning an income I shall walk off from him,

> *The Major revives,*

BOOTH. You will do nothing of the sort, Beatrice.

BEATRICE. [*Unruffled.*] How will you stop me, Booth?

BOOTH. I shall tell Hugh he must command you to stay.

BEATRICE. [*With a little smile.*] Now that might make a difference. It was one of the illusions of my girlhood that I should love a man who would master me.

BOOTH. Hugh must assert himself.

He begins to walk about, giving some indication of how it should be done. BEATRICE'S *smile has vanished.*

BEATRICE. Don't think I've enjoyed taking the lead in everything throughout my married life. But someone had to plan and scheme and be foreseeing . . we weren't sparrows or lilies of the field . . someone had to get up and do something. [*She becomes conscious of his strutting, and smiles rather mischievously.*] Ah . . if I'd married you, Booth!

BOOTH'S *face grows beatific.*

BOOTH. Well, I must own to thinking that I am a masterful man . . that is the duty of every man to be so. [*He adds forgivingly.*] Poor old Hugh!

BEATRICE. [*Unable to resist temptation.*] If I'd tried to leave you, Booth, you'd have whipped me . . wouldn't you?

BOOTH. [*Ecstatically complacent.*] Ha . . well . . !

BEATRICE. Do say yes. Think how it'll frighten Emily.

The Major strokes his moustache, and is most friendly.

BOOTH. Hugh's been a worry to me all my life. And now as Head of the Family . . Well, I suppose I'd better go and give the dear old chap another talking to. I quite see your point of view, Beatrice.

BEATRICE. Why disturb him at his book?

MAJOR BOOTH *leaves them, squaring his shoulders as becomes a lord of creation. The two sisters-in-law*

go on with their work silently for a moment; then
BEATRICE *adds . .*

BEATRICE.   Do you find Booth difficult to manage, Emily?

EMILY.   [*Putting down her knitting to consider the matter.*]   No.   It's best to allow him to talk himself out.
When he's done that he'll often come to me for advice.   I
let him get his own way as much as possible . . or think
he's getting it.   Otherwise he becomes so depressed.

BEATRICE.   [*Quietly amused.*]   Edward shouldn't hear
this.   What has he to do with women's secrets?

EDWARD.   I won't tell . . and I'm a bachelor.

EMILY.   [*Solemnly, as she takes up her knitting again.*]
Do you really mean to leave Hugh?

BEATRICE.   [*Slightly impatient.*]   Emily, I've said so.

They are joined by ALICE MAITLAND, *who comes in
gaily.*

ALICE.   What's Booth shouting about in the billiard
room?

EMILY.   [*Pained.*]   On Christmas Eve, too!

BEATRICE.   Don't you take any interest in my matrimonial affairs?

MRS. VOYSEY *shuts up the Nineteenth Century and
removes her spectacles.*

MRS. VOYSEY.   That's a very interesting article.   The
Chinese Empire must be in a shocking state!   Is it ten
o'clock yet?

EDWARD.   Past.

MRS. VOYSEY.   [*As* EDWARD *is behind her.*]   Can anyone
see the clock?

ALICE.   It's past ten, Auntie.

MRS. VOYSEY.   Then I think I'll go to my room.

EMILY.   Shall I come and look after you, Mother?

MRS. VOYSEY.   If you'd find Honor for me, Emily.

EMILY *goes in search of the harmless, necessary*

HONOR, *and* MRS. VOYSEY *begins her nightly chant of departure.*

MRS. VOYSEY. Good-night, Alice. Good-night, Edward.

EDWARD. Good-night, Mother.

MRS. VOYSEY. [*With sudden severity.*] I'm not pleased with you, Beatrice.

BEATRICE. I'm sorry, Mother.

But, without waiting to be answered, the old lady has sailed out of the room. BEATRICE, EDWARD *and* ALICE *are attuned to each other enough to be able to talk with ease.*

BEATRICE. Hugh is right about his family. It'll never make any new life for itself.

EDWARD. There are Booth's children.

BEATRICE. Poor little devils!

ALICE. [*Judicially.*] Emily is an excellent mother.

BEATRICE. Yes . . they'll grow up good men and women. And one will go into the Army and one into the Navy and one into the Church . . and perhaps one to the Devil and the Colonies. They'll serve their country, and govern it, and help to keep it like themselves . . dull and respectable . . hopelessly middle-class. [*She puts down her work now and elevates an oratorical fist.*] Genius and Poverty may exist in England, if they'll hide their heads. For show days we've our aristocracy. But never let us forget, gentlemen, that it is the plain, solid middle-class man who has made us . . what we are.

EDWARD. [*In sympathetic derision.*] Hear! hear . . ! and cries of bravo!

BEATRICE. Now that is out of my book . . the next one. [*She takes up her work again.*] You know, Edward . . without wishing to open up Painful Streets . . however scandalous it has been, your father left you a man's work to do.

EDWARD. [*His face cloudy.*] An outlaw's!

BEATRICE. [*Whimsical, after a moment.*] I meant that. At all events you've not had to be your Father's right arm . . or the instrument of justice . . or a representative of the people . . or anything second hand of that sort, have you?

EDWARD. [*With sudden excitement.*] Do you know what I discovered the other day about [*he nods at the portrait*] . . him?

BEATRICE. [*Enquiring calmly.*] Innocence or guilt?

EDWARD. He saved his firm once . . that was true. A most capable piece of heroism. Then, fifteen years afterwards . . he started again.

BEATRICE. [*Greatly interested.*] Did he, now?

EDWARD. One can't believe it was merely through weakness . .

BEATRICE. [*With artistic enthusiasm.*] Of course not. He was a great financier . . a man of imagination. He had to find scope for his abilities, or die. He despised these fat little clients living so snugly on their unearned incomes . . and put them and their money to the best use he could.

EDWARD. [*Shaking his head solemnly.*] That's all a fine phrase for robbery.

BEATRICE *turns her clever face to him and begins to follow up her subject keenly.*

BEATRICE. My dear Edward . . I understand you've been robbing your rich clients for the benefit of the poor ones?

ALICE. [*Who hasn't missed a word.*] That's true.

EDWARD. [*Gently.*] Well . . we're all a bit in debt to the poor, aren't we?

BEATRICE. Quite so. And you don't possess, and your father didn't possess that innate sense of the sacredness of property . . . [*she enjoys that phrase*] which alone can make a truly honest man. Nor did the man possess it who picked my pocket last Friday week . . nor does the tax-gatherer . . . nor do I. Your father's freedom from prejudice was tempered by a taste for Power and Display. Yours is by Charity. But that's all the difference I'll admit between you. Robbery! . . it's a beautiful word.

EDWARD. [*A little pained by as much of this as he takes to be serious.*] I think he might have told me the truth.

BEATRICE. Perhaps he didn't know it! Would you have believed him?

EDWARD. Perhaps not. But I loved him.

BEATRICE *looks again at the gentle, earnest face.*

BEATRICE. After as well as before?

EDWARD. Yes. And not from mere force of habit, either.

BEATRICE. [*With reverence in her voice now.*] That should silence a bench of judges. Well . . well . .

> *Her sewing finished, she stuffs the things into her basket, gets up, in her abrupt, unconventional way, and goes without another word. Her brain is busy with the Voysey Inheritance.* EDWARD *and* ALICE *are left in chairs by the fire, facing each other like an old domestic couple.*

EDWARD. Stay and speak to me.

ALICE. I want to. Something more serious has happened since dinner.

EDWARD. I'm glad you can see that.

ALICE. What is it?

EDWARD. [*With sudden exultation.*] The smash has come . . and not by my fault. Old George Booth——

ALICE. Has he been here?

EDWARD. Can you imagine it? That old man forced me into telling him the truth. I told him to take what money of his there was, and prosecute. He won't prosecute, but he bargains to take the money . . and further to bleed us, sovereign by sovereign, as I earn sovereign by sovereign with the sweat of my soul. I'll see him in his Christian Heaven first . . the Jew!

ALICE. [*Keeping her head.*] You can't reason with him?

EDWARD. He thinks he has the whip hand, and he means to use it. Also the Vicar has been told . . who has told his wife. She knows how not to keep a secret. The smash has come at last.

ALICE. So you're glad?

EDWARD. Thankful. My conscience is clear. I've done my best. [*Then, as usual with him, his fervour collapses.*] And oh, Alice . . has it been worth doing?

ALICE. [*Encouragingly.*] Half a dozen people pulled out of the fire.

EDWARD. If only that isn't found out! I've bungled this job, Alice. I feared all along I should. It was work for a strong man . . not for me.

ALICE. Work for a patient man.

EDWARD. You use kind words. But I've never shirked the truth about myself. My father said mine was a weak nature. He knew.

ALICE. You have a religious nature.

EDWARD. [*Surprised.*] Oh, no!

ALICE. [*Proceeding to explain.*] Therefore you're not fond of creeds and ceremonies. Therefore . . as the good things of this worldly world don't satisfy you, you shirk contact with it all you can. I understand this temptation to neglect and despise practical things. But if one yields to it one's character narrows and cheapens. That's a pity . . but it's so.

EDWARD. [*His eyes far away.*] D'you ever feel that there aren't enough windows in a house?

ALICE. [*Prosaically.*] In this weather . . too many.

EDWARD. Well, then . . in a house—especially in a big city—in my office, at work, then . . one is out of hearing of all the music of the world. And when one does get back to Nature, instead of being all curves to her roundness, one is all corners.

ALICE. [*Smiling at him.*] Yes, you love to think idly
. . just as Hugh does. You do it quite well, too. [*Then
briskly.*] Edward, may I scold you?

EDWARD. For that?

ALICE. Because of that. You're grown to be a sloven
lately . . deliberately letting yourself be unhappy.

EDWARD. Is happiness under one's control?

ALICE. My friend, you shouldn't neglect your happiness
any more than you neglect to wash your face. Here has
the squalour of your work been making you poor. Because
it was liable to be stopped at any moment, uncompleted . .
why should that let your life be incomplete? Edward, for
the last eighteen months you've been more like a moral
portent than a man. You've not had a smile to throw to
a friend . . or an opinion upon any subject. You've
dropped your volunteering. [*He protests.*] I know there's
something comic in volunteering . . though Heaven knows
what it is! I suppose you found it out of keeping with
your unhappy fate. And how slack you were in your politics last November. I don't believe you even voted . .

EDWARD. [*Contrite at this.*] That was wrong of me!

ALICE. Yes, I expect a man to be a good citizen. And
you don't even eat properly.

> *With that she completes the accusation, and* EDWARD
> *searches round for a defence.*

EDWARD. Alice, it was always an effort with me to do
all those things . . and lately every effort has had to go to
my work.

ALICE. You did them . . on principle.

EDWARD. Don't laugh at me.

ALICE. [*Whispering the awful words.*] Then truthfully, Edward, once upon a time you were a bit of a prig.

EDWARD. [*With enough sense of humour to whisper
back.*] Was I?

ALICE. I'm afraid so. But the prig fell ill when your

father died . . and had to be buried in his grave. [*Then her voice rises stirringly.*] Oh, don't you see what a blessing this cursed work was meant to be to you? Why must you stand stiff against it?

EDWARD. [*Without a smile now.*] But lately, Alice, I've hardly known myself. Once or twice I've lost my temper . . I've been brutal.

ALICE. That's the best news in the world. There's your own wicked nature coming out. That's what we've been waiting for . . that's what we want. That's you.

EDWARD. [*Still serious.*] I'm sorry for it.

ALICE. Oh, Edward, be a little proud of poor humanity . . take your own share in it gladly. It so discourages the rest of us if you don't.

Suddenly he breaks down completely.

EDWARD. I can't let myself be glad and live. There's the future to think of. And I'm so afraid of that. I must pretend I don't care . . even to myself . . even to you.

ALICE. [*Her mocking at an end.*] What is it you fear most about the future . . not just the obviously unpleasant things?

EDWARD. They'll put me in prison.

ALICE. Perhaps.

EDWARD. Who'll be the man who comes out?

ALICE. Yourself.

EDWARD. No, no! I'm a coward. I can't stand alone, it's too lonely. I need affection . . I need friends. I cling to people that I don't care for deeply . . just for the comfort of it. I've no home of my own. Every house that welcomes me now I like to think of as something of a home. And I know that this disgrace in store will leave me for a long time or a short time . . homeless.

There he sits, shaken. ALICE *waits a moment, not taking her eyes from him; then speaks.*

ALICE. There's something else I want to scold you for.

You've still given up proposing to me. Certainly that shows a lack of courage . . and of perseverance. Or is it the loss of what I always considered a very laudable ambition?

> EDWARD *is hardly able to trust his ears. Then he looks into her face, and his thankfulness frames itself into a single sentence.*

EDWARD. Will you marry me?

ALICE. Yes, Edward.

> *For a minute he just holds his breath with happiness. But he shakes himself free of it, almost savagely.*

EDWARD. No! no! no! We mustn't be stupid. I'm sorry I asked for that.

ALICE. [*With serene strength.*] I'm glad that you want me. While I live . . where I am will be Home.

EDWARD. [*Struggling with himself.*] No, it's too late. If you'd said Yes before I came into my inheritance . . perhaps I shouldn't have given myself to the work. So be glad that it's too late. I am.

ALICE. [*Happily.*] There was never any chance of my marrying you when you were only a well-principled prig. I didn't want you . . and I don't believe you really wanted me. Now you do. And you must always take what you want.

EDWARD. [*Turning to her again.*] My dear, what have we to start life upon . . to build our house upon? Poverty . . and prison for me.

ALICE. [*Mischievous.*] Edward, you seem to think that all the money in the world was invested in your precious firm. I have four hundred a year of my own. At least let that tempt you.

> EDWARD *catches her in his arms with a momentary little burst of passion.*

EDWARD. You're tempting me.

*She did not resist, but nevertheless he breaks away
from her, disappointed with himself. She goes on,
quietly, serenely.*

ALICE. Am I? Am I playing upon your senses in any
way? Am I a silly child, looking to you for protection in
return for your favour? Shall I hinder or help your life?
If you don't think me your equal as woman to man, we'll
never speak of this again. But if you do . . look at me,
and make your choice. To refuse me my work and happiness in life and to cripple your own nature . . or to take
my hand.

*She puts out her hand frankly, as a friend should.
With only a second's thought he, happy, too, now,
takes it as frankly. Then she sits beside him, and
quite cheerfully changes the subject.*

ALICE. Now, referring to the subject of Mr. George
Booth. What will he do?

EDWARD. [*Responsive though impatient.*] He'll do nothing. I shall be before him.

ALICE. What about his proposal?

EDWARD. That needs no answer.

ALICE. Yes, it does. I know the temptation to hit back
at him mock-heroically . . it's natural. Well, we'll consider it done. But he's a silly old man, and he doesn't
know what he's talking about. I think we can bargain
with him to keep the firm going somehow . . and if we
can we must.

*At this EDWARD makes a last attempt to abandon
himself to his troubles.*

EDWARD. No, Alice, no . . let it end here. It has done
for me . . I'm broken. And of course we can't be married . . that's absurd.

ALICE. [*With firmness enough for two.*] We shall be
married. And nothing's broken . . except our pride and
righteousness . . and several other things we're better

without. And now we must break our dignity in to bargaining.

EDWARD. [*Struggling in the toils of virtue.*] But it'll be so useless. Colpus'll be round in a day or two to make his conditions . . he'll tell some intimate friend. They'll all come after their money like wasps after honey. And if they know I won't lift a finger in my own defence . . what sort of mercy will they have?

ALICE. [*Triumphantly completing her case.*] No, Edward, if you surrender yourself entirely, you'll find them powerless against you. You see, you had something to hope or fear from Mr. Booth . . you hoped in your heart he'd end your trouble. But when you've conquered that last little atom of the selfishness which gets in one's way, I think you'll find you can do what you wish with these selfish men. [*And she adds, fervently.*] Oh, it's a power so seldom used. But the man who is able, and cares deeply, and yet has nothing to hope or fear is all powerful . . even in little things.

EDWARD. Will nothing ever happen to set me free? Shall I never be able to rest for a moment . . turn round and say I've succeeded or I've failed?

ALICE. That isn't what matters.

EDWARD. If they could all meet, and agree, they might syndicate themselves, and keep me at it for life.

ALICE. What more could you wish for?

EDWARD. Than that dreary round!

ALICE. My dear, the world must be put tidy. That's the work which splendid criminals . . and others leave about for us poor commonplace people to do.

EDWARD. [*With a little laugh.*] And I don't believe in Heaven, either.

ALICE. [*Close to him.*] But there's to be our life. What's wrong with that?

EDWARD. My dear, when they put me in prison for swindling—— [*He makes the word sound its worst.*]

ALICE. I think they won't. But if they are so stupid . . I must be very careful.

EDWARD. Of what?

ALICE. To avoid false pride. I shall be foolishly proud of you.

EDWARD. It's good to be praised sometimes . . by you.

ALICE. My heart praises you. Good-night.

EDWARD. Good-night.

She kisses his forehead. But he puts up his face like a child, so she bends down, and for the first time their lips meet. Then she steps back from him, adding happily, with perhaps just a touch of shyness.

ALICE. Till to-morrow.

EDWARD. [*Echoing in gratitude the hope and promise in her voice.*] Till to-morrow.

She leaves him to sit there by the table for a few moments longer, looking into his future, streaked as it is to be with trouble and joy. As whose is not? From above . . from above the mantelpiece, that is to say . . the face of the late MR. VOYSEY *seems to look down upon his son not unkindly, though with that curious buccaneering twist of the eyebrows which distinguished his countenance in life.*

Waste

1906-7

WASTE

At Shapters, GEORGE FARRANT's house in Hertfordshire.
Ten o'clock on a Sunday evening in summer.

*Facing you at her piano by the window, from which she
is protected by a little screen, sits* MRS. FARRANT; *a
woman of the interesting age, clear-eyed and all her
face serene, except for a little pucker of the brows
which shows a puzzled mind upon some important
matters. To become almost an ideal hostess has been
her achievement; and in her own home, as now, this
grace is written upon every movement. Her eyes
pass over the head of a girl, sitting in a low chair by
a little table, with the shaded lamplight falling on her
face. This is* LUCY DAVENPORT; *twenty-three, undefeated in anything as yet, and so unsoftened. The
book on her lap is closed, for she has been listening
to the music. It is possibly some German philoso-
pher, whom she reads with a critical appreciation of
his shortcomings. On the sofa near her lounges*
MRS. O'CONNELL; *a charming woman, if by charming
you understand a woman who converts every quality
she possesses into a means of attraction, and has no
use for any others. On the sofa opposite sits* MISS
TREBELL. *In a few years, when her hair is quite
grey, she will assume as by right the dignity of an
old maid. Between these two, in a low armchair, is*
LADY DAVENPORT. *She has attained to many digni-
ties. Mother and grandmother, she has brought into*

215

the world and nourished not merely life but charac-
ter. A wonderful face she has, full of proud memo-
ries and fearless of the future. Behind her, on a
sofa between the windows, is WALTER KENT. *He is*
just what the average English father would like his
son to be. You can see the light shooting out through
the windows and mixing with moonshine upon a
smooth lawn. On your left is a door. There are
many books in the room, hardly any pictures, a stat-
uette perhaps. The owner evidently sets beauty of
form before beauty of colour. It is a woman's room,
and it has a certain delicate austerity. By the time
you have observed everything, MRS. FARRANT *has*
played Chopin's prelude opus 28, number 20, from
beginning to end.

LADY DAVENPORT. Thank you, my dear Julia.

WALTER KENT. [*Protesting.*] No more?

MRS. FARRANT. I won't play for a moment longer than
I feel musical.

MISS TREBELL. Do you think it right, Julia, to finish
with that after an hour's Bach?

MRS. FARRANT. I suddenly came over Chopinesque,
Fanny; . . what's your objection? [*As she sits by her.*]

FRANCES TREBELL. What . . when Bach has raised me
to the heights of unselfishness!

AMY O'CONNELL. [*Grimacing sweetly, her eyes only half
lifted.*] Does he? I'm glad that I don't understand him.

FRANCES TREBELL. [*Putting mere prettiness in its place.*]
One may prefer Chopin when one is young.

AMY O'CONNELL. And is that a reproach or a compliment?

WALTER KENT. [*Boldly.*] I do.

FRANCES TREBELL. Or a man may . . unless he's a phi-
losopher.

LADY DAVENPORT. [*To the rescue.*] Miss Trebell, you're very hard on mere humanity.

FRANCES TREBELL. [*Completing the reproof.*] That's my wretched training as a schoolmistress, Lady Davenport . . one grew to fear it above all things.

LUCY DAVENPORT. [*Throwing in the monosyllable with sharp, youthful enquiry.*] Why?

FRANCES TREBELL. There were no text books on the subject.

MRS. FARRANT. [*Smiling at her friend.*] Yes, Fanny . . I think you escaped to look after your brother only just in time.

FRANCES TREBELL. In another year I might have been head-mistress, which commits you to approve of the system for ever.

LADY DAVENPORT. [*Shaking her wise head.*] I've watched the Education fever take England . . .

FRANCES TREBELL. If I hadn't stopped teaching things I didn't understand . . !

AMY O'CONNELL. [*Not without mischief.*] And what was the effect on the pupils?

LUCY DAVENPORT. I can tell you that.

AMY O'CONNELL. Frances never taught you.

LUCY DAVENPORT. No, I wish she had. But I was at her sort of a school before I went to Newnham. I know.

FRANCES TREBELL. [*Very distastefully.*] Up-to-date, it was described as.

LUCY DAVENPORT. Well, it was like a merry-go-round at top speed. You felt things wouldn't look a bit like that when you came to a standstill.

AMY O'CONNELL. And they don't?

LUCY DAVENPORT. [*With great decision.*] Not a bit.

AMY O'CONNELL. [*In her velvet tone.*] I was taught the whole duty of woman by a parson-uncle who disbelieved in his Church.

WALTER KENT. When a man at Jude's was going to take orders . . .

AMY O'CONNELL. Jude's?

WALTER KENT. At Oxford. The dons went very gingerly with him over bits of science and history.

> [*This wakes a fruitful thought in* JULIA FARRANT'S *brain.*]

MRS. FARRANT. Mamma, have you ever discussed so-called anti-Christian science with Lord Charles?

FRANCES TREBELL. . . Cantelupe?

MRS. FARRANT. Yes. It was over appointing a teacher for the schools down here . . he was staying with us. The Vicar's his fervent disciple. However, we were consulted.

LUCY DAVENPORT. Didn't Lord Charles want you to send the boys there till they were ready for Harrow?

MRS. FARRANT. Yes.

FRANCES TREBELL. Quite the last thing in Toryism!

MRS. FARRANT. Mamma made George say we were too *nouveau riche* to risk it.

LADY DAVENPORT. [*As she laughs.*] I couldn't resist that.

MRS. FARRANT. [*Catching something of her subject's dry, driving manner.*] Lord Charles takes the superior line, and says . . that with his consent the Church may teach the unalterable Truth in scientific language or legendary, whichever is easier understood of the people.

LADY DAVENPORT. Is it the prospect of Disestablishment suddenly makes him so accommodating?

FRANCES TREBELL. [*With large contempt.*] He needn't be. The majority of people believe the world was made in an English week.

LUCY DAVENPORT. Oh, no!

FRANCES TREBELL. No Bishop dare deny it.

MRS. FARRANT. [*From the heights of experience.*] Dear Lucy, do you seriously think that the English spirit—the nerve that runs down the backbone—is disturbed by new theology . . or new anything?

LADY DAVENPORT. [*Enjoying her epigram.*] What a waste of persecution history shows us!

　　　WALTER KENT *now captures the conversation with a very young politician's fervour.*

WALTER KENT. Once they're disestablished they must make up their minds what they do believe.

LADY DAVENPORT. I presume Lord Charles thinks it'll hand the Church over to him and his . . dare I say "Sect"?

WALTER KENT. Won't it? He knows what he wants.

MRS. FARRANT. [*Subtly.*] There's the election to come yet.

WALTER KENT. But now both parties are pledged to a bill of some sort.

MRS. FARRANT. Political prophecies have a knack of not coming true; but, d'you know, Cyril Horsham warned me to watch this position developing . . nearly four years ago.

FRANCES TREBELL. Sitting on the opposite bench sharpens the eyesight.

WALTER KENT. [*Ironically.*] Has he been pleased with the prospect?

MRS. FARRANT. [*With perfect diplomacy.*] If the Church must be disestablished . . better done by its friends than its enemies.

FRANCES TREBELL. Still, I don't gather he's pleased with his dear cousin Charles's conduct.

MRS. FARRANT. [*Shrugging.*] Oh, lately, Lord Charles has never concealed his tactics.

FRANCES TREBELL. And that speech at Leeds was the crowning move, I suppose; just asking the Nonconformists to bring things to a head?

MRS. FARRANT. [*Judicially.*] I think that was precipitate.

WALTER KENT. [*Giving them* LORD CHARLES's *oratory.*] Gentlemen, in these latter days of Radical opportunism!— You know, I was there . . sitting next to an old gentleman who shouted "Jesuit."

FRANCES TREBELL. But supposing Mallaby and the Non-conformists hadn't been able to force the Liberals' hand?

MRS. FARRANT. [*Speaking as of inferior beings.*] Why, they were glad of any cry going to the country!

FRANCES TREBELL. [*As she considers this.*] Yes . . and Lord Charles would still have had as good a chance of forcing Lord Horsham's. It has been clever tactics.

LUCY DAVENPORT. [*Who has been listening, sharp-eyed.*] Contrariwise, he wouldn't have liked a Radical Bill, though, would he?

WALTER KENT. [*With aplomb.*] He knew he was safe from that. The government must have dissolved before Christmas, anyway . . and the swing of the pendulum's a sure thing.

MRS. FARRANT. [*With her smile.*] It's never a sure thing.

WALTER KENT. Oh, Mrs. Farrant, look how unpopular the Liberals are.

FRANCES TREBELL. What made them bring in Resolutions?

WALTER KENT. [*Overflowing with knowledge of the subject.*] I was told Mallaby insisted on their showing they meant business. I thought he was being too clever . . and it turns out he was. Tommy Luxmore told me there was a fearful row in the Cabinet about it. But on their last legs, you know, it didn't seem to matter, I suppose. Even then, if Prothero had mustered up an ounce of tact . . I believe they could have pulled them through . .

FRANCES TREBELL. Not the Spoliation one,

WALTER KENT. Well, Mr. Trebell dished that!

FRANCES TREBELL. Henry says his speech didn't turn a vote.

MRS. FARRANT. [*With charming irony.*] How disinterested of him!

WALTER KENT. [*Enthusiastic.*] That speech did if ever a speech did.

FRANCES TREBELL. Is there any record of a speech that ever did? He just carried his own little following with him.

MRS. FARRANT. But the crux of the whole matter is, and has always been . . what's to be done with the Church's money.

LUCY DAVENPORT. [*Visualising sovereigns.*] A hundred millions or so . . think of it!

FRANCES TREBELL. There has been from the start a good deal of anti-Nonconformist feeling against applying the money to secular uses.

MRS. FARRANT. [*Deprecating false modesty, on anyone's behalf.*] Oh, of course the speech turned votes . . twenty of them at least.

LUCY DAVENPORT. [*Determined on information.*] Then I was told Lord Horsham had tried to come to an understanding himself with the Nonconformists about Disestablishment—oh—a long time ago . . over the Education Bill.

FRANCES TREBELL. Is that true, Julia?

MRS. FARRANT. How should I know?

FRANCES TREBELL. [*With some mischief.*] You might.

MRS. FARRANT. [*Weighing her words.*] I don't think it would have been altogether wise to make advances. They'd have asked more than a Conservative government could possibly persuade the Church to give up.

WALTER KENT. I don't see that Horsham's much better off now. He only turned the Radicals out on the Spoliation question by the help of Trebell. And so far . . I mean till this election is over, Trebell counts still as one of them, doesn't he, Miss Trebell? Oh . . perhaps he doesn't.

FRANCES TREBELL. He'll tell you he never has counted as one of them.

MRS. FARRANT. No doubt Lord Charles would sooner have done without his help. And that's why I didn't ask the gentle Jesuit this week-end, if anyone wants to know.

WALTER KENT. [*Stupent at this lack of party spirit.*] What . . he'd rather have had the Liberals go to the country undefeated!

MRS. FARRANT. [*With finesse.*] The election may bring us back independent of Mr. Trebell and anything he stands for.

WALTER KENT. [*Sharply.*] But you asked Lord Horsham to meet him.

MRS. FARRANT. [*With still more finesse.*] I had my reasons. Votes aren't everything.

> LADY DAVENPORT *has been listening with rather a doubtful smile; she now caps the discussion.*

LADY DAVENPORT. I'm relieved to hear you say so, my dear Julia. On the other hand, democracy seems to have brought itself to a pretty pass. Here's a measure, which the country as a whole neither demands nor approves of, will certainly be carried, you tell me, because a minority on each side is determined it shall be . . for totally different reasons.

MRS. FARRANT. [*Shrugging again.*] It isn't our business to prevent popular government looking foolish, Mamma.

LADY DAVENPORT. Is that Tory cynicism or feminine?

> *At this moment* GEORGE FARRANT *comes through the window; a good-natured man of forty-five. He would tell you that he was educated at Eton and Oxford. But the knowledge which saves his life comes from the thrusting upon him of authority and experience; ranging from the management of an*

estate which he inherited at twenty-four, through the chairmanship of a newspaper syndicate, through a successful marriage, to a minor post in the last Tory cabinet and the prospect of one in the near-coming next. Thanks to his agents, editors, permanent officials, and his own common sense, he always acquits himself creditably. He comes to his wife's side and waits for a pause in the conversation.

LADY DAVENPORT. I remember Mr. Disraeli once said to me . . Clever women are as dangerous to the State as dynamite.

FRANCES TREBELL. [*Not to be impressed by Disraeli.*] Well, Lady Davenport, if men will leave our intellects lying loose about . .

FARRANT. Blackborough's going, Julia.

MRS. FARRANT. Yes, George.

LADY DAVENPORT. [*Concluding her little apologue to* MISS TREBELL.] Yes, my dear, but power without responsibility isn't good for the character that wields it, either.

There follows FARRANT *through the window a man of fifty. He has about him that unmistakable air of acquired wealth and power which distinguishes many Jews, and has therefore come to be regarded as a solely Jewish characteristic. He speaks always with that swift decision which betokens a narrowed view. This is* RUSSELL BLACKBOROUGH, *manufacturer, politician . . statesman, his own side calls him.*

BLACKBOROUGH. [*To his hostess.*] If I start now, they tell me, I shall get home before the moon goes down. I'm sorry I must get back to-night. It's been a most delightful week-end.

MRS. FARRANT. [*Gracefully giving him a good-bye hand.*] And a successful one, I hope.

FARRANT. We talked Education for half an hour.

MRS. FARRANT. [*Her eyebrows lifting a shade.*] Education!

FARRANT. Then Trebell went away to work.

BLACKBOROUGH. I've missed the music, I fear.

MRS. FARRANT. But it's been Bach.

BLACKBOROUGH. No Chopin?

MRS. FARRANT. For a minute only.

BLACKBOROUGH. Why don't these new Italian men write things for the piano? Good-night, Lady Davenport.

LADY DAVENPORT. [*As he bows over her hand.*] And what has Education to do with it?

BLACKBOROUGH. [*Non-committal himself.*] Perhaps it was a subject that compromised nobody.

LADY DAVENPORT. Do you think my daughter has been wasting her time and her tact?

FARRANT. [*Clapping him on the shoulder.*] Blackborough's frankly flabbergasted at the publicity of this intrigue.

MRS. FARRANT. Intrigue! Mr. Trebell walked across the House . . actually into your arms.

BLACKBOROUGH. [*With a certain dubious grimness.*] Well . . we've had some very interesting talks since. And his views upon Education are quite . . Utopian. Goodbye, Miss Trebell.

FRANCES TREBELL. Good-bye.

MRS. FARRANT. I wouldn't be so haughty till after the election, if I were you, Mr. Blackborough.

BLACKBOROUGH. [*Indifferently.*] Oh, I'm glad he's with us on the Church question . . so far.

MRS. FARRANT. So far as you've made up your minds? The electoral cat will jump soon.

BLACKBOROUGH. [*A little beaten by such polite cynicism.*] Well . . our conservative principles! After all, we know what they are. Good-night, Mrs. O'Connell.

AMY O'CONNELL. Good-night.

FARRANT. Your neuralgia better?

AMY O'CONNELL. By fits and starts.

FARRANT. [*Robustly.*] Come and play billiards. Horsham and Maconochie started a game. They can neither of them play. We left them working out a theory of angles on bits of paper.

WALTER KENT. Professor Maconochie lured me on to golf yesterday. He doesn't suffer from theories about that.

BLACKBOROUGH. [*With approval.*] Started life as a caddie.

WALTER KENT. [*Pulling a wry face.*] So he told me after the first hole.

BLACKBOROUGH. What's this, Kent, about Trebell's making you his secretary?

WALTER KENT. He thinks he'll have me.

BLACKBOROUGH. [*Almost reprovingly.*] No question of politics?

FARRANT. More intrigue, Blackborough.

WALTER KENT. [*With disarming candour.*] The truth is, you see, I haven't any as yet. I was Socialist at Oxford . . but of course that doesn't count. I think I'd better learn my job under the best man I can find . . and who'll have me.

BLACKBOROUGH. [*Gravely.*] What does your father say?

WALTER KENT. Oh, as long as Jack will inherit the property in a Tory spirit! My father thinks it my wild oats.

A Footman has come in.

THE FOOTMAN. Your car is round, sir.

BLACKBOROUGH. Ah! Good-night, Miss Davenport. Good-bye again, Mrs. Farrant . . a charming week-end.

He makes a business-like departure. FARRANT *follows him.*

THE FOOTMAN. A telephone message from Dr. Wedgecroft, ma'am. His thanks; they stopped the express for him at Hitchin, and he has reached London quite safely.

MRS. FARRANT. Thank you.

The Footman goes out. MRS. FARRANT *exhales delicately, as if the air were a little refined by* BLACKBOROUGH'S *removal.*

MRS. FARRANT. Mr. Blackborough and his patent turbines and his gas engines and what not are the motive power of our party nowadays, Fanny.

FRANCES TREBELL. Yes, you claim to be steering plutocracy. Do you never wonder if it isn't steering you?

MRS. O'CONNELL, *growing restless, has wandered round the room, picking at the books in their cases.*

AMY O'CONNELL. I always like your books, Julia. It's an intellectual distinction to know someone who has read them.

MRS. FARRANT. That's the Communion I choose.

FRANCES TREBELL. Aristocrat . . fastidious aristocrat.

MRS. FARRANT. No, now. Learning's a great leveller.

FRANCES TREBELL. But Julia . . books are quite unreal. D'you think life is a bit like them?

MRS. FARRANT. They bring me into touch with . . Oh, there's nothing more deadening than to be boxed into a set in Society! Speak to a woman outside it . . she doesn't understand your language.

FRANCES TREBELL. And do you think by prattling Hegel with Gilbert Wedgecroft when he comes to physic you——

MRS. FARRANT. [*Joyously.*] Excellent physic that is. He never leaves a prescription.

LADY DAVENPORT. Don't you think an aristocracy of brains is the best aristocracy, Miss Trebell?

FRANCES TREBELL. [*With a little more bitterness than the abstraction of the subject demands.*] I'm sure it is just as out of touch with humanity as any other . . more so, perhaps. If I were a country I wouldn't be governed by arid intellects.

MRS. FARRANT. Manners, Frances.

FRANCES TREBELL. I'm one myself, and I know. They're either dead or dangerous.

> GEORGE FARRANT *comes back and goes straight to* MRS. O'CONNELL.

FARRANT. [*Still robustly.*] Billiards, Mrs. O'Connell?

AMY O'CONNELL. [*Declining sweetly.*] I think not.

FARRANT. Billiards, Lucy?

LUCY DAVENPORT. [*As robust as he.*] Yes, Uncle George. You shall mark while Walter gives me twenty-five and I beat him.

WALTER KENT. [*With a none-of-your-impudence air.*] I'll give you ten yards start and race you to the billiard room.

LUCY DAVENPORT. Will you wear my skirt? Oh . . Grandmamma's thinking me vulgar.

LADY DAVENPORT. [*Without prejudice.*] Why, my dear, freedom of limb is worth having . . and perhaps it fits better with freedom of tongue.

FARRANT. [*In the proper avuncular tone.*] I'll play you both . . and I'd race you both if you weren't so disgracefully young.

> AMY O'CONNELL *has reached an open window.*

AMY O'CONNELL. I shall go for a walk with my neuralgia.

MRS. FARRANT. Poor thing!

AMY O'CONNELL. The moon's good for it.

LUCY DAVENPORT. Shall you come, Aunt Julia?

MRS. FARRANT. [*In flat protest.*] No, I will not sit up while you play billiards.

> MRS. O'CONNELL *goes out through the one window, stands for a moment, wistfully romantic, gazing at the moon, then disappears.* FARRANT *and* WALTER

KENT *are standing at the other, looking across the lawn.*

FARRANT. Horsham still arguing with Maconochie. They've got to Botany now.

WALTER KENT. Demonstrating something with a . . what's that thing?

WALTER goes out.

FARRANT. [*With a throw of his head towards the distant* HORSHAM.] He was so bored with our politics . . having to give his opinion, too. We could just hear your piano.

And he follows WALTER.

MRS. FARRANT. Take Amy O'Connell that lace thing, will you, Lucy?

LUCY DAVENPORT. [*Her tone expressing quite wonderfully her sentiments towards the owner.*] Don't you think she'd sooner catch cold?

She catches it up and follows the two men; then after looking round impatiently, swings off in the direction MRS. O'CONNELL *took. The three women now left together are at their ease.*

FRANCES TREBELL. Did you expect Mr. Blackborough to get on well with Henry?

MRS. FARRANT. He has become a millionaire by appreciating clever men when he met them.

LADY DAVENPORT. Yes, Julia, but his political conscience is comparatively new-born.

MRS. FARRANT. Well, Mamma, can we do without Mr. Trebell?

LADY DAVENPORT. Everyone seems to think you'll come back with something of a majority.

MRS. FARRANT. [*A little impatient.*] What's the good of that? The Bill can't be brought into the Lords . . and who's going to take Disestablishment through the Commons for us? Not Eustace Fowler . . not Mr. Black-borough . . not Lord Charles . . not George!

LADY DAVENPORT. [*Warningly.*] Not all your brilliance as a hostess will keep Mr. Trebell in a Tory Cabinet.

MRS. FARRANT. [*With wilful avoidance of the point.*] Cyril Horsham is only too glad.

LADY DAVENPORT. Because you tell him he ought to be.

FRANCES TREBELL. [*Coming to the rescue.*] There is this. Henry has never exactly called himself a Liberal. He really is elected independently.

MRS. FARRANT. I wonder will all the garden-cities become pocket-boroughs?

FRANCES TREBELL. I think he has made a mistake.

MRS. FARRANT. It makes things easier now . . his having kept his freedom.

FRANCES TREBELL. I think it's a mistake to stand outside a system. There's an inhumanity in that amount of detachment . .

MRS. FARRANT. [*Brilliantly.*] I think a statesman may be a little inhuman.

LADY DAVENPORT. [*With keenness.*] Do you mean superhuman? It's not the same thing, you know.

MRS. FARRANT. I know.

LADY DAVENPORT. Most people don't know.

MRS. FARRANT. [*Proceeding with her cynicism.*] Humanity achieves . . what? Housekeeping and children.

FRANCES TREBELL. As far as a woman's concerned.

MRS. FARRANT. [*A little mockingly.*] Now, Mamma, say that is as far as a woman's concerned.

LADY DAVENPORT. My dear, you know I don't think so.

MRS. FARRANT. We may none of us think so. But there's our position . . bread and butter and a certain satisfaction until . . Oh, Mamma, I wish I were like you . . beyond all the passions of life.

LADY DAVENPORT. [*With great vitality.*] I'm nothing of

the sort. It's my egoism's dead . . that's an intimation of mortality.

MRS. FARRANT. I accept the snub, but I wonder what I'm to do with myself for the next thirty years.

FRANCES TREBELL. Help Lord Horsham to govern the country.

> JULIA FARRANT *gives a little laugh and takes up the subject this time.*

MRS. FARRANT. Mamma . . how many people, do you think, believe that Cyril's *grande passion* for me takes that form?

LADY DAVENPORT. Everyone who knows Cyril and most people who know you.

MRS. FARRANT. Otherwise I seem to have fulfilled my mission in life. The boys are old enough to go to school. George and I have become happily unconscious of each other.

FRANCES TREBELL. [*With sudden energy of mind.*] Till I was forty I never realised the fact that most women must express themselves through men.

MRS. FARRANT. [*Looking at* FRANCES *a little curiously.*] Didn't your instinct lead you to marry . . or did you fight against it?

FRANCES TREBELL. I don't know. Perhaps I had no vitality to spare.

LADY DAVENPORT. That boy is a long time proposing to Lucy.

> *This effectually startles the other two from their conversational reverie.*

MRS. FARRANT. Walter? I'm not sure that he means to. She means to marry him if he does.

FRANCES TREBELL. Has she told you so?

MRS. FARRANT. No. I judge by her business-like interest in his welfare.

FRANCES TREBELL. He's beginning to feel the responsibility of manhood . . doesn't know whether to be frightened or proud of it.

LADY DAVENPORT. It's a pretty thing to watch young people mating. When they're older, and marry from disappointment or deliberate choice, thinking themselves so worldly-wise . .

MRS. FARRANT. [*Back to her politely cynical mood.*] Well . . then at least they don't develop their differences at the same fire-side, regretting the happy time when neither possessed any character at all.

LADY DAVENPORT. [*Giving a final douche of common sense.*] My dear, any two reasonable people ought to be able to live together.

FRANCES TREBELL. Granted three sitting rooms. That'll be the next middle-class political cry . . when women are heard.

MRS. FARRANT. [*Suddenly as practical as her mother.*] Walter's lucky . . Lucy won't stand any nonsense. She'll have him in the Cabinet by the time he's fifty.

LADY DAVENPORT. And are you the power behind your brother, Miss Trebell?

FRANCES TREBELL. [*Gravely.*] He ignores women. I've forced enough good manners on him to disguise the fact decently. His affections are two generations ahead.

MRS. FARRANT. People like him in an odd sort of way.

FRANCES TREBELL. That's just respect for work done . . one can't escape from it.

> *There is a slight pause in their talk. By some not very devious route* MRS. FARRANT'S *mind travels to the next subject.*

MRS. FARRANT. Fanny . . how fond are you of Amy O'Connell?

FRANCES TREBELL. She says we're great friends.

MRS. FARRANT. She says that of me.

FRANCES TREBELL. It's a pity about her husband.

MRS. FARRANT. [*Almost provokingly.*] What about him?

FRANCES TREBELL. It seems to be understood that he treats her badly.

LADY DAVENPORT. [*A little malicious.*] Is there any particular reason he should treat her well?

FRANCES TREBELL. Don't you like her, Lady Davenport?

LADY DAVENPORT. [*Dealing out justice.*] I find her quite charming to look at and talk to . . but why shouldn't Justin O'Connell live in Ireland for all that? I'm going to bed, Julia.

>   *She collects her belongings and gets up.*

MRS. FARRANT. I must look in at the billiard room.

FRANCES TREBELL. I won't come, Julia.

MRS. FARRANT. What's your brother working at?

FRANCES TREBELL. I don't know. Something we shan't hear of for a year, perhaps.

MRS. FARRANT. On the Church business, I daresay.

FRANCES TREBELL. Did you hear Lord Horsham at dinner on the lack of dignity in an irreligious state?

MRS. FARRANT. Poor Cyril . . he'll have to find a way round that opinion of his now.

FRANCES TREBELL. Does he like leading his party?

MRS. FARRANT. [*After due consideration.*] It's an intellectual exercise. He's the right man, Fanny. You see it isn't a party in the active sense at all, except now and then when it's captured by someone with an axe to grind.

FRANCES TREBELL. [*Humorously.*] Such as my brother.

MRS. FARRANT. [*As humorous.*] Such as your brother. It expresses the thought of the men who aren't taken in by the claptrap of progress.

FRANCES TREBELL. Sometimes they've a queer way of expressing their love for the people of England.

MRS. FARRANT. But one must use democracy. Wellington wouldn't . . Disraeli did.

LADY DAVENPORT. [*At the door.*] Good-night, Miss Trebell.

FRANCES TREBELL. I'm coming . . it's past eleven.

MRS. FARRANT. [*At the window.*] What a gorgeous night! I'll come in and kiss you, Mamma.

> FRANCES *follows* LADY DAVENPORT *and* MRS. FARRANT *starts across the lawn to the billiard room . .*
>
> *An hour later you can see no change in the room except that only one lamp is alight on the table in the middle.* AMY O'CONNELL *and* HENRY TREBELL *walk past one window and stay for a moment in the light of the other. Her wrap is about her shoulders. He stands looking down at her.*

AMY O'CONNELL. There goes the moon . . it's quieter than ever now. [*She comes in.*] Is it very late?

TREBELL. [*As he follows.*] Half-past twelve.

> TREBELL *is hard-bitten, brainy, forty-five and very sure of himself. He has a cold, keen eye, which rather belies a sensitive mouth; hands which can grip, and a figure that is austere.*

AMY O'CONNELL. I ought to be in bed. I suppose everyone has gone.

TREBELL. Early trains to-morrow. The billiard room lights are out.

AMY O'CONNELL. The walk has just tired me comfortably.

TREBELL. Sit down. [*She sits by the table. He sits by her, and says with the air of a certain buyer at a market.*] You're very pretty.

AMY O'CONNELL. As well here as by moonlight? Can't you see any wrinkles?

TREBELL. One or two . . under the eyes. But they give character, and bring you nearer my age. Yes, Nature hit on the right curve in making you.

> *She stretches herself, cat-like.*

AMY O'CONNELL.   Praise is the greatest of luxuries, isn't it, Henry? . . Henry . . [*She caresses the name.*]

TREBELL.   Quite right . . Henry.

AMY O'CONNELL.   Henry . . Trebell.

TREBELL.   Having formally taken possession of my name . .

AMY O'CONNELL.   I'll go to bed.

> *His eyes have never moved from her. Now she breaks the contact and goes towards the door.*

TREBELL.   I wouldn't . . my spare time for love making is so limited.

> *She turns back, quite at ease, her eyes challenging him.*

AMY O'CONNELL.   That's the first offensive thing you've said.

TREBELL.   Why offensive?

AMY O'CONNELL.   I may flirt.   Making love's another matter.

TREBELL.   Sit down, and explain the difference . . Mrs. O'Connell.

> *She sits down.*

AMY O'CONNELL.   Quite so.   "Mrs. O'Connell."   That's the difference.

TREBELL.   [*Provokingly.*]   But I doubt if I'm interested in the fact that your husband doesn't understand you, and that your marriage was a mistake . . and how hard you find it to be strong.

AMY O'CONNELL.   [*Kindly.*]   I'm not quite a fool, though you think so on a three months' acquaintance.   But tell me this . . what education besides marriage does a woman get?

TREBELL.   [*His head lifting quickly.*]   Education . .

AMY O'CONNELL.   Don't be business-like.

TREBELL.   I beg your pardon.

AMY O'CONNELL.   Do you think the things you like to

have taught in schools are any use to one when one comes to deal with you?

TREBELL.   [*After a little scrutiny of her face.*]   Well, if marriage is only the means to an end . . what's the end? Not flirtation.

AMY O'CONNELL.   [*With an air of self-revelation.*]   I don't know. To keep one's place in the world, I suppose, one's self-respect and a sense of humour.

TREBELL.   Is that difficult?

AMY O'CONNELL.   To get what I want, without paying more than it's worth to me . . ?

TREBELL.   Never to be reckless.

AMY O'CONNELL.   [*With a side-glance.*]   One isn't so often tempted.

TREBELL.   In fact . . to flirt with life generally. Now, what made your husband marry you?

AMY O'CONNELL.   [*Dealing with the impertinence in her own fashion.*]   What would make you marry me? Don't say: Nothing on earth.

TREBELL.   [*Speaking apparently of someone else.*]   A prolonged fit of idleness might make me marry . . a clever woman. But I've never been idle for more than a week. And I've never met a clever woman . . worth calling a woman.

AMY O'CONNELL.   [*Bringing their talk back to herself, and fastidiously.*]   Justin has all the natural instincts.

TREBELL.   He's Roman Catholic, isn't he?

AMY O'CONNELL.   So am I . . by profession.

TREBELL.   It's a poor religion unless you really believe in it.

AMY O'CONNELL.   [*Appealing to him.*]   If I were to live at Linaskea, and have as many children as God sent, I should manage to make Justin pretty miserable! And what would be left of me at all, I should like to know?

TREBELL.   So Justin lives at Linaskea alone?

AMY O'CONNELL. I'm told now there's a pretty house-maid. . . [*She shrugs.*]

TREBELL. Does he drink, too?

AMY O'CONNELL. Oh, no. You'd like Justin, I daresay. He's clever. The thirteenth century's what he knows about. He has done a book on its statutes . . has been doing another.

TREBELL. And after an evening's hard work I find you here, ready to flirt with.

AMY O'CONNELL. What have you been working at?

TREBELL. A twentieth century statute, perhaps. That's not any concern of yours, either.

She does not follow his thought.

AMY O'CONNELL. No. I prefer you in your unprofessional moments.

TREBELL. Real flattery. I didn't know I had any.

AMY O'CONNELL. That's why you should flirt with me . . Henry . . to cultivate them. I'm afraid you lack imagination.

TREBELL. One must choose something to lack in this life.

AMY O'CONNELL. Not develop your nature to its utmost capacity.

TREBELL. And then?

AMY O'CONNELL. Well, if that's not an end in itself . . [*With a touch of romantic piety.*] I suppose there's the hereafter.

TREBELL. [*Grimly material.*] What! more developing? I watch people wasting time on themselves with amazement . . I refuse to look forward to wasting eternity.

AMY O'CONNELL. [*Shaking her head.*] You are very self-satisfied.

TREBELL. Not more so than any machine that runs smoothly. And I hope not self-conscious.

AMY O'CONNELL. [*Rather attractively treating him as a child.*] It would do you good to fall really desperately in

love with me . . to give me the power to make you unhappy.

> *He suddenly becomes very definite.*

TREBELL.   At twenty-three I engaged myself to be married to a charming and virtuous fool. I broke it off.

AMY O'CONNELL.   Did she mind much?

TREBELL.   We both minded. But I had ideals of womanhood that I wouldn't sacrifice to any human being. Then
I fell in with a woman who seduced me, and for a whole
year led me the life of a French novel . . played about
with my emotion as I had tortured that other poor girl's
brains. Education you'd call it in the one case as I called
it in the other. What a waste of time!

AMY O'CONNELL.   And what has become of your ideal?

TREBELL.   [*Relapsing to his former mood.*]   It's no
longer a personal matter.

AMY O'CONNELL.   [*With coquetry.*]   You're not interested in my character?

TREBELL.   Oh, yes, I am . . up to kissing point.

> *She does not shrink, but speaks with just a shade of
> contempt.*

AMY O'CONNELL.   You get that far more easily than a
woman. That's one of my grudges against men. Why
can't women take love-affairs so lightly?

TREBELL.   There are reasons. But make a good beginning with this one. Kiss me at once.

> *He leans towards her. She considers him quite
> calmly.*

AMY O'CONNELL.   No.

TREBELL.   When will you, then?

AMY O'CONNELL.   When I can't help myself . . if that
time ever comes.

TREBELL.   [*Accepting the postponement in a business-
like spirit.*]   Well . . I'm an impatient man.

AMY O'CONNELL.   [*Confessing engagingly.*]   I made up

my mind to bring you within arms' length of me when
we'd met at Lady Percival's. Do you remember? [*His
face shows no sign of it.*] It was the day after your
speech on the Budget.

TREBELL. Then I remember. But I haven't observed
the process.

AMY O'CONNELL. [*Subtly.*] Your sister grew to like me
very soon. That's all the cunning there has been.

TREBELL. The rest is just mutual attraction?

AMY O'CONNELL. And opportunities.

TREBELL. Such as this.

> At the drop of their voices they become conscious
> of the silent house.

AMY O'CONNELL. Do you really think everyone has gone
to bed?

TREBELL. [*Disregardful.*] And what is it makes my
pressing attentions endurable . . if one may ask?

AMY O'CONNELL. Some spiritual need or other, I suppose, which makes me risk unhappiness . . in fact, wel-
come it.

TREBELL. [*With great briskness.*] Your present need is
a good shaking . . I seriously mean that. You get to attach importance to these shades of emotion. A slight
physical shock would settle them all. That's why I asked
you to kiss me just now.

AMY O'CONNELL. You haven't very nice ideas, have you?

TREBELL. There are three facts in life that call up emotion . . Birth, Death, and the Desire for Children. The
niceties are shams.

AMY O'CONNELL. Then why do you want to kiss me?

TREBELL. I don't . . seriously. But I shall in a minute,
just to finish the argument. Too much diplomacy always
ends in a fight.

AMY O'CONNELL. And if I don't fight . . it'd be no fun
for you, I suppose?

TREBELL. You would get that much good out of me. For it's my point of honour . . to leave nothing I touch as I find it.

He is very close to her.

AMY O'CONNELL. You're frightening me a little . .

TREBELL. Come and look at the stars again. Come along.

AMY O'CONNELL. Give me my wrap. [*He takes it up, but holds it.*] Well, put it on me. [*He puts it round her, but does not withdraw his arms.*] Be careful; the stars are looking at you.

TREBELL. No, they can't see so far as we can. That's the proper creed.

AMY O'CONNELL. [*Softly, almost shyly.*] Henry.

TREBELL. [*Bending closer to her.*] Yes, pretty thing.

AMY O'CONNELL. Is this what you call being in love?

He looks up and listens.

TREBELL. Here's somebody coming.

AMY O'CONNELL. Oh! . .

TREBELL. What does it matter?

AMY O'CONNELL. I'm untidy, or something . .

She slips out, for they are close to the window. The FOOTMAN *enters, stops suddenly.*

THE FOOTMAN. I beg your pardon, sir. I thought everyone had gone.

TREBELL. I've just been for a walk. I'll lock up if you like.

THE FOOTMAN. I can easily wait up, sir.

TREBELL. [*At the window.*] I wouldn't. What do you do . . just slide the bolt?

THE FOOTMAN. That's all, sir.

TREBELL. I see. Good-night.

THE FOOTMAN. Good-night, sir.

He goes. TREBELL'S *demeanour suddenly changes, becomes alert, with the alertness of a man doing something in secret. He leans out of the window and whispers.*

TREBELL. Amy!

There is no answer, so he gently steps out. For a moment the room is empty, and there is silence. Then AMY *has flown from him into the safety of lights. She is flushed, trembling, but rather ecstatic, and her voice has lost all affectation now.*

AMY O'CONNELL. Oh . . oh . . you shouldn't have kissed me like that!

TREBELL *stands in the window-way, a light in his eyes, and speaks low but commandingly.*

TREBELL. Come here.

Instinctively she moves towards him. They speak in whispers.

AMY O'CONNELL. He was locking up.

TREBELL. I've sent him to bed.

AMY O'CONNELL. He won't go.

TREBELL. Never mind him.

AMY O'CONNELL. We're standing full in the light . . anyone could see us.

TREBELL. [*With fierce egotism.*] Think of me . . not of anyone else. [*He draws her from the window; then does not let her go.*] May I kiss you again?

AMY O'CONNELL. [*Her eyes closed.*] Yes.

He kisses her. She stiffens in his arms; then laughs almost joyously, and is commonplace.

AMY O'CONNELL. Well . . let me get my breath.

TREBELL. [*Letting her stand free.*] Now . . go along.

Obediently she turns to the door, but sinks on the nearest chair.

AMY O'CONNELL. In a minute. I'm a little faint. [*He goes to her quickly.*] No, it's nothing.

TREBELL. Come into the air again. [*Then half seriously.*] I'll race you across the lawn.

AMY O'CONNELL. [*Still breathless and a little hysterical.*] Thank you!

TREBELL. Shall I carry you?

AMY O'CONNELL. Don't be silly. [*She recovers her self-possession, gets up and goes to the window, then looks back at him and says very beautifully.*] But the night's beautiful, isn't it?

> *He has her in his arms again, more firmly this time.*

TREBELL. Make it so.

AMY O'CONNELL. [*Struggling . . with herself.*] Oh, why do you rouse me like this?

TREBELL. Because I want you.

AMY O'CONNELL. Want me to . . ?

TREBELL. Want you to . . kiss me just once.

AMY O'CONNELL. [*Yielding.*] If I do . . don't let me go mad, will you?

TREBELL. Perhaps. [*He bends over her, her head drops back.*] Now.

AMY O'CONNELL. Yes!

> *She kisses him on the mouth. Then he would release her, but suddenly she clings again.*

Oh . . don't let me go!

TREBELL. [*With fierce pride of possession.*] Not yet.
> *She is fragile beside him. He lifts her in his arms and carries her out into the darkness.*

THE SECOND ACT

TREBELL's house in Queen Anne Street, London. Eleven
o'clock on an October morning.

TREBELL's *working room is remarkable chiefly for the love
of sunlight it evidences in its owner. The walls are
white; the window which faces you is bare of all but
the necessary curtains. Indeed, lack of draperies
testifies also to his horror of dust. There faces you
besides a double door; when it is opened another
door is seen. When that is opened you discover a
writing table, and beyond can discern a book-case
filled with heavy volumes—law reports, perhaps.
The little room beyond is, so to speak, an under-
study. Between the two rooms a window, again
barely curtained, throws light down the staircase.
But in the big room, while the books are many, the
choice of them is catholic; and the book-cases are
low, running along the wall. There is an armchair
before the bright fire, which is on your right. There
is a sofa. And in the middle of the room is an enor-
mous double writing table, piled tidily with much
appropriate impedimenta, blue books and pamphlets,
and with an especial heap of unopened letters and
parcels. At the table sits* TREBELL *himself, in good
health and spirits, but eyeing askance the work to
which he has evidently just returned. His sister
looks in on him. She is dressed to go out, and has a
housekeeping air.*

FRANCES.   Are you busy, Henry?

TREBELL.   More or less. Come in.

FRANCES.   You'll dine at home?

TREBELL.   Anyone coming?

FRANCES.   Julia Farrant and Lucy have run up to town,
I think. I thought of going round and asking them to
come in . . but perhaps your young man will be going
there. Amy O'Connell said something vague about our
going to Charles Street . . but she may be out of town
by now.

TREBELL.   Well . . I'll be in anyhow.

FRANCES.   [*Going to the window as she buttons her
gloves.*] Were you on deck early this morning? It must
have been lovely.

TREBELL.   No, I turned in before we got out of le Havre.
I left Kent on deck, and found him there at six.

FRANCES.   I don't think autumn means to come at all
this year . . it'll be winter one morning. September has
been like a hive of bees, busy and drowsy. By the way,
Cousin Mary has another baby . . a girl.

TREBELL.   [*Indifferent to the information.*] That's the
fourth.

FRANCES.   Fifth. They asked me down for the christening . . but I really couldn't.

TREBELL.   September's the month for Tuscany. The car
chose to break down one morning just as we were starting
North again; so we climbed one of the little hills, and sat
for a couple of hours, while I composed a fifteenth century
electioneering speech to the citizens of Siena.

FRANCES.   [*With a half smile.*] Have you a vein of
romance for holiday time?

TREBELL.   [*Dispersing the suggestion.*] Not at all romantic . . nothing but figures and fiscal questions. That
was the hardest commercial civilisation there has been,
though you only think of its art and its murders now.

FRANCES. The papers on both sides have been very full
of you . . saying you hold the moral balance . . or deny-
ing it.

TREBELL. An interviewer caught me at Basle. I offered
to discuss the state of the Swiss navy.

FRANCES. Was that before Lord Horsham wrote to you?

TREBELL. Yes. His letter came to Innsbruck. He
"expressed" it somehow. Why . . it isn't known that he
will definitely ask me to join?

FRANCES. The Whitehall had a leader before the Elections were will over to say that he must . . but, of course,
that was Mr. Farrant.

TREBELL. [Knowingly.] Mrs. Farrant. I saw it in
Paris . . it just caught me up.

FRANCES. The Times is very shy over the whole question . . has a letter from a fresh bishop every day . .
doesn't talk of you very kindly yet.

TREBELL. Tampering with the Establishment, even Cantelupe's way, will be a pill to the real old Tory right to
the bitter end.

WALTER KENT comes in, very fresh and happy-look-
ing. A young man started in life. TREBELL hails him.

TREBELL. Hullo . . you've not been long getting shaved.

KENT. How do you do, Miss Trebell? Lucy turned me
out.

FRANCES. My congratulations. I've not seen you since
I heard the news.

KENT. [Glad and unembarrassed.] Thank you. I do
deserve them, don't I? Mrs. Farrant didn't come down . .
she left us to breakfast together. But I've a message for
you . . her love and she is in town. I went and saw Lord
Charles, sir. He will come to you, and be here at half
past eleven.

TREBELL. Look at these.

He smacks on the back, so to speak, the pile of parcels and letters.

KENT. Oh, Lord! . . I'd better start on them.

FRANCES. [*Continuing in her smooth, oldmaidish manner.*] Thank you for getting engaged just before you went off with Henry . . it has given me my only news of him, through Lucy and your postcards.

TREBELL. Oh, what about Wedgecroft?

KENT. I think it was he spun up just as I'd been let in.

TREBELL. Oh, well . . [*And he rings at the telephone which is on his table.*]

KENT. [*Confiding in* MISS TREBELL.] We're a common sense couple, aren't we? I offered to ask to stay behind. but she . . .

SIMPSON, *the maid, comes in.*

SIMPSON. Dr. Wedgecroft, sir.

WEDGECROFT *is on her heels. If you have an eye for essentials you may tell at once that he is a doctor, but if you only notice externals you will take him for anything else. He is over forty, and in perfect health of body and spirit. His enthusiasms are his vitality, and he has too many of them ever to lose one. He squeezes* MISS TREBELL's *hand with an air of fearless affection, which is another of his characteristics, and not the least lovable.*

WEDGECROFT. How are you?

FRANCES. I'm very well, thanks.

WEDGECROFT. [*To* TREBELL, *as they shake hands.*] You're looking fit.

TREBELL. [*With tremendous emphasis.*] I am!

WEDGECROFT. You've got the motor eye, though.

TREBELL. Full of dust?

WEDGECROFT. Look at Kent's. [*He takes* WALTER's *arm.*] It's a slight but serious contraction of the pupil . . which I charge fifty guineas to cure.

FRANCES. It's the eye of faith in you and your homeopathic doses. Don't you interfere with it.

> FRANCES TREBELL, *housekeeper, goes out.* KENT *has seized on the letters and is carrying them to his room.*

KENT. This looks like popularity and the great heart of the people, doesn't it?

WEDGECROFT. Trebell, you're not ill, and I've work to do.

TREBELL. I want ten minutes. Keep anybody out, Kent.

KENT. I'll switch that speaking tube arrangement to my room.

> TREBELL, *overflowing with vitality, starts to pace the floor.*

TREBELL. I've seen the last of Pump Court, Gilbert.

WEDGECROFT. The Bar ought to give you a testimonial . . to the man who not only could retire on twenty years' briefs, but h a s.

TREBELL. Fifteen. But I bled the City sharks with a good conscience . . quite freely.

WEDGECROFT. [*With a pretence of grumbling.*] I wish I could retire.

TREBELL. No you don't. Doctoring's a priestcraft . . you've taken vows.

WEDGECROFT. Then why don't you establish o u r church instead of . .

TREBELL. Yes, my friend . . but you're a heretic. I'd have to give the Medical Council power to burn you at the stake.

KENT. [*With the book packages.*] Parcel from the S. P. C. K., sir.

TREBELL. I know . . Disestablishment a crime against God; sermon preached by the Vicar of something Parva in eighteen seventy-three. I hope you're aware it's your duty to read all those.

KENT. Suppose they convert me? Lucy wanted to know if she could see you.

TREBELL. [*His eyebrows up.*]   Yes, I'll call at Mrs. Farrant's. Oh, wait. Aren't they coming to dinner?

KENT.   To-night? No, I think they go back to Shapters by the five o'clock. I told her she might come round about twelve, on the chance.

TREBELL.   Yes . . if Cantelupe's punctual . . I'd sooner not have too long with him.

KENT.   All right, then.

> *He goes, shutting the door; then you hear the door of his room shut, too. The two friends face each other, glad of a talk.*

TREBELL.   Well?

WEDGECROFT.   Well . . you'll never do it.

TREBELL.   Yes, I shall.

WEDGECROFT.   You can't carry any bill to be a credit to you with the coming Tory cabinet on your back. You know the Government is cursing you with its dying breath.

TREBELL.   [*Rubbing his hands.*]   Of course. They've been beaten out of the House and in now. I suppose they will meet Parliament.

WEDGECROFT.   They must, I think. It's over a month since——

TREBELL.   [*His thoughts running quickly.*]   There'll only be a nominal majority of sixteen against them. The Labour lot are committed on their side . . and now that the Irish have gone——

WEDGECROFT.   But they'll be beaten on the Address, first go.

TREBELL.   Yes . . Horsham hasn't any doubt of it.

WEDGECROFT.   He'll be in office within a week of the King's speech.

TREBELL.   [*With another access of energy.*]   I'll pull the bill that's in my head through a Horsham cabinet and the House. Then I'll leave them . . they'll go to the country——

WEDGECROFT.   You know Percival's pledge about that at Bristol wasn't very definite.

TREBELL.   Horsham means to.

WEDGECROFT.   [*With friendly contempt.*] Oh, Horsham!

TREBELL.   Anyway, it's about Percival I want you. How ill is he?

WEDGECROFT.   Not very.

TREBELL.   Is he going to die?

WEDGECROFT.   Well, I'm attending him.

TREBELL.   [*Pinked.*] Yes . . that's a good answer. How does he stomach me in prospect as a colleague, so far?

WEDGECROFT.   Sir, professional etiquette forbids me to disclose what a patient may confess in the sweat of his agony.

TREBELL.   He'll be Chancellor again, and lead the House.

WEDGECROFT.   Why not? He only grumbles that he's getting old.

TREBELL.   [*Thinking busily again.*] The difficulty is I shall have to stay through one budget with them. He'll have a surplus . . well, it looks like it . . and my only way of agreeing with him will be to collar it.

WEDGECROFT.   But . . good heavens! . . you'll have a hundred million or so to give away when you've disendowed.

TREBELL.   Not to give away. I'll sell every penny.

WEDGECROFT.   [*With an incredulous grin.*] You're not going back to extending old-age pensions after turning the unfortunate Liberals out on it, are you?

TREBELL.   No, no . . none of your half crown measures. They can wait to round off their solution of that till they've the courage to make one big bite of it.

WEDGECROFT.   We shan't see the day.

TREBELL.   [*Lifting the subject off its feet.*] Not if I come out of the cabinet and preach revolution?

WEDGECROFT.   Or will they make a Tory of you?

TREBELL. [*Acknowledging that stroke with a return grin.*] It'll be said they have when the bill is out.

WEDGECROFT. It's said so already.

TREBELL. Who knows a radical bill when he sees it!

WEDGECROFT. I'm not pleased you have to be running a tilt against the party system. [*He becomes a little dubious.*] My friend . . it's a nasty windmill. Oh, you've not seen that article in the Nation on Politics and Society . . it's written at Mrs. Farrant and Lady Lurgashall and that set. They hint that the Tories would never have had you if it hadn't been for this bad habit of opposite party men meeting each other.

TREBELL. [*Unimpressed.*] Excellent habit! What we really want in this country is a coalition of all the shibboleths with the rest of us in opposition . . for five years only.

WEDGECROFT. [*Smiling generously.*] Well, it's a sensation to see you become arbiter. The Tories are owning they can't do without you. Percival likes you personally . . Townsend don't matter . . Cantelupe you buy with a price, I suppose . . Farrant you can put in your pocket. I tell you I think the man you may run up against is Blackborough.

TREBELL. No, all he wants is to be let look big . . and to have an idea given him when he's going to make a speech, which isn't often.

WEDGECROFT. Otherwise . . I suppose . . now I may go down to history as having been in your confidence. I'm very glad you've arrived.

TREBELL. [*With great seriousness.*] I've sharpened myself as a weapon to this purpose.

WEDGECROFT. [*Kindly.*] And you're sure of yourself, aren't you?

TREBELL. [*Turning his wrist.*] Try.

WEDGECROFT. [*Slipping his doctor's fingers over the pulse.*] Seventy, I should say.

TREBELL. I promise you it hasn't varied a beat these three big months.

WEDGECROFT. Well, I wish it had. Perfect balance is most easily lost. How do you know you've the power of recovery? . . and it's that gets one up in the morning, day by day.

TREBELL. Is it? My brain works steadily on . . hasn't failed me yet. I keep it well fed. [*He breathes deeply.*] But I'm not sure one shouldn't have been away from England for five years instead of five weeks . . to come back to a job like this with a fresh mind. D'you know why really I went back on the Liberals over this question? Not because they wanted the church money for their pensions . . but because all they can see in Disestablishment is destruction. Any fool can destroy! I'm not going to let a power like the Church get loose from the State. A thirteen hundred years' tradition of service . . and all they can think of is to cut it adrift!

WEDGECROFT. I think the Church is moribund.

TREBELL. Oh, yes, of course you do . . you sentimental agnostic anarchist. Nonsense! The supernatural's a bit blown upon . . till we re-discover what it means. But it's not essential. Nor is the Christian doctrine. Put a Jesuit in a corner, and shut the door, and he'll own that. No . . the tradition of self-sacrifice and fellowship in service for its own sake . . that's the spirit we've to capture and keep.

WEDGECROFT. [*Really struck.*] A secular Church!

TREBELL. [*With reasoning in his tone.*] Well . . why not? Listen here. In drafting an act of Parliament one must alternately imagine oneself God Almighty and the most ignorant, prejudiced little blighter who will be affected by what's passed. God says: Let's have done with Heaven and Hell . . it's the Earth that shan't pass away.

WEDGECROFT. Instead of spending your brains in explaining it. Yes, I agree.

TREBELL. [*With full voice.*] But in the creed I'll lay down as unalterable there shall be neither Jew nor Greek . . What do you think of St. Paul, Gilbert?

WEDGECROFT. I'd make him the head of a college.

TREBELL. I'll make the Devil himself head of a college, if he'll undertake to teach honestly all he knows.

WEDGECROFT. And he'll conjure up Comte and Robespierre for you to assist in this little *rechauffée* of their schemes.

TREBELL. Hullo! Comte I knew about. Have I stolen from Robespierre, too?

WEDGECROFT. [*Giving out the epigram with an air.*] Property to him who can make the best use of it.

TREBELL. And then what we must do is to give the children power over their teachers?

　　Now he is comically enigmatic. WEDGECROFT *echoes*
　　him.

WEDGECROFT. And what exactly do you mean by that?

TREBELL. [*Serious again.*] How positive a pedagogue would you be if you had to prove your cases and justify your creed every century or so to the pupils who had learnt just a little more than you could teach them? Give power to the future, my friend . . not to the past. Give responsibility . . even if you give it for your own discredit. What's beneath trust deeds and last wills and testaments, and even acts of Parliament and official creeds? Fear of the verdict of the next generation . . fear of looking foolish in their eyes. Ah, we . . doing our best now . . must be ready for every sort of death. And to provide the means of change and disregard of the past is a secret of statesmanship. Presume that the world will come to an end every thirty years if it's not reconstructed.

Therefore give responsibility . . give responsibility . . give the children power.

WEDGECROFT. [*Disposed to whistle.*] Those statutes will want some framing.

TREBELL. [*Relapsing to a chuckle.*] There's an incidental change to foresee. Disappearance of the parson into the schoolmaster . . and the Archdeacon into the Inspector . . and the Bishop into—I rather hope he'll stick to his mitre, Gilbert.

WEDGECROFT. Some Ruskin will arise and make him.

TREBELL. [*As he paces the room and the walls of it fade away to him.*] What a church could be made of the best brains in England, sworn only to learn all they could, teach what they knew without fear of the future or favour to the past . . sworn upon their honour as seekers after truth, knowingly to tell no child a lie. It will come.

WEDGECROFT. A priesthood of women, too? There's the tradition of service with them.

TREBELL. [*With the sourest look yet on his face.*] Slavery . . not quite the same thing. And the paradox of such slavery is that they're your only tyrants.

> *At this moment the bell of the telephone upon the table rings. He goes to it, talking the while.*

One has to be very optimistic not to advocate the harem. That's simple and wholesome . . Yes?

> KENT *comes in.*

KENT. Does it work?

TREBELL. [*Slamming down the receiver.*] You and your new toy! What is it?

KENT. I'm not sure about the plugs of it . . I thought I'd got them wrong. Mrs. O'Connell has come to see Miss Trebell, who is out, and she says will we ask y o u if any message has been left for her.

TREBELL. No. Oh, about dinner? Well, she's round at Mrs. Farrant's.

KENT. I'll ring them up.

He goes back into his room to do so, leaving TRE-
BELL's *door open. The two continue their talk.*

TREBELL. My difficulties will be with Percival.

WEDGECROFT. Not over the Church.

TREBELL. You see I must discover how keen he'd be on
settling the Education quarrel, once and for all . . what
there is left of it.

WEDGECROFT. He's not sectarian.

TREBELL. It'll cost him his surplus. When'll he be up
and about?

WEDGECROFT. Not for a week or more.

TREBELL. [*Knitting his brow.*] And I've to deal with
Cantelupe. Curious beggar, Gilbert.

WEDGECROFT. Not my sort. He'll want some dealing
with over your bill as introduced to me.

TREBELL. I've not cross-examined company promoters
for ten years without learning how to do business with a
professional high churchman.

WEDGECROFT. Providence limited . . eh?

They are interrupted by MRS. O'CONNELL's *appearance in the doorway. She is rather pale, very calm,
but there is pain in her eyes, and her voice is un-
naturally steady.*

AMY. Your maid told me to come up, and I'm interrupting business . . I thought she was wrong.

TREBELL. [*With no trace of self-consciousness.*] Well
. . how are you, after this long time?

AMY. How do you do? [*Then she sees* WEDGECROFT,
and has to control a shrinking from him.] Oh!

WEDGECROFT. How are you, Mrs. O'Connell?

TREBELL. Kent is telephoning to Frances. He knows
where she is.

AMY. How are you, Dr. Wedgecroft? [*Then to* TRE-

BELL.] Did you have a good holiday? London pulls one
to pieces wretchedly. I shall give up living here at all.

WEDGECROFT. You look very well.

AMY. Do I?

TREBELL. A very good holiday. Sit down . . he won't
be a minute.

She sits on the nearest chair.

AMY. You're not ill . . interviewing a doctor?

TREBELL. The one thing Wedgecroft's no good at is
doctoring. He keeps me well by sheer moral suasion.

KENT *comes out of his room and is off downstairs.*
TREBELL *calls to him.*

TREBELL. Mrs. O'Connell is here.

KENT. Oh! [*He comes back and into the room.*] Miss
Trebell hasn't got there yet.

WEDGECROFT *has suddenly looked at his watch.*

WEDGECROFT. I must fly. Good-bye, Mrs. O'Connell.

AMY. [*Putting her hand, constrained by its glove, into
his open hand.*] I am always a little afraid of you.

WEDGECROFT. That isn't the feeling a doctor wants to
inspire.

KENT. [*To* TREBELL.] David Evans——

TREBELL. Evans?

KENT. The reverend one . . is downstairs, and wants
to see you.

WEDGECROFT. [*As he comes to them.*] Hampstead Road
Tabernacle . . Oh, the mammon of righteousness!

TREBELL. Shut up! How long have I before Lord
Charles——?

KENT. Only ten minutes.

MRS. O'CONNELL *goes to sit at the big table, and apparently idly takes a sheet of paper to scribble on.*

TREBELL. [*Half thinking, half questioning.*] He's a man
I can say nothing to politely.

WEDGECROFT. I'm off to Percival's now. Then I've an-

other case, and I'm due back at twelve. If there's anything helpful to say I'll look in again for two minutes . .
not more.

TREBELL.　You're a good man.

WEDGECROFT.　[*As he goes.*]　Congratulations, Kent.

KENT.　[*Taking him to the stairs.*]　Thank you very
much.

AMY.　[*Beckoning with her eyes.*]　What's this, Mr.
Trebell?

TREBELL.　Eh?　I beg your pardon.

He goes behind her and reads over her shoulder
what she has written.　KENT *comes back.*

KENT.　Shall I bring him up here?

TREBELL *looks up, and for a moment stares at his*
secretary rather sharply, then speaks in a matter-
of-fact voice.

TREBELL.　See him yourself, downstairs.　Talk to him
for five minutes . . find out what he wants.　Tell him it
will be as well for the next week or two if he can say he
hasn't seen me.

KENT.　Yes.

He goes.　TREBELL *follows him to the door, which*
he shuts.　Then he turns to face AMY, *who is tear-*
ing up the paper she wrote on.

TREBELL.　What is it?

AMY.　[*Her steady voice breaking, her carefully calcu-*
lated control giving way.]　Oh, Henry . . Henry!

TREBELL.　Are you in trouble?

AMY.　You'll hate me, but . . oh, it's brutal of you to
have been away so long!

TREBELL.　Is it with your husband?

AMY.　Perhaps.　Oh, come nearer to me . . do!

TREBELL.　[*Coming nearer, without haste or excitement.*]
Well?　[*Her eyes are closed.*]　My dear girl, I'm too busy

for love-making now. If there are any facts to be faced,
let me have them . . quite quickly.

> *She looks up at him for a moment; then speaks
> swiftly and sharply, as one speaks of disaster.*

AMY. There's a danger of my having a child . . your
child . . some time in April. That's all.

TREBELL. [*A sceptic who has seen a vision.*] Oh . .
it's impossible!

AMY. [*Flashing at him, revengefully.*] Why?

TREBELL. [*Brought to his mundane self.*] Well . . are
you sure?

AMY. [*In sudden agony.*] D'you think I want it to be
true? D'you think I—? You don't know what it is to
have a thing happening in spite of you.

TREBELL. [*His face set in thought.*] Where have you
been since we met?

AMY. Not to Ireland . . I haven't seen Justin for a
year.

TREBELL. All the easier for you not to see him for another year.

AMY. That wasn't what you meant.

TREBELL. It wasn't . . but never mind.

> *They are silent for a moment . . miles apart . .
> Then she speaks dully.*

AMY. We do hate each other . . don't we?

TREBELL. Nonsense! Let's think of what matters.

AMY. [*Aimlessly.*] I went to a man at Dover . . picked
him out of the directory . . didn't give my own name . .
pretended I was off abroad. He was a kind old thing . .
said it was all most satisfactory. Oh, my God!

TREBELL. [*He goes to bend over her kindly.*] Yes,
you've had a torturing month or two. That's been wrong.
I'm sorry.

AMY. Even now I have to keep telling myself that it's
so . . otherwise I couldn't understand it. Any more than

one really believes one will ever die . . one doesn't believe that, you know.

TREBELL. [*On the edge of a sensation that is new to him.*] I am told that a man begins to feel unimportant from this moment forward. Perhaps it's true.

AMY. What has it to do with you, anyhow? We don't belong to each other. How long were we together that night? Half an hour! You didn't seem to care a bit until after you'd kissed me, and . . this is an absurd consequence.

TREBELL. Nature's a tyrant.

AMY. Oh, it's my punishment . . I see that well enough . . for thinking myself so clever . . forgetting my duty and religion . . not going to confession, I mean. [*Then hysterically.*] God can make you believe in Him when He likes, can't He?

TREBELL. [*With comfortable strength.*] My dear girl, this needs your pluck. [*And he sits by her.*] All we have to do is to prevent it being found out.

AMY. Yes . . the scandal would smash you, wouldn't it?

TREBELL. There isn't going to be any scandal.

AMY. No . . if we're careful. You'll tell me what to do, won't you? Oh, it's a relief to be able to talk about it.

TREBELL. For one thing, you must take care of yourself, and stop worrying.

> *It soothes her to feel that he is concerned; but it is not enough to be soothed.*

AMY. Yes, I wouldn't like to have been the means of smashing you, Henry . . especially as you don't care for me.

TREBELL. I intend to care for you.

AMY. Love me, I mean. I wish you did . . a little; then perhaps I shouldn't feel so degraded.

TREBELL. [*A shade impatiently, a shade contemptuously.*] I can say I love you, if that'll make things easier.

AMY. [*More helpless than ever.*] If you'd said it at
first I should be taking it for granted . . though it wouldn't
be any more true, I daresay, than now . . when I should
know you weren't telling the truth.

TREBELL. Then I'd do without so much confusion.

AMY. Don't be so heartless.

TREBELL. [*As he leaves her.*] We seem to be attaching
importance to such different things.

AMY. [*Shrill even at a momentary desertion.*] What do
you mean? I want affection now just as I want food. I
can't do without it . . I can't reason things out as you can.
D'you think I haven't tried? [*Then in sudden rebellion.*]
Oh, the physical curse of being a woman . . no better
than any savage in this condition . . worse off than an
animal. It's unfair.

TREBELL. Never mind . . you're here now to hand me
half the responsibility, aren't you?

AMY. As if I could! If I have to lie through the night,
simply shaking with bodily fear, much longer . . I believe
I shall go mad.

> *This aspect of the matter is meaningless to him. He
> returns to the practical issue.*

TREBELL. There's nobody that need be suspecting, is
there?

AMY. My maid sees I'm ill and worried, and makes
remarks . . only to me, so far. Don't I look a wreck? I
nearly ran away when I saw Dr. Wedgecroft . . some of
these men are so clever.

TREBELL. [*Calculating.*] Someone will have to be
trusted.

AMY. [*Burrowing into her little tortured self again.*]
And I ought to feel as if I had done Justin a great wrong
. . but I don't. I hate you now; now and then. I was
being myself. You've brought me down. · I feel worthless.

> *The last word strikes him. He stares at her.*

TREBELL. Do you?

AMY. [*Pleadingly.*] There's only one thing I'd like you to tell me, Henry . . it isn't much. That night we were together . . it was for a moment different to everything that has ever been in your life before, wasn't it?

TREBELL. [*Collecting himself as if to explain to a child.*] I must make you understand . . I must get you to realise that for a little time to come you're above the law . . above even the shortcomings and contradictions of a man's affection.

AMY. But let us have one beautiful memory to share.

TREBELL. [*Determined she shall face the cold logic of her position.*] Listen. I look back on that night as one looks back on a fit of drunkenness.

AMY. [*Neither understanding nor wishing to; only shocked and hurt.*] You beast!

TREBELL. [*With bitter sarcasm.*] No, don't say that. Won't it comfort you to think of drunkenness as a beautiful thing? There are precedents enough . . classic ones.

AMY. You mean I might have been any other woman.

TREBELL. [*Quite inexorable.*] Wouldn't any other woman have served the purpose . . and is it less of a purpose because we didn't know we had it? Does my unworthiness then . . if you like to call it so . . make you unworthy now? I must make you see that it doesn't.

AMY. [*Petulantly hammering at her idée fixe.*] But you didn't love me . . and you don't love me.

TREBELL. [*Keeping his patience.*] No . . only within the last five minutes have I really taken the smallest interest in you. And now I believe I'm half jealous. Can you understand that? You've been talking a lot of nonsense about your emotions and your immortal soul. Don't you see it's only now that you've become a person of some importance to the world . . and why?

AMY. [*Losing her patience, childishly.*] What do you

mean by the World? You don't seem to have any personal
feelings at all. It's horrible you should have thought of
me like that. There has been no other man than you that
I would have let come anywhere near me . . not for more
than a year.

> *He realises that she will never understand.*

TREBELL. My dear girl, I'm sorry to be brutal. Does
it matter so much to you that I should have w i s h e d to
be the father of your child?

AMY. [*Ungracious, but pacified by his change of tone.*]
It doesn't matter now.

TREBELL. [*Friendly still.*] On principle, I don't make
promises. But I think I can promise you that if you keep
your head, and will keep your health, this shall all be made
as easy for you as if everyone could know. And let's
think what the child may mean to you . . just the fact
of his birth. Nothing to me, of course! Perhaps that
accounts for the touch of jealousy. I've forfeited my
rights because I hadn't honourable intentions. You can't
forfeit yours. Even if you never see him, and he has to
grow up among strangers . . just to have had a child must
make a difference to you. Of course, it may be a girl.
I wonder.

> *As he wanders on so optimistically she stares at him
> and her face changes. She realises . .*

AMY. Do you expect me to go through with this?
Henry! . . I'd sooner kill myself.

> *There is silence between them. He looks at her as
> one looks at some unnatural thing. Then after a
> moment he speaks, very coldly.*

TREBELL. Oh . . indeed. Don't get foolish ideas into
your head. You've no choice now . . no reasonable choice.

AMY. [*Driven to bay; her last friend an enemy.*] I
won't go through with it.

TREBELL. It hasn't been so much the fear of scandal, then——

AMY. That wouldn't break my heart. You'd marry me, wouldn't you? We could go away somewhere. I could be very fond of you, Henry.

TREBELL. [*Marvelling at these tangents.*] Marry you! I should murder you in a week.

> *This sounds only brutal to her; she lets herself be shamed.*

AMY. You've no more use for me than the use you've made of me.

TREBELL. [*Logical again.*] Won't you realise that there's a third party to our discussion . . that I'm of no importance beside him, and you of very little. Think of the child.

> AMY *blazes into desperate rebellion.*

AMY. There's no child, because I haven't chosen there shall be; and there shan't be, because I don't choose. You'd have me first your plaything and then Nature's, would you?

TREBELL. [*A little abashed.*] Come now, you knew what you were about.

AMY. [*Thinking of those moments.*] Did I? I found myself wanting you, belonging to you suddenly. I didn't stop to think and explain. But are we never to be happy and irresponsible . . never for a moment?

TREBELL. Well . . one can't pick and choose consequences.

AMY. Your choices in life have made you what you want to be, haven't they? Leave me mine.

TREBELL. But it's too late to argue like that.

AMY. If it is, I'd better jump into the Thames. I've thought of it.

> *He considers how best to make a last effort to bring her to her senses. He sits by her.*

TREBELL. Amy . . if you were my wife——

AMY. [*Unresponsive to him now.*] I was Justin's wife,
and I went away from him sooner than bear him children.
Had I the right to choose, or had I not?

TREBELL. [*Taking another path.*] Shall I tell you something I believe? If we were left to choose, we should
stand for ever deciding whether to start with the right
foot or the left. We blunder into the best things in life.
Then comes the test . . have we faith enough to go on . .
to go through with the unknown thing?

AMY. [*So bored by these metaphysics.*] Faith in what?

TREBELL. Our vitality . . I don't give a fig for beauty,
happiness, or brains. All I ask of myself is . . can I pay
Fate on demand?

AMY. Yes . . in imagination. But I've got physical
facts to face.

> *But he has her attention now, and pursues the
> advantage.*

TREBELL. Very well, then . . let the meaning of them
go. Look forward simply to a troublesome illness. In a
little while you can go abroad quietly and wait patiently.
We're not fools, and we needn't find fools to trust in.
Then come back to England . . .

AMY. And forget. That seems simple enough, doesn't
it?

TREBELL. If you don't want the child, let it be mine . .
not yours.

AMY. [*Wondering suddenly at this bond between them.*]
Yours! What would you do with it?

TREBELL. [*Matter-of-fact.*] Provide for it, of course.

AMY. Never see it, perhaps.

TREBELL. Perhaps not. If there were anything to be
gained . . for the child. I'll see that he has his chance
as a human being.

AMY. How hopeful! [*Now her voice drops. She is*

looking back, perhaps at a past self.] If you loved me . .
perhaps I might learn to love the thought of your child.

TREBELL. [*As if half his life depended on her answer.*]
Is that true?

AMY. [*Irritably.*] Why are you picking me to pieces?
I think that is true. If you had been loving me for a long,
long time—— [*The agony rushes back on her.*] But now
I'm only afraid. You might have some pity for me . . I'm
so afraid.

TREBELL. [*Touched.*] Indeed . . indeed, I'll take what
share of this I can.

　　She shrinks from him unforgivingly.

AMY. No, let me alone. I'm nothing to you. I'm a sick
beast in danger of my life, that's all . . cancerous!

　　*He is roused for the first time, roused to horror and
　　protest.*

TREBELL. Oh, you unhappy woman! . . . if life is like
death to you . . .

AMY. [*Turning on him.*] Don't lecture me! If you're
so clever put a stop to this horror. Or you might at least
say you're sorry.

TREBELL. Sorry! [*The bell on the table rings jar-
ringly.*] Cantelupe!

　　*He goes to the telephone. She gets up, cold and
　　collected, steadied merely by the unexpected sound.*

AMY. I mustn't keep you from governing the country.
I'm sure you'll do it very well.

TREBELL. [*At the telephone.*] Yes, bring him up, of
course . . isn't Mr. Kent there? [*Then to her.*] I may
be ten minutes with him or half an hour. Wait, and we'll
come to a conclusion.

　　KENT *comes in, an open letter in his hand.*

KENT. This note, sir. Had I better go round myself
and see him?

TREBELL. [*As he takes the note.*] Cantelupe's come.

KENT. [*Glancing at the telephone.*] Oh, has he!

TREBELL. [*As he reads.*] Yes, I think you had.

KENT. Evans was very serious.

> *He goes back into his room.* AMY *moves swiftly to where* TREBELL *is standing, and whispers.*

AMY. Won't you tell me whom to go to?

TREBELL. No.

AMY. Oh, really . . what unpractical, sentimental children you men are! You and your consciences . . you and your laws. You drive us to distraction and sometimes to death by your stupidities. Poor women——!

> *The Maid comes in to announce* LORD CHARLES CAN-TELUPE, *who follows her.* CANTELUPE *is forty, unathletic, and a gentleman in the best and worst sense of the word. He moves always with a caution which may betray his belief in the personality of the Devil. He speaks cautiously, too, and as if not he but something inside him were speaking. One feels that before strangers he would not, if he could help it, move or speak at all. A pale face: the mouth would be hardened by fanaticism were it not for the elements of Christianity in his religion; and he has the limpid eye of the enthusiast.*

TREBELL. Glad to see you. You know Mrs. O'Connell.

CANTELUPE *bows in silence.*

AMY. We have met.

> *She offers her hand. He silently takes it and drops it.*

TREBELL. Then you'll wait for Frances?

AMY. Is it worth while?

> KENT, *with his hat on, leaves his room and goes downstairs.*

TREBELL. Have you anything better to do?

AMY. There's somewhere I can go. But I mustn't keep you chatting of my affairs. Lord Charles is impatient to disestablish the Church.

CANTELUPE. [*Unable to escape a remark.*] Forgive me, since that is also your affair.

AMY. Oh . . but I was received at the Oratory when I was married.

CANTELUPE. [*With contrition.*] I beg your pardon.
    Then he makes for the other side of the room. TRE-
    BELL *and* MRS. O'CONNELL *stroll to the door, their
    eyes full of meaning.*

AMY. I think I'll go on to this place that I've heard of. If I wait . . for your sister . . she may disappoint me again.

TREBELL. Wait.

    KENT'S *room is vacant.*

AMY. Well . . in here?

TREBELL. If you like law-books.

AMY. I haven't been much of an interruption now, have I?

TREBELL. Please wait.

AMY. Thank you.

    TREBELL *shuts her in, for a moment seems inclined to
    lock her in, but he comes back into his own room
    and faces* CANTELUPE, *who, having primed and
    trained himself on his subject like a gun, fires off a
    speech, without haste, but also apparently without
    taking breath.*

CANTELUPE. I was extremely thankful, Mr. Trebell, to hear last week from Horsham that you will see your way to join his cabinet and undertake the disestablishment bill in the House of Commons. Any measure of mine, I have always been convinced, would be too much under the suspicion of blindly favouring Church interests to command the allegiance of that heterogeneous mass of thought . . in some cases, alas, of free thought . . which now-a-days composes the Conservative party. I am more than content to exercise what influence I may from a seat in the cabinet which will authorise the bill.

TREBELL. Yes. That chair's uncomfortable.

CANTELUPE *takes another.*

CANTELUPE. Horsham forwarded to me your memorandum upon the conditions you held necessary, and I incline to think I may accept them in principle on behalf of those who honour me with their confidences.

He fishes some papers from his pocket. TREBELL *sits squarely at his table to grapple with the matter.*

TREBELL. Horsham told me you did accept them . . it's on that I'm joining.

CANTELUPE. Yes . . in principle.

TREBELL. Well . . we couldn't carry a bill you disapproved of, could we?

CANTELUPE. [*With finesse.*] I hope not.

TREBELL. [*A little dangerously.*] And I have no intention of being made the scapegoat of a wrecked Tory compromise with the Nonconformists.

CANTELUPE. [*Calmly ignoring the suggestion.*] So far as I am concerned I meet the Nonconformists on their own ground . . that Religion had better be free from all compromise with the State.

TREBELL. Quite so . . if you're set free you'll look after yourselves. My discovery must be what to do with the men who think more of the state than their Church . . the majority of parsons, don't you think? . . if the question's really put and they can be made to understand it.

CANTELUPE. [*With sincere disdain.*] There are more profitable professions.

TREBELL. And less. Will you allow me that it is statecraft to make a profession profitable?

CANTELUPE *picks up his papers, avoiding theoretical discussion.*

CANTELUPE. Well, now . . will you explain to me this project for endowing Education with your surplus?

TREBELL. Putting Appropriation, the Buildings and the Representation question on one side for the moment?

CANTELUPE. Candidly, I have yet to master your figures . . .

TREBELL. The roughest figures so far.

CANTELUPE. Still I have yet to master them on the first two points.

TREBELL. [*Firmly premising.*] We agree that this is not diverting Church money to actually secular uses.

CANTELUPE. [*As he peeps from under his eyelids.*] I can conceive that it might not be. You know that we hold Education to be a Church function. But . . .

TREBELL. Can you accept thoroughly now the secular solution for all Primary Schools?

CANTELUPE. Haven't we always preferred it to the undenominational? Are there to be facilities for a n y of the teachers giving dogmatic instruction?

TREBELL. I note your emphasis on any. I think we can put the burden of that decision on local authorities. Let us come to the question of Training Colleges for your teachers. It's on that I want to make my bargain.

CANTELUPE. [*Alert and cautious.*] You want to endow colleges?

TREBELL. Heavily.

CANTELUPE. Under public control?

TREBELL. Church colleges under Church control.

CANTELUPE. There'd be others?

TREBELL. To preserve the necessary balance in the schools.

CANTELUPE. Not founded with Church money?

TREBELL. Think of the grants in aid that will be released. I must ask the Treasury for a further lump sum, and with that there may be sufficient for secular colleges

. . if you can agree with me upon the statutes of those over which you'd otherwise have free control.

TREBELL *is weighing his words.*

CANTELUPE. "You" meaning, for instance . . what authorities in the Church?

TREBELL. Bishops, I suppose . . and others. [CANTELUPE *permits himself to smile.*] On that point I shall be weakness itself, and . . may I suggest . . your seat in the Cabinet will give you some control.

CANTELUPE. Statutes?

TREBELL. To be framed in the best interests of educational efficiency.

CANTELUPE. [*Finding an opening.*] I doubt if we agree upon the meaning to be attached to that term.

TREBELL. [*Forcing the issue.*] What meaning do you attach to it?

CANTELUPE. [*Smiling again.*] I have hardly a sympathetic listener.

TREBELL. You have an unprejudiced one . . the best you can hope for. I was not educated myself. I learnt certain things that I desired to know . . from reading my first book—Don Quixote it was—to mastering Company Law. You see, as a man without formulas, either for education or religion, I am perhaps peculiarly fitted to settle the double question. I have no grudges . . no revenge to take.

CANTELUPE. [*Suddenly congenial.*] Shelton's translation of Don Quixote, I hope . . the modern ones have no flavour. And you took all the adventures as seriously as the Don did?

TREBELL. [*Not expecting this.*] I forget.

CANTELUPE. It's the finer attitude . . the child's attitude. And it would enable you immediately to comprehend mine towards an education consisting merely of practical knowledge. The life of Faith is still the happy one. What is more crushingly finite than knowledge? Moral discipline is a nation's only safety. How much of your science tends in support of the great spiritual doctrine of sacrifice?

TREBELL *returns to his subject as forceful as ever.*

TREBELL. The Church has assimilated much in her time. Do you think it wise to leave agnostic science at the side of the plate? I think, you know, that this craving for common knowledge is a new birth in the mind of man; and if your Church won't recognise that soon, by so much will she be losing her grip for ever over men's minds. What's the test of godliness but your power to receive the new idea in whatever form it comes, and give it life? It is blasphemy to pick and choose your good. [*For a moment his thoughts seem to be elsewhere.*] That's an unhappy man or woman or nation . . I know it if it has only come to me this minute . . and I don't care what their brains or their riches or their beauty or any of their triumphs may be . . they're unhappy and useless if they can't tell life from death.

CANTELUPE. [*Interested in the digression.*] Remember that the Church's claim has ever been to know that difference.

TREBELL. [*Fastening to his subject again.*] My point is this: A man's demand to know the exact structure of a fly's wing, and his assertion that it degrades any child in the street not to know such a thing, is a religious revival . . a token of spiritual hunger. What else can it be? And we commercialise our teaching!

CANTELUPE. I wouldn't have it so.

TREBELL. Then I'm offering you the foundation of a new Order of men and women who'll serve God by teaching his children. Now shall we finish the conversation in prose?

CANTELUPE. [*Not to be put down.*] What is the prose for God?

TREBELL. [*Not to be put down, either.*] That's what we
irreligious people are giving our lives to discover. [*He
plunges into detail.*] I'm proposing to found about seventy-
two new colleges, and of course to bring the ones there
are up to the new standard. Then we must gradually
revise all teaching salaries in government schools . . to a
scale I have in mind. Then the course must be compul-
sory and the training time doubled——

CANTELUPE. Doubled! Four years?

TREBELL. Well, a minimum of three . . a university
course. Remember we're turning a trade into a calling.

CANTELUPE. There's more to that than taking a degree.

TREBELL. I think so. You've fought for years for your
tests and your atmosphere with plain business men not
able to understand such lunacy. Quite right . . atmosphere's all that matters. If one and one don't make two
by God's grace . . .

CANTELUPE. Poetry again!

TREBELL. I beg your pardon. Well . . you've no further
proof. If you can't plant your thumb on the earth and
your little finger on the pole star you know nothing of dis-
tances. We must do away with text-book teachers.

CANTELUPE *is opening out a little in spite of himself.*

CANTELUPE. I'm waiting for our opinions to differ.

TREBELL. [*Businesslike again.*] I'll send you a draft of
the statutes I propose, within a week. Meanwhile shall
I put the offer this way: If I accept your tests will you
accept mine?

CANTELUPE. What are yours?

TREBELL. I believe if one provides for efficiency one
provides for the best part of truth . . honesty of statement. I shall hope for a little more elasticity in your dog-
mas than Becket or Cranmer or Laud would have allowed.
When you've a chance to re-formulate the reasons of your
faith for the benefit of men teaching mathematics and sci-

ence and history and political economy, you won't neglect to answer or allow for criticisms and doubts. I don't see why . . in spite of all the evidence to the contrary . . such a thing as progress in a definite religious faith is impossible.

CANTELUPE. Progress is a soiled word. [*And now he weighs his words.*] I shall be very glad to accept on the Church's behalf control of the teaching of teachers in these colleges.

TREBELL. Good. I want the best men.

CANTELUPE. You are surprisingly inexperienced if you think that creeds can ever become mere forms except to those who have none.

TREBELL. But teaching—true teaching—is learning, and the wish to know is going to prevail against any creed . . so I think. I wish you cared as little for the form in which a truth is told as I do. On the whole, you see, I think I shall manage to plant your theology in such soil this spring that the garden will be fruitful. On the whole, I'm a believer in Churches of all sorts and their usefulness to the State. Your present use is out-worn. Have I found you in this the beginnings of a new one?

CANTELUPE. The Church says: Thank you, it is a very old one.

TREBELL. [*Winding up the interview.*] To be sure, for practical politics our talk can be whittled down to your accepting the secular solution for Primary Schools, if you're given these colleges under such statutes as you and I shall agree upon.

CANTELUPE. And the country will accept.

TREBELL. The country will accept any measure if there's enough money in it to bribe all parties fairly.

CANTELUPE. You expect very little of the constancy of my Church to her faith, Mr. Trebell.

TREBELL. I have only one belief myself. That is in

human progress—yes, progress—over many obstacles and by many means. I have no ideals. I believe it is statesmanlike to use all the energy you find . . turning it into the nearest channel that points forward.

CANTELUPE.   Forward to what?

TREBELL.   I don't know . . and my caring doesn't matter. We do know . . and if we deny it it's only to be encouraged by contradiction . . that the movement is forward and with some gathering purpose. I'm friends with any fellow traveller.

> CANTELUPE *has been considering him very curiously.*
> *Now he gets up to go.*

CANTELUPE.   I should like to continue our talk when I've studied your draft of the statutes. Of course the political position is favourable to a far more comprehensive bill than we had ever looked for . . and you've the advantage now of having held yourself very free from party ties. In fact, not only will you give us the bill we shall most care to accept, but I don't know what other man would give us a bill we and the other side could accept at all.

TREBELL.   I can let you have more Appropriation figures by Friday. The details of the Fabrics scheme will take a little longer.

CANTELUPE.   In a way, there's no such hurry. We're not in office yet.

TREBELL.   When I'm building with figures I like to give the foundations time to settle. Otherwise they are the inexactest things.

CANTELUPE.   [*Smiling to him for the first time.*] We shall have you finding Faith the only solvent of all problems some day.

TREBELL.   I hope my mind is not afraid . . even of the Christian religion.

CANTELUPE.   I am sure that the needs of the human soul

. . be it dressed up in whatever knowledge . . do not alter
from age to age . .

> *He opens the door, to find* WEDGECROFT *standing out-*
> *side, watch in hand.*

TREBELL.　Hullo . . . waiting?

WEDGECROFT.　I was giving you two minutes by my watch.
How are you, Cantelupe?

> CANTELUPE, *with a gesture which might be mistaken*
> *for a bow, folds himself up.*

TREBELL.　Shall I bring you the figures on Friday . .
that might save time.

> CANTELUPE, *by taking a deeper fold in himself,*
> *seems to assent.*

TREBELL.　Will the afternoon do? Kent shall fix the hour.

CANTELUPE.　[*With an effort.*]　Kent?

TREBELL.　My secretary.

CANTELUPE.　Friday. Any hour before five. I know
my way.

> *The three phrases having meant three separate ef-*
> *forts,* CANTELUPE *escapes.* WEDGECROFT *has walked*
> *to the table, his brows a little puckered. Now* TRE-
> BELL *notices that* KENT'S *door is open; he goes*
> *quickly into the room, and finds it empty. Then he*
> *stands for a moment irritable and undecided before*
> *returning.*

TREBELL.　Been here long?

WEDGECROFT.　Five minutes . . more, I suppose.

TREBELL.　Mrs. O'Connell gone?

WEDGECROFT.　To her dressmaker's.

TREBELL.　Frances forgot she was coming, and went out.

WEDGECROFT.　Pretty little fool of a woman! D'you
know her husband?

TREBELL.　No.

WEDGECROFT.　Says she's been in Ireland with him since
we met at Shapters. He has trouble with his tenantry.

TREBELL.   Won't he sell, or won't they purchase?

WEDGECROFT.   Curious chap.   A Don at Balliol when I first knew him.   Warped of late years . . perhaps by his marriage.

TREBELL.   [*Dismissing that subject.*]   Well . . how's Percival?

WEDGECROFT.   Better this morning.   I told him I'd seen you . . and in a little calculated burst of confidence what I'd reason to think you were after.   He said you and he could get on though you differed on every point; but he didn't see how you'd pull with such a blasted weak-kneed lot as the rest of the Horsham's cabinet would be.   He'll be up in a week or ten days.

TREBELL.   Can I see him?

WEDGECROFT.   You might.   I admire the old man . . the way he sticks to his party, though they misrepresent now most things he believes in!

TREBELL.   What a damnable state to arrive at . . doubly damned by the fact you admire it.

WEDGECROFT.   And to think that at this time of day you should need instructing in the ethics of party government. But I'll have to do it.

TREBELL.   Not now.   I've been at ethics with Cantelupe.

WEDGECROFT.   Certainly not now.   What about my man with the stomach-ache at twelve o'clock sharp!   Good-bye.

He is gone.   TREBELL *battles with uneasiness and at last mutters,* "Oh . . why didn't she wait?" *Then the telephone bell rings.   He goes quickly, as if it were an answer to his anxiety.*   "Yes?"   *Of course it isn't . .*   "Yes."   *He paces the room, impatient, wondering what to do.   The Maid comes in to announce* MISS DAVENPORT.   LUCY *follows her.   She has gained lately perhaps a little of the joy which was lacking, and at least she brings now into this room a breath of very wholesome womanhood.*

LUCY. It's very good of you to let me come; I'm not going to keep you more than three minutes.

TREBELL. Sit down.

> *Only women unused to busy men would call him rude.*

LUCY. What I want to say is . . don't mind my being engaged to Walter. It shan't interfere with his work for you. If you want a proof that it shan't . . it was I got Aunt Julia to ask you to take him . . Though he didn't know . . so don't tell him that.

TREBELL. You weren't engaged then.

LUCY. I . . thought that we might be.

TREBELL. [*With cynical humour.*] Which I'm not to tell him, either?

LUCY. Oh, that wouldn't matter.

TREBELL. [*With decision.*] I'll make sure you don't interfere.

LUCY. [*Deliberately . . not to be treated as a child.*] You couldn't, you know, if I wanted to.

TREBELL. Why, is Walter a fool?

LUCY. He's very fond of me, if that's what you mean.

> TREBELL *looks at her for the first time, and changes his tone a little.*

TREBELL. If it was what I meant . . I'm disposed to withdraw the suggestion.

LUCY. And because I'm fond of his work as well, I shan't, therefore, ask him to tell me things . . secrets.

TREBELL. [*Reverting to his humour.*] It'll be when you're a year or two married that danger may occur . . in his desperate effort to make conversation.

> LUCY *considers this and him quite seriously.*

LUCY. You're rather hard on women, aren't you . . just because they don't have the chances men do.

TREBELL. Do you want the chances?

LUCY.   I think I'm as clever as most men I meet, though
I know less, of course.

TREBELL.   Perhaps I should have offered you the secre-
taryship instead.

LUCY.   [*Readily.*] Don't you think I'm taking it in a
way . . by marrying Walter? That's fanciful, of course.
But marriage is a very general and complete sort of partnership, isn't it? At least, I'd like to make mine so.

TREBELL.   He'll be more under your thumb in some
things if you leave him free in others.

> *She receives the sarcasm in all seriousness, and then
> speaks to him as she would to a child.*

LUCY.   Oh . . I'm not explaining what I mean quite
well, perhaps. Walter has been everywhere and done
everything. He speaks three languages . . which all
makes him an ideal private secretary.

TREBELL.   Quite.

LUCY.   Do you think he'd develop into anything else . .
but for me?

TREBELL.   So I have provided just a first step, have I?

LUCY.   [*With real enthusiasm.*] Oh, Mr. Trebell, it's a
great thing for us. There isn't anyone worth working
under but you. You'll make him think and give him ideas
instead of expecting them from him. But just for that
reason he'd get so attached to you and be quite content to
grow old in your shadow . . if it wasn't for me.

TREBELL.   True . . I should encourage him in nothingness. What's more, I want extra brains and hands. It's
not altogether a pleasant thing, is it . . the selfishness of
the hard worked man?

LUCY.   If you don't grudge your own strength, why
should you be tender of other people's?

> *He looks at her curiously.*

TREBELL.   Y o u r ambition is making for only second-
hand satisfaction, though.

LUCY. What's a woman to do? She must work through men, mustn't she?

TREBELL. I'm told that's degrading . . the influencing of husbands and brothers and sons.

LUCY. [*Only half humorously.*] But what else is one to do with them? Of course, I've enough money to live on . . so I could take up some woman's profession . . . What are you smiling at?

TREBELL. [*Who has smiled very broadly.*] As you don't mean to . . don't stop while I tell you.

LUCY. But I'd sooner get married. I want to have children. [*The words catch him and hold him. He looks at her reverently this time. She remembers she has transgressed convention; then, remembering that it is only convention, proceeds quite simply.*] I hope we shall have children.

TREBELL. I hope so.

LUCY. Thank you. That's the first kind thing you've said.

TREBELL. Oh . . you can do without compliments, can't you?

She considers for a moment.

LUCY. Why have you been talking to me as if I were someone else?

TREBELL. [*Startled.*] Who else?

LUCY. No one particular. But you've shaken a moral fist, so to speak. I don't think I provoked it.

TREBELL. It's a bad parliamentary habit. I apologise.

She gets up to go.

LUCY. Now I shan't keep you longer . . you're always busy. You've been so easy to talk to. Thank you very much.

TREBELL. Why . . I wonder?

LUCY. I knew you would be, or I shouldn't have come. You think Life's an important thing, don't you? That's

priggish, isn't it? Good-bye. We're coming to dinner . .
Aunt Julia and I. Miss Trebell arrived to ask us just as
I left.

TREBELL.   I'll see you down.

LUCY.   What waste of time for you. I know how the
door opens.

> *As she goes out* WALTER KENT *is on the way to his*
> *room. The two nod to each other like old friends.*
> TREBELL *turns away with something of a sigh.*

KENT.   Just come?

LUCY.   Just going.

KENT.   I'll see you at dinner.

LUCY.   Oh, are you to be here? . . that's nice.

> LUCY *departs as purposefully as she came.* KENT
> *hurries to* TREBELL, *whose thoughts are away again*
> *by now.*

KENT.   I haven't been long there and back, have I? The
Bishop gave me these letters for you. He hasn't answered
the last . . but I've his notes of what he means to say.
He'd like them back to-night. He was just going out.
I've one or two notes of what Evans said. Bit of a char-
latan, don't you think?

TREBELL.   Evans?

KENT.   Well, he talked of his Flock. There are quite
fifteen letters you'll have to deal with yourself, I'm afraid.

> TREBELL *stares at him; then, apparently making up*
> *his mind . .*

TREBELL.   Ring up a messenger, will you . . I must
write a note and send it.

KENT.   Will you dictate?

TREBELL.   I shall have done it while you're ringing . .
it's only a personal matter. Then we'll start work.

> KENT *goes into his room and tackles the telephone*
> *there.* TREBELL *sits down to write the note, his face*
> *very set and anxious.*

THE THIRD ACT

AT LORD HORSHAM's house in Queen Anne's Gate, in the evening, a week later.

If rooms express their owners' character, the grey and black of LORD HORSHAM's *drawing room, the faded brocade of its furniture, reveal him as a man of delicate taste and somewhat thin intellectuality. He stands now before a noiseless fire, contemplating with a troubled eye either the pattern of the Old French carpet, or the black double doors of the library opposite, or the moulding on the Adams ceiling, which the flicker of all the candles casts into deeper relief. His grey hair and black clothes would melt into the decoration of his room, were the figure not rescued from such oblivion by the British white glaze of his shirt front and—to a sympathetic eye— by the lovable perceptive face of the man. Sometimes he looks at the sofa in front of him, on which sits* WEDGECROFT, *still in the frock coat of a busy day, depressed and irritable. With his back to them, on a sofa with its back to them, is* GEORGE FARRANT, *planted with his knees apart, his hands clasped, his head bent; very glum. And sometimes* HORSHAM *glances at the door, as if waiting for it to open. Then his gaze will travel back, up the long, shiny, black piano, with a volume of the Well Tempered Clavichord open on its desk, to where* CANTELUPE *is perched uncomfortably on the bench; paler than*

*ever; more self-contained than ever, looking, to one
who knows him as well as* HORSHAM *does, a little
dangerous. So he returns to contemplation of the
ceiling or the carpet. They wait there as men wait
who have said all they want to say upon an unpleasant subject and yet cannot dismiss it. At last*
FARRANT *breaks the silence.*

FARRANT. What time did you ask him to come, Horsham?

HORSHAM. Eh . . O'Connell? I didn't ask him directly. What time did you say, Wedgecroft?

WEDGECROFT. Any time after half past ten, I told him.

FARRANT. [*Grumbling.*] It's a quarter to eleven.
Doesn't Blackborough mean to turn up at all?

HORSHAM. He was out of town . . my note had to be
sent after him. I couldn't wire, you see.

FARRANT. No.

CANTELUPE. It was by the merest chance your man
caught me, Cyril. I was taking the ten fifteen to Ton-
bridge, and happened to go to James Street first for some
papers.

The conversation flags again.

CANTELUPE. But since Mrs. O'Connell is dead what is
the excuse for a scandal?

*At this unpleasant dig into the subject of their
thoughts the three other men stir uncomfortably.*

HORSHAM. Because the inquest is unavoidable . . apparently.

WEDGECROFT. [*Suddenly letting fly.*] I declare I'd have
risked penal servitude, and given a certificate, but just before the end O'Connell would call in old Fielding Andrews,
who has moral scruples about everything—it's his trade-
mark—and of course about this . . !

FARRANT. Was he told of the whole business?

WEDGECROFT. No . . O'Connell kept things up before
him. Well . . the woman was dying.

HORSHAM. Couldn't you have kept the true state of the case from Sir Fielding?

WEDGECROFT. And been suspected of the malpractice myself if he'd found it out? . . which he would have done . . he's no fool. Well . . I thought of trying that . . .

FARRANT. My dear Wedgecroft . . how grossly quixotic! You have a duty to yourself.

HORSHAM. [*Rescuing the conversation from unpleasantness.*] I'm afraid I feel that our position to-night is most irregular, Wedgecroft.

WEDGECROFT. Still, if you can make O'Connell see reason. And if you all can't . . [*He frowns at the alternative.*]

CANTELUPE. Didn't you say she came to you first of all?

WEDGECROFT. I met her one morning at Trebell's.

FARRANT. Actually a t Trebell's?

WEDGECROFT. The day he came back from abroad.

FARRANT. Oh! No one seems to have noticed them together much at any time. My wife . . . No matter!

WEDGECROFT. She tackled me as a doctor with one part of her trouble . . added she'd been with O'Connell in Ireland, which, of course, it turns out wasn't true . . asked me to help her. I had to say I couldn't.

HORSHAM. [*Echoing rather than querying.*] You couldn't.

FARRANT. [*Shocked.*] My dear Horsham!

WEDGECROFT. Well, if she'd told me the truth! . . No, anyhow I couldn't. I'm sure there was no excuse. One can't run these risks.

FARRANT. Quite right, quite right.

WEDGECROFT. There are men who do on one pretext or another.

FARRANT. [*Not too shocked to be curious.*] Are there really.

WEDGECROFT. Oh, yes, men well known . . in other directions. I could give you four addresses . . but of course I wasn't going to give her one. Though there again . . if she'd told me the whole truth! . . My God, women are such fools! And they prefer quackery . . look at the decent doctors they simply turn into charlatans. Though, there again, that all comes of letting a trade work mysteriously under the thumb of a benighted oligarchy . . which is beside the question. But one day I'll make you sit up on the subject of the Medical Council, Horsham.

> HORSHAM *assumes an impenetrable air of states-*
> *manship.*

HORSHAM. I know. Very interesting . . very important . . very difficult to alter the status quo.

WEDGECROFT. Then the poor little liar said she'd go off to an appointment with her dressmaker; and I heard nothing more till she sent for me a week later, and I found her almost too ill to speak. Even then she didn't tell me the truth! So when O'Connell arrived, of course I spoke to him quite openly, and all he told me in reply was that it wouldn't have been his child.

FARRANT. Poor devil!

WEDGECROFT. O'Connell?

FARRANT. Yes, of course.

WEDGECROFT. I wonder. Perhaps she didn't realize he'd been sent for . . or felt then she was dying, and didn't care . . or lost her head. I don't know.

FARRANT. Such a pretty little woman!

WEDGECROFT. If I could have made him out, and dealt with him, of course I shouldn't have come to you. Farrant's known him even longer than I have.

FARRANT. I was with him at Harrow.

WEDGECROFT. So I went to Farrant first.

> *That part of the subject drops.* CANTELUPE, *who*
> *has not moved, strikes in again.*

CANTELUPE. How was Trebell's guilt discovered?

FARRANT. He wrote her one letter which she didn't destroy. O'Connell found it.

WEDGECROFT. Picked it up from her desk . . it wasn't even locked up.

FARRANT. Not twenty words in it . . quite enough, though.

HORSHAM. His habit of being explicit . . of writing things down . . I know!

He shakes his head, deprecating all rashness. There is another pause. FARRANT, *getting up to pace about, breaks it.*

FARRANT. Look here, Wedgecroft, one thing is worrying me. Had Trebell any foreknowledge of what she did and the risk she was running, and could he have stopped it?

WEDGECROFT. [*Almost ill-temperedly.*] How could he have stopped it?

FARRANT. Because . . well, I'm not a casuist . . but I know by instinct when I'm up against the wrong thing to do; and if he can't be cleared on that point I won't lift a finger to save him.

HORSHAM. [*With nice judgment.*] In using the term Any Foreknowledge, Farrant, you may be more severe on him than you wish to be.

FARRANT, *unappreciative, continues.*

FARRANT. Otherwise . . well, we must admit, Cantelupe, that if it hadn't been for the particular consequence of this it wouldn't be anything to be so mightily shocked about.

CANTELUPE. I disagree.

FARRANT. My dear fellow, it's our business to make laws, and we know the difference of saying in one of 'em you m a y or you m u s t. Who ever proposed to insist on pillorying every case of spasmodic adultery? One would never have done! Some of these attachments do more harm . . to the third party, I mean . . some less. But it's only when a menage becomes socially impossible that a sensible man will interfere. [*He adds, quite unnecessarily.*] I'm speaking quite impersonally, of course.

CANTELUPE. [*As coldly as ever.*] Trebell is morally responsible for every consequence of the original sin.

WEDGECROFT. That is a hard saying.

FARRANT. [*Continuing his own remarks quite independently.*] And I put aside the possibility that he deliberately helped her to her death to save a scandal, because I don't believe it is a possibility. But if that were so I'd lift my finger to help him to his. I'd see him hanged with pleasure.

WEDGECROFT. [*Settling this part of the matter.*] Well, Farrant, to all intents and purposes he didn't know, and he'd have stopped it if he could.

FARRANT. Yes, I believe that. But what makes you so sure?

WEDGECROFT. I asked him, and he told me.

FARRANT. That's no proof.

WEDGECROFT. You read the letter that he sent her . . unless you think it was written as a blind.

FARRANT. Oh . . to be sure . . yes. I might have thought of that.

> *He settles down again. Again no one has anything to say.*

CANTELUPE. What is to be said to Mr. O'Connell when he comes?

HORSHAM. Yes . . what exactly do you propose we shall say to O'Connell, Wedgecroft?

WEDGECROFT. Get him to open his oyster of a mind, and . . .

FARRANT. So it is, and his face like a stone wall yesterday. Absolutely refused to discuss the matter with me!

CANTELUPE. May I ask, Cyril, why are we concerning ourselves with this wickedness at all?

HORSHAM. Just at this moment, when we have official weight without official responsibility, Charles . .

WEDGECROFT. I wish I could have let Percival out of bed, but these first touches of autumn are dangerous to a convalescent of his age.

HORSHAM. But you saw him, Farrant . . and he gave you his opinion, didn't he?

FARRANT. Last night . . yes.

HORSHAM. I suppose it's a pity Blackborough hasn't turned up.

FARRANT. Never mind him.

HORSHAM. He gets people to agree with him. That's a gift.

FARRANT. Wedgecroft, what is the utmost O'Connell will be called upon to do for us . . for Trebell?

WEDGECROFT. Probably only to hold his tongue at the inquest to-morrow. As far as I know, there's no one but her maid to prove that Mrs. O'Connell didn't meet her husband some time in the summer. He'll be called upon to tell a lie or two by implication.

FARRANT. Cantelupe . . what does perjury to that extent mean to a Roman Catholic?

> CANTELUPE'S *face melts into an expression of mild*
> *amazement.*

CANTELUPE. Your asking such a question shows that you would not understand my answer to it.

FARRANT. [*Leaving the fellow to his subtleties.*] Well, what about the maid?

WEDGECROFT. She may suspect facts but not names, I think. Why should they question her on such a point if O'Connell says nothing?

HORSHAM. He's really very late. I told . . [*He stops.*] Charles, I've forgotten that man's name again.

CANTELUPE. Edmunds you said it was.

HORSHAM. Edmunds. Everybody's down at Lympne . .

I've been left with a new man here, and I don't know his name. [*He is very pathetic.*] I told him to put O'Connell in the library there. I thought that either Farrant or I might perhaps see him first and——

> *At this moment* EDMUNDS *comes in, and, with that air of discreet tact which he considers befits the establishment of a Prime Minister, announces,* "Mr. O'Connell, my lord." *As* O'CONNELL *follows him,* HORSHAM *can only try not to look too disconcerted.* O'CONNELL, *in his tightly buttoned frock coat, with his shaven face and close-cropped iron grey hair, might be mistaken for a Catholic priest; except that he has not also acquired the easy cheerfulness which professional familiarity with the mysteries of that religion seems to give. For the moment, at least, his features are so impassive that they may tell either of the deepest grief or the purest indifference; or it may be, merely of reticence on entering a stranger's room. He only bows towards* HORSHAM'S *half-proffered hand. With instinctive respect for the situation of this tragically made widower the men have risen, and stand in various uneasy attitudes.*

HORSHAM. Oh . . how do you do? Let me see . . do you know my cousin, Charles Cantelupe? Yes . . we were expecting Russell Blackborough. Sir Henry Percival is ill. Do sit down.

> O'CONNELL *takes the nearest chair, and gradually the others settle themselves,* FARRANT *seeking an obscure corner. But there follows an uncomfortable silence, which* O'CONNELL *at last breaks.*

O'CONNELL. You have sent for me, Lord Horsham?

HORSHAM. I hope that by my message I conveyed no impression of sending for you.

O'CONNELL. I am always in some doubt as to by what person or persons in or out of power this country is gov-

erned, but from all I hear you are at the present moment
approximately entitled to send for me.

> *The level music of his Irish tongue seems to give*
> *finer edge to his sarcasm.*

HORSHAM. Well, Mr. O'Connell . . you know our request before we make it.

O'CONNELL. Yes, I understand that if the fact of Mr.
Trebell's adultery with my wife were made as public as its
consequences to her must be to-morrow, public opinion
would make it difficult for you to include him in your
cabinet.

HORSHAM. Therefore we ask you . . though we have
no right to ask you . . to consider the particular circumstances, and forget the man in the statesman, Mr. O'Connell.

O'CONNELL. My wife is dead. What have I to do at all
with Mr. Trebell as a man? As a statesman I am, in any
case, uninterested in him.

> *Upon this throwing of cold water,* EDMUNDS *returns*
> *to mention, even more discreetly . . .*

EDMUNDS. Mr. Blackborough is in the library, my lord.

HORSHAM. [*Patiently impatient.*] No, no . . here.

WEDGECROFT. Let me go.

HORSHAM. [*To the injured* EDMUNDS.] Wait . . wait!

WEDGECROFT. I'll put him *au fait.* I shan't come back.

HORSHAM. [*Gratefully.*] Yes, yes. [*Then to* EDMUNDS,
who is waiting, with perfect dignity.] Yes . . yes . . yes.

> EDMUNDS *departs, and* WEDGECROFT *makes for the*
> *library door, glad to escape.*

O'CONNELL. If you are not busy at this hour, Wedgecroft, I should be grateful if you'd wait for me. I shall
keep you, I think, but a very few minutes.

WEDGECROFT. [*In his most matter-of-fact tone.*] All
right, O'Connell.

> *He goes into the library.*

CANTELUPE. Don't you think, Cyril, it would be wiser to prevent your man coming into the room at all while we're discussing this?

HORSHAM. [*Collecting his scattered tact.*] Yes, I thought I had arranged that he shouldn't. I'm very sorry. He's a fool. However, there's no one else to come. Once more, Mr. O'Connell . . [*He frames no sentence.*]

O'CONNELL. I am all attention, Lord Horsham.

>   CANTELUPE, *with a self-denying effort, has risen to his feet.*

CANTELUPE. Mr. O'Connell, I remain here almost against my will. I cannot think quite calmly about this double and doubly heinous sin. Don't listen to us while we make light of it. If we think of it as a political bother and ask you to smooth it away . . I am ashamed. But I believe I may not be wrong if I put it to you, that, looking to the future, and for the sake of your own Christian dignity, it may become you to be merciful. And I pray, too . . I think we may believe . . that Mr. Trebell is feeling need of your forgiveness. I have no more to say. [*He sits down again.*]

O'CONNELL. It may be. I have never met Mr. Trebell.

HORSHAM. I tell you, Mr. O'Connell, putting aside Party, that your country has need of this man just at this time.

>   *They hang upon* O'CONNELL'S *reply. It comes with deliberation.*

O'CONNELL. I suppose my point of view must be an unusual one. I notice, at least, that twenty-four hours and more has not enabled Farrant to grasp it.

FARRANT. For God's sake, O'Connell, don't be so cold-blooded. You have the life or death of a man's reputation to decide on.

O'CONNELL. [*With a cold flash of contempt.*] That's a petty enough thing now-a-days, it seems to me. There are

so many clever men . . and they are all so alike . . surely
one will not be missed.

CANTELUPE. Don't you think that is only sarcasm, Mr.
O'Connell?

> *The voice is so gently reproving that* O'CONNELL
> *must turn to him.*

O'CONNELL. Will you please to make allowance, Lord
Charles, for a mediæval scholar's contempt of modern
government? Y o u, at least, will partly understand his
horror as a Catholic at the modern superstitions in favour
of popular opinion and control which it encourages. You
see, Lord Horsham, I am not a party man, only a little less
enthusiastic for the opposite cries than for his own. You
appealed very strangely to my feelings of patriotism for
this country; but you see even my own is—in the twentieth century—foreign to me. From my point of view,
neither Mr. Trebell, nor you, nor the men you have just
defeated, nor any discoverable man or body of men will
make laws which matter . . or differ in the slightest. You
are all part of your age, and you all voice—though in separate keys, or even tunes they may be—only the greed and
follies of your age. That you should do this, and nothing
more, is, of course, the democratic ideal. You will forgive
my thinking tenderly of the statesmanship of the f i r s t
Edward.

> *The library door opens, and* RUSSELL BLACKBOROUGH
> *comes in. He has on evening clothes, complicated
> by a long silk comforter and the motoring cap
> which he carries.*

HORSHAM. You know Russell Blackborough.

O'CONNELL. I think not.

BLACKBOROUGH. How d'you do?

> O'CONNELL *having bowed,* BLACKBOROUGH *having
> nodded, the two men sit down,* BLACKBOROUGH *with*

an air of great attention, O'CONNELL *to continue his*
interrupted speech.

O'CONNELL. And you are as far from me in your code of
personal morals as in your politics. In neither do you seem
to realise that such a thing as passion can exist. No doubt
you use the words Love and Hatred; but do you know that
love and hatred for principles or persons should come from
beyond a man? I notice you speak of forgiveness as if it
were a penny in my pocket. You have been endeavouring
for these two days to rouse me from my indifference towards Mr. Trebell. Perhaps you are on the point of suc-
ceeding . . but I do not know what you may rouse.

HORSHAM. I understand. We are much in agreement,
Mr. O'Connell. What can a man be—who has any pre-
tensions to philosophy—but helplessly indifferent to the
thousands of his fellow creatures whose fates are inter-
twined with his?

O'CONNELL. I am glad that you understand. But, again
. . have I been wrong to shrink from personal relations
with Mr. Trebell? Hatred is as sacred a responsibility as
love. And you will not agree with me when I say that
punishment can be the salvation of a man's soul.

FARRANT. [*With aggressive common sense.*] Look here,
O'Connell, if you're indifferent, it doesn't hurt you to let
him off. And if you hate him . . ! Well, one shouldn't
hate people . . there's no room for it in this world.

CANTELUPE. [*Quietly as ever.*] We have some authority for thinking that the punishment of a secret sin is
awarded by God secretly.

O'CONNELL. We have very poor authority, sir, for using
God's name merely to fill up the gaps in an argument,
though we may thus have our way easily with men who
fear God more than they know Him. I am not one of those.
Yes, Farrant, you and your like have left little room in
this world except for the dusty roads on which I notice

you beginning once more to travel. The rule of them is the same for all, is it not . . from the tramp and the labourer to the plutocrat in his car? This is the age of equality; and it's a fine, practical equality . . the equality of the road. But you've fenced the fields of human joy and turned the very hillsides into hoardings. Commercial opportunity is painted on them, I think.

FARRANT. [*Not to be impressed.*] Perhaps it is, O'Connell. My father made his money out of newspapers, and I ride in a motor car, and you came from Holyhead by train. What has all that to do with it? Why can't you make up your mind? You know in this sort of case one talks a lot . . and then does the usual thing. You must let Trebell off, and that's all about it.

O'CONNELL. Indeed. And do they still think it worth while to administer an oath to your witnesses?

> *He is interrupted by the flinging open of the door and the triumphant right-this-time-anyhow voice in which* EDMUNDS *announces* "Mr. Trebell, my lord." *The general consternation expresses itself through* HORSHAM, *who complains aloud and unreservedly.*

HORSHAM. Good God . . No! Charles, I must give him notice at once . . he'll have to go. [*He apologises to the company.*] I beg your pardon.

> *By this time* TREBELL *is in the room, and has discovered the stranger, who stands to face him, without emotion or anger.* BLACKBOROUGH'S *face wears the grimmest of smiles,* CANTELUPE *is sorry,* FARRANT *recovers from the fit of choking which seemed imminent, and* EDMUNDS, *dimly perceiving by now some fly in the perfect amber of his conduct, departs. The two men still face each other.* FARRANT *is prepared to separate them should they come to blows, and indeed is advancing in that anticipation when* O'CONNELL *speaks.*

o'CONNELL. I am Justin O'Connell.

TREBELL. I guess that.

o'CONNELL. There's a dead woman between us, Mr. Trebell.

> *A tremor sweeps over* TREBELL; *then he speaks simply.*

TREBELL. I wish she had not died.

o'CONNELL. I am called upon by your friends to save you from the consequences of her death. What have you to say about that?

TREBELL. I have been wondering what sort of expression the last of your care for her would find . . but not much. My wonder is at the power over me that has been given to something I despised.

> *Only* o'CONNELL *grasps his meaning. But he, stirred for the first time, and to his very depths, drives it home.*

o'CONNELL. Yes . . If I wanted revenge, I have it. She was a worthless woman. First my life and now yours! Dead because she was afraid to bear your child, isn't she?

TREBELL. [*In agony.*] I'd have helped that if I could.

o'CONNELL. Not the shame . . not the wrong she had done me . . but just fear—fear of the burden of her womanhood. And because of her my children are bastards, and cannot inherit my name. And I must live in sin against my Church, as—God help me—I can't against my nature. What are men to do when this is how women use the freedom we have given them? Is the curse of barrenness to be nothing to a man? And that's the death in life to which you gentlemen, with your fine civilisation, are bringing us. I think we are brothers in misfortune, Mr. Trebell.

TREBELL. [*Far from responding.*] Not at all, sir. If you wanted children, you did the next best thing when she left you. My own problem is neither so simple, nor is it

yet anyone's business but my own. I apologise for allud-
ing to it.

> HORSHAM *takes advantage of the silence that fol-*
> *lows.*

HORSHAM. Shall we . .

O'CONNELL. [*Measuring* TREBELL *with his eyes.*] And
by which shall I help you to a solution . . telling lies or
the truth to-morrow?

TREBELL. [*Roughly, almost insolently.*] If you want my
advice . . I should do the thing that comes more easily to
you, or that will content you most. If you haven't yet
made up your mind as to the relative importance of my
work and your conscience, it's too late to begin now.
Nothing you may do can affect m e.

HORSHAM. [*Fluttering fearfully into this strange dis-*
pute.] O'Connell . . if you and I were to join Wedgecroft . .

O'CONNELL. You value your work more than anything
else in the world?

TREBELL. Have I anything else in the world?

O'CONNELL. Have you not? [*With grim ambiguity.*]
Then I am sorry for you, Mr. Trebell. [*Having said all*
he had to say, he notices HORSHAM.] Yes, Lord Horsham,
by all means . .

> Then HORSHAM *opens the library door and sees him*
> *safely through. He passes* TREBELL *without any sal-*
> *utation, nor does* TREBELL *turn after him; but when*
> HORSHAM *also is in the library, and the door is*
> *closed, comments viciously.*

TREBELL. The man's a sentimentalist . . like all men
who live alone or shut away. [*Then surveying his three*
glum companions, bursts out.] Well . . ? We can stop
thinking of this dead woman, can't we? It's a waste
of time.

FARRANT. Trebell, what did you want to come here for?

TREBELL.   Because you thought I wouldn't.   I knew
you'd be sitting round, incompetent with distress, calculating to a nicety the force of a scandal . .

BLACKBOROUGH.   [*With the firmest of touches.*]   Horsham has called some of us here to discuss the situation.
I am considering my opinion.

TREBELL.   You are not, Blackborough.   You haven't recovered yet from the shock of your manly feelings.   Oh,
cheer up.   You know we're an adulterous and sterile generation.   Why should you cry out at a proof now and then
of what's always in the hearts of most of us?

FARRANT.   [*Plaintively.*]   Now, for God's sake, Trebell
. . O'Connell has been going on like that.

TREBELL.   Well, then . . think of what matters.

BLACKBOROUGH.   Of you and your reputation in fact.

FARRANT.   [*Kindly.*]   Why do you pretend to be callous?
He strokes TREBELL'S *shoulder, who shakes him off
impatiently.*

TREBELL.   Do you all mean to out-face the British Lion
with me after to-morrow . . dare to be Daniels·?

BLACKBOROUGH.   Bravado won't carry this off.

TREBELL.   Blackborough . . it would immortalise you.
I'll stand up in my place in the House of Commons and tell
everything that has befallen, soberly and seriously.   Why
should I flinch?

FARRANT.   My dear Trebell, if your name comes out at
the inquest——

TREBELL.   If it does! . . whose has been the real offence
against Society . . hers or mine?   It's I who am most
offended . . if I choose to think so.

BLACKBOROUGH.   You seem to forget the adultery.

TREBELL.   Isn't Death divorce enough for her?   And . .
oh, wasn't I right? . . What do you start thinking of once
the shock's over?   Punishment . . revenge . . uselessness
. . waste of me.

FARRANT. [*With finality.*] If your name comes out at the inquest, to talk of anything but retirement from public life is perfect lunacy . . and you know it.

> HORSHAM *comes back from the passage. He is a little distracted; then the more so at finding himself again in a highly-charged atmosphere.*

HORSHAM. He's gone off with Wedgecroft.

TREBELL. [*Including* HORSHAM *now in his appeal.*] Does anyone think he knows me now to be a worse man . . less fit, less able . . than he did a week ago?

> *From the piano-stool comes* CANTELUPE'S *quiet voice.*

CANTELUPE. Yes, Trebell . . I do.

> TREBELL *wheels round at this, and ceases all bluster.*

TREBELL. On what grounds?

CANTELUPE. Unarguable ones.

HORSHAM. [*Finding refuge again in his mantelpiece.*] You know, he has gone off without giving me his promise.

FARRANT. That's your own fault, Trebell.

HORSHAM. The fool says I didn't give him explicit instructions.

FARRANT. What fool?

HORSHAM. That man . . [*The name fails him.*] . . my new man. One of those touches of Fate's little finger, really.

> *He begins to consult the ceiling and the carpet once more.* TREBELL *tackles* CANTELUPE *with gravity.*

TREBELL. I have only a logical mind, Cantelupe. I know that to make myself a capable man I've purged myself of all the sins . . I never was idle enough to commit. I know that if your God didn't make use of men, sins and all . . what would ever be done in the world? That one natural action, which the slight shifting of a social law could have made as negligible as eating a meal, can make me incapable . . takes the linch-pin out of one's brain, doesn't it?

HORSHAM. Trebell, we've been doing our best to get

you out of this mess. Your remarks to O'Connell weren't
of any assistance, and . .

> CANTELUPE *stands up, so momentously that* HOR-
> SHAM'S *gentle flow of speech dries up.*

CANTELUPE. Perhaps I had better say at once that,
whatever hushing up you may succeed in, it will be impossible for me to sit in a cabinet with Mr. Trebell.

> *It takes even* FARRANT *a good half minute to recover
> his power of speech on this new issue.*

FARRANT. What perfect nonsense, Cantelupe! I hope
you don't mean that.

BLACKBOROUGH. Complication number one, Horsham.

FARRANT. [*Working up his protest.*] Why on earth
not? You really mustn't drag your personal feelings and
prejudices into important matters like this . . matters of
state.

CANTELUPE. I think I have no choice, when Trebell
stands convicted of a mortal sin, of which he has not even
repented.

TREBELL. [*With bitterest cynicism.*] Dictate any form
of repentance you like . . my signature is yours.

CANTELUPE. Is this a matter for intellectual jugglery?

TREBELL. [*His defence failing at last.*] I offered to
face the scandal from my place in the House. That was
mad, wasn't it?

> BLACKBOROUGH—*his course mapped out—changes
> the tone of the discussion.*

BLACKBOROUGH. Horsham, I hope Trebell will believe I
have no personal feelings in this matter, but we may as
well face the fact even now that O'Connell holding his
tongue to-morrow won't stop gossip in the House, club
gossip, gossip in drawing rooms. What do the Radicals
really care so long as a scandal doesn't get into the papers!
There's an inner circle with its eye on us.

FARRANT. Well, what does that care as long as scandal's

its own copyright? Do you know, my dear father refused a peerage because he felt it meant putting blinkers on his best newspaper.

BLACKBOROUGH. [*A little subtly.*] Still . . now you and Horsham are cousins, aren't you ?

FARRANT. [*Off the track, and explanatory.*] No, no . . my wife's mother . . .

BLACKBOROUGH. I'm inaccurate, for I'm not one of the family circle myself. My money gets me here, and any skill I've used in making it. It wouldn't keep me at a pinch. And Trebell . . [*he speaks through his teeth*] . . do you think your accession to power in the party is popular at the best? Who is going to put out a finger to make it less awkward for Horsham to stick to you if there's a chance of your going under?

　　　　TREBELL *smiles at some mental picture he is making.*

TREBELL. Can your cousins and aunts make it so awkward for you, Horsham?

HORSHAM. [*Repaying humour with humour.*] I bear up against their affectionate intentions.

TREBELL. But I quite understand how uncongenial I may be. What made you take up with me at all?

FARRANT. Your brains, Trebell.

TREBELL. He should have enquired into my character first, shouldn't he, Cantelupe?

CANTELUPE. [*With crushing sincerity.*] Yes.

TREBELL. Oh, the old unnecessary choice . . Wisdom or Virtue. We all think we must make it . . and we all discover we can't. But if you've to choose between Cantelupe and me, Horsham, I quite see you've no choice.

　　　　HORSHAM *now takes the field, using his own
　　　　weapons.*

HORSHAM. Charles, it seems to me that we are somewhat in the position of men who have overheard a private conversation. Do you feel justified in making public use of it?

CANTELUPE. It is not I who am judge. God knows I would not sit in judgment upon anyone.

TREBELL. Cantelupe, I'll take your personal judgment, if you can give it me.

FARRANT. Good Lord, Cantelupe, didn't you sit in a cabinet with . . Well, we're not here to rake up old scandals.

BLACKBOROUGH. I am concerned with the practical issue.

HORSHAM. We know, Blackborough. [*Having quelled the interruption, he proceeds.*] Charles, you spoke, I think, of a mortal sin.

CANTELUPE. In spite of your lifted eyebrows at the childishness of the word.

HORSHAM. Theoretically, we must all wish to guide ourselves by eternal truths. But you would admit, wouldn't you, that we can only deal with temporal things?

CANTELUPE. [*Writhing slightly under the sceptical cross-examination.*] There are divine laws laid down for our guidance . . I admit no disbelief in them.

HORSHAM. Do they place any time-limit to the effect of a mortal sin? If this affair were twenty years old would you do as you are doing? Can you forecast the opinion you will have of it six months hence?

CANTELUPE. [*Positively.*] Yes.

HORSHAM. Can you? Nevertheless, I wish you had postponed your decision even till to-morrow.

> *Having made his point he looks round almost for approval.*

BLACKBOROUGH. What had Percival to say on the subject, Farrant?

FARRANT. I was only to make use of his opinion under certain circumstances.

BLACKBOROUGH. So it isn't favourable to your remaining with us, Mr. Trebell.

FARRANT. [*Indignantly emerging from the trap.*] I never said that.

　　　Now TREBELL *gives the matter another turn, very forcefully.*

TREBELL. Horsham . . I don't bow politely and stand aside at this juncture, as a gentleman should, because I want to know how the work's to be done if I leave you what I was to do.

BLACKBOROUGH. Are we so incompetent?

TREBELL. I daresay not. I want to know . . that's all.

CANTELUPE. Please understand, Mr. Trebell, that I have in no way altered my good opinion of your proposals.

BLACKBOROUGH. Well, I beg to remind you, Horsham, that from the first I've reserved myself liberty to criticise fundamental points in the scheme.

HORSHAM. [*Pacifically.*] Quite so.

BLACKBOROUGH. That nonsensical new standard of teachers' salaries, for one thing . . you'd never pass it.

HORSHAM. Quite easily. It's an administrative point, so leave the legislation vague. Then, as the appropriation money falls in, the qualifications rise and the salaries rise. No one will object, because no one will appreciate it but administrators, past or future . . and they never cavil at money. [*He remains lost in the beauty of this prospect.*]

TREBELL. Will you take charge of the bill, Blackborough?

BLACKBOROUGH. Are you serious?

HORSHAM. [*Brought to earth.*] Oh, no! [*He corrects himself, smiling.*] I mean, my dear Blackborough, why not stick to the colonies?

BLACKBOROUGH. You see, Trebell, there's still the possibility that O'Connell may finally spike your gun to-morrow. You realise that, don't you?

TREBELL. Thank you. I quite realise that.

CANTELUPE. Can nothing further be done?

BLACKBOROUGH. Weren't we doing our best?

HORSHAM. Yes . . if we were bending our thoughts to that difficulty now . . .

TREBELL. [*Hardly.*] May I ask you to interfere on my behalf no further?

FARRANT. My dear Trebell!

TREBELL. I assure you that I am interested in the Disestablishment Bill.

> *So they turn readily enough from the more uncomfortable part of their subject.*

BLACKBOROUGH. Well . . here's Farrant.

FARRANT. I'm no good. Give me agriculture.

BLACKBOROUGH. Pity you're in the Lords, Horsham.

TREBELL. Horsham, I'll devil for any man you choose to name . . feed him sentence by sentence. . .

HORSHAM. That's impossible.

TREBELL. Well, what's to become of my bill? I want to know.

BLACKBOROUGH. [*Casting his care on Providence.*] We shall manage somehow. Why, if you had died suddenly . . or, let us say, never been born . . .

TREBELL. Then, Blackborough . . speaking as a dying man . . if you go back on the integrity of this scheme, I'll haunt you. [*Having said this, with some finality, he turns his back.*]

CANTELUPE. Cyril, I agree with what Trebell is saying. Whatever happens, there must be no tampering with the comprehensiveness of the scheme. Remember you are in the hands of the extremists . . on both sides. I won't support a compromise on one . . nor will they on the other.

HORSHAM. Well, I'll confess to you candidly, Trebell, that I don't know of any man available for this piece of work but you.

TREBELL.   Then I should say it would be almost a relief to you if O'Connell tells on me to-morrow.

FARRANT.   We seem to have got off that subject altogether. [*There comes a portentous tap at the door.*] Good Lord! . . I'm getting jumpy.

HORSHAM.   Excuse me.

> *A note is handed to him through the half opened door; and obviously it is at* EDMUNDS *whom he frowns. Then he returns, fidgetting for his glasses.*

Oh, it turns out . . I'm so sorry you were blundered in here, Trebell . . this man . . what's his name . . Edwards . . had been reading the papers, and thought it was a cabinet council . . seemed proud of himself. This is from Wedgecroft . . scribbled in a messenger office. I never can read his writing . . it's like prescriptions. Can you?

> *It has gradually dawned on the three men, and then on* TREBELL, *what this note may have in it.* FARRANT'S *hand even trembles a little as he takes it. He gathers the meaning himself and looks at the others with a smile before he reads the few words aloud.*

FARRANT.   "All right. He has promised."

BLACKBOROUGH.   O'Connell?

FARRANT.   Thank God. [*He turns enthusiastically to* TREBELL, *who stands rigid.*] My dear fellow . . I hope you know how glad I am.

CANTELUPE.   I am very glad.

BLACKBOROUGH.   Of course we're all very glad indeed, Trebell . . very glad we persuaded him.

FARRANT.   That's dead and buried now, isn't it?

> TREBELL *moves away from them all, and leaves them wondering. When he turns round, his face is as hard as ever; his voice, if possible, harder.*

TREBELL.   But, Horsham, returning to the more important question . . you've taken trouble, and O'Connell's to perjure himself, for nothing, if you still can't get me into your child's puzzle .. to make the pretty picture that a cabinet should be.

HORSHAM *looks at* BLACKBOROUGH *and scents danger.*

HORSHAM. We shall all be glad, I am sure, to postpone any further discussion . . .

TREBELL. I shall not.

BLACKBOROUGH. [*Encouragingly.*] Quite so, Trebell. We're on the subject, and it won't discount our pleasure that you're out of this mess to continue it. This habit of putting off the hour of disagreement is .. well, Horsham, it's contrary to my business instincts.

TREBELL. If one time's as good as another for you .. this moment is better than most for me.

HORSHAM. [*A little irritated at the wantonness of this dispute.*] There is nothing before us on which we are capable of coming to any decision .. in a technical sense.

BLACKBOROUGH. That's a quibble. [*Poor* HORSHAM *gasps.*] I'm not going to pretend, either now or in a month's time, that I think Trebell anything but a most dangerous acquisition to the party. I pay you a compliment in that, Trebell. Now, Horsham proposes that we should go to the country when Disestablishment's through.

HORSHAM. It's the condition of Nonconformist support.

BLACKBOROUGH. One condition. Then you'd leave us, Trebell?

HORSHAM. I hope not.

BLACKBOROUGH. And carry with you the credit of our one big measure. Consider the effect upon our reputation with the Country.

FARRANT. [*Waking to* BLACKBOROUGH'S *line of action.*] Why on earth should you leave us, Trebell? You've hardly been a Liberal, even in name.

BLACKBOROUGH. [*Vigorously making his point.*] Then what would be the conditions of your remaining? You're not a party man, Trebell. You haven't the true party feeling. You are to be bought. Of course you take your price in measures, not in money. But you are preeminently a man of ideas . . an expert. And a man of ideas is often a grave embarrassment to a government.

HORSHAM. And vice-versa . . vice-versa!

TREBELL. [*Facing* BLACKBOROUGH *across the room.*] Do I understand that you, for the good of the Tory party . . just as Cantelupe for the good of his soul . . will refuse to sit in a cabinet with me?

BLACKBOROUGH. [*Unembarrassed.*] I don't commit myself to saying that.

CANTELUPE. No, Trebell . . it's that I must believe your work could not prosper . . in God's way.

TREBELL *softens to his sincerity.*

TREBELL. Cantelupe, I quite understand. You may be right . . it's a very interesting question. Blackborough, I take it that you object, first of all, to the scheme that I'm bringing you.

BLACKBOROUGH. I object to those parts of it which I don't think you'll get through the House.

FARRANT. [*Feeling that he must take part.*] For instance?

BLACKBOROUGH. I've given you one already.

CANTELUPE. [*His eye on* BLACKBOROUGH.] Understand, there are things in that scheme we must stand or fall by.

Suddenly TREBELL *makes for the door.* HORSHAM *gets up concernedly.*

TREBELL. Horsham, make up your mind to-night whether you can do with me or not. I have to see Percival again to-morrow . . we cut short our argument at the important point. Good-bye . . don't come down. Will you decide to-night?

HORSHAM. I have made up my own mind.

TREBELL. Is that sufficient?

HORSHAM.   A collective decision is a matter of development.

TREBELL.   Well, I shall expect to hear.

HORSHAM.   By hurrying one only reaches a rash conclusion.

TREBELL.   Then be rash for once, and take the consequences.   Good-night.

He is gone before HORSHAM *can compose another epigram.*

BLACKBOROUGH.   [*Deprecating such conduct.*]   Lost his temper!

FARRANT.   [*Ruffling considerably.*]   Horsham, if Trebell is to be hounded out of your cabinet . . he won't go alone.

HORSHAM.   [*Bitter-sweet.*]   My dear Farrant . . I have yet to form my cabinet.

CANTELUPE.   You are forming it to carry disestablishment, are you not, Cyril?   Therefore you will form it in the best interests of the best scheme possible.

HORSHAM.   Trebell was and is the best man I know of for the purpose.   I'm a little weary of saying that.

He folds his arms and awaits further developments. After a moment CANTELUPE *gets up as if to address a meeting.*

CANTELUPE.   Then if you would prefer not to include me . . I shall feel justified in giving independent support to a scheme I have great faith in.   [*And he sits down again.*]

BLACKBOROUGH.   [*Impatiently.*]   My dear Cantelupe, if you think Horsham can form a disestablishment cabinet to include Trebell and exclude you, you're vastly mistaken. I for one . . .

FARRANT.   But do both of you consider how valuable, how vital, Trebell is to us just at this moment?   The Radicals trust him.

BLACKBOROUGH.   They hate him.

HORSHAM. [*Elucidating.*] Their front bench hates him because he turned them out. The rest of them hate their front bench. After six years of office who wouldn't?

BLACKBOROUGH. That's true.

FARRANT. Oh, of course, we must stick to Trebell, Blackborough.

> BLACKBOROUGH *is silent; so* HORSHAM *turns his attention to his cousin.*

HORSHAM. Well, Charles, I won't ask you for a decision now. I know how hard it is to accept the dictates of other men's consciences . . but a necessary condition of all political work, believe me.

CANTELUPE. [*Uneasily.*] You can form your cabinet without me, Cyril.

> *At this* BLACKBOROUGH *charges down on them, so to speak.*

BLACKBOROUGH. No, I tell you, I'm damned if he can. Leaving the whole high church party to blackmail all they can out of us and vote how they like! Here . . I've got my Yorkshire people to think of. I can bargain for them with you in a cabinet . . not if you've the pull of being out of it.

HORSHAM. [*With charming insinuation.*] And have you calculated, Blackborough, what may become of us if Trebell has the pull of being out of it?

> BLACKBOROUGH *makes a face.*

BLACKBOROUGH. Yes . . I suppose he might turn nasty.

FARRANT. I should hope he would.

BLACKBOROUGH. [*Tackling* FARRANT *with great ease.*] I should hope he would consider the matter not from the personal, but from the political point of view . . as I am trying to do.

HORSHAM. [*Tasting his epigram with enjoyment.*] Introspection is the only bar to such an honourable endeavour. [BLACKBOROUGH *gapes.*] You don't suffer from that as—for instance—Charles here, does.

BLACKBOROUGH. [*Pugnaciously.*] D'you mean I'm just pretending not to attack him personally?

HORSHAM. [*Safe on his own ground.*] It's only a curious metaphysical point. Have you never noticed your distaste for the colour of a man's hair translate itself ultimately into an objection to his religious opinions . . or what not? I am sure—for instance—I could trace Charles's scruples about sitting in a cabinet with Trebell back to a sort of academic reverence for women generally which he possesses. I am sure I could . . if he were not probably now doing it himself. But this does not make the scruples less real, less religious, or less political. We must be humanly biased in expression . . or not express ourselves.

BLACKBOROUGH. [*Whose thoughts have wandered.*] The man's less of a danger than he was . . I mean he'll be alone. The Liberals won't have him back. He smashed his following there to come over to us.

FARRANT. [*Giving a further meaning to this.*] Yes, Blackborough, he did.

BLACKBOROUGH. To gain his own ends! Oh, my dear Horsham, can't you see that if O'Connell had blabbed to-morrow it really would have been a blessing in disguise? I don't pretend to Cantelupe's standard . . but there must be something radically wrong with a man who could get himself into such a mess as that . . now mustn't there? Ah! . . you have a fatal partiality for clever people. I tell you . . though this might be patched up . . Trebell would fail us in some other way before we were six months older.

This speech has its effect; but HORSHAM *looks at him a little sternly.*

HORSHAM. And am I to conclude that you don't want Charles to change his mind?

BLACKBOROUGH. [*On another tack.*] Farrant has not yet allowed us to hear Percival's opinion.

FARRANT *looks rather alarmed.*

FARRANT. It has very little reference to the scandal.

BLACKBOROUGH. As that is at an end . . all the more reason we should hear it.

HORSHAM. [*Ranging himself with* FARRANT.] I called this quite informal meeting, Blackborough, only to dispose of the scandal, if possible.

BLACKBOROUGH. Well, of course, if Farrant chooses to insult Percival so gratuitously by burking his message to us . . .

There is an unspoken threat in this. HORSHAM *sees it, and without disguising his irritation.*

HORSHAM. Let us have it, Farrant.

FARRANT. [*With a sort of puzzled discontent.*] Well . . I never got to telling him of the O'Connell affair at all. He started talking to me . . saying that he couldn't for a moment agree to Trebell's proposals for the finance of his bill . . I couldn't get a word in edgeways. Then his wife came up . .

HORSHAM *takes something in this so seriously that he actually interrupts.*

HORSHAM. Does he definitely disagree? What is his point?

FARRANT. He says Disestablishment's a bad enough speculation for the party as it is.

BLACKBOROUGH. It is inevitable.

FARRANT. He sees that. But then he says . . to go to the Country again, having bolstered up Education and quarrelled with everybody, will be bad enough . . to go having spent fifty millions on it will dish us for all our lifetimes.

HORSHAM. What does he propose?

FARRANT. He'll offer to draft another bill, and take it

through himself. He says . . do as many good turns as we can with the money . . don't put it all on one horse.

BLACKBOROUGH. He's your man, Horsham. That's one difficulty settled.

> HORSHAM'S *thoughts are evidently beyond* BLACK-BOROUGH, *beyond the absent* PERCIVAL *even.*

HORSHAM. Oh . . any of us could carry that sort of a bill.

> CANTELUPE *has heard this last passage with nothing less than horror and pale anger, which he contains no longer.*

CANTELUPE. I won't have this. I won't have this opportunity frittered away for party purposes.

BLACKBOROUGH. [*Expostulating reasonably.*] My dear Cantelupe . . you'll get whatever you think it right for the Church to have. You carry a solid thirty-eight votes with you.

> HORSHAM'S *smooth voice intervenes. He speaks with finesse.*

HORSHAM. Percival, as an old campaigner, expresses himself very roughly. The point is, that we are, after all, only the trustees of the party. If we know that a certain step will decimate it . . clearly we have no right to take the step.

CANTELUPE. [*Glowing to white heat.*] Is this a time to count the consequences to ourselves?

HORSHAM. [*Unkindly.*] By your action this evening, Charles, you evidently think not. [*He salves the wound.*] No matter, I agree with you . . the bill should be a comprehensive one, whoever brings it in.

BLACKBOROUGH. [*Not without enjoyment of the situation.*] Whoever brings it in will have to knuckle under to Percival over its finance.

FARRANT. Trebell won't do that. I warned Percival.

HORSHAM. Then what did he say?

FARRANT. He only swore.

HORSHAM *suddenly becomes peevish.*

HORSHAM. I think, Farrant, you should have given me this message before.

FARRANT. My dear Horsham, what had it to do with our request to O'Connell?

HORSHAM. [*Scolding the company generally.*] Well, then, I wish he hadn't sent it. I wish we were not discussing these points at all. The proper time for them is at a cabinet meeting. And when we have actually assumed the responsibilities of government . . then threats of resignation are not things to be played about with.

FARRANT. Did you expect Percival's objection to the finance of the scheme.

HORSHAM. Perhaps . . perhaps. I knew Trebell was to see him last Tuesday. I expect everybody's objections to any parts of every scheme to come at a time when I am in a proper position to reconcile them . . not now.

> *Having vented his grievances, he sits down to recover.* BLACKBOROUGH *takes advantage of the ensuing pause.*

BLACKBOROUGH. It isn't so easy for me to speak against Trebell, since he evidently dislikes me personally as much as I dislike him . . but I'm sure I'm doing my duty. Horsham . . here you have Cantelupe who won't stand in with the man, and Percival, who won't stand in with his measure, while I would sooner stand in with neither. Isn't it better to face the situation now than take trouble to form the most makeshift of cabinets, and if that doesn't go to pieces, be voted down in the House by your own party?

> *There is an oppressive silence.* HORSHAM *is sulky. The matter is beyond* FARRANT. CANTELUPE, *whose agonies have expressed themselves in slight writhings, at last, with an effort, writhes himself to his feet.*

CANTELUPE. I think I am prepared to reconsider my decision.

FARRANT. That's all right, then!

He looks round wonderingly for the rest of the chorus, to find that neither BLACKBOROUGH *nor* HORSHAM *have stirred.*

BLACKBOROUGH. [*stealthily.*] Is it, Horsham?

HORSHAM. [*Sotto voce.*] Why did you ever make it?

BLACKBOROUGH *leaves him for* CANTELUPE.

BLACKBOROUGH. You're afraid for the integrity of the bill.

CANTELUPE. It must be comprehensive . . that's vital.

BLACKBOROUGH. [*Very forcefully.*] I give you my word to support its integrity, if you'll keep with me in persuading Horsham that the inclusion of Trebell in his cabinet will be a blow to the whole Conservative Cause. Horsham, I implore you not to pursue this short-sighted policy. All parties have made up their minds to Disestablishment . . surely nothing should be easier than to frame a bill which will please all parties.

FARRANT. [*At last perceiving the drift of all this.*] But good Lord, Blackborough . . now Cantelupe has come round and will stand in . . .

BLACKBOROUGH. That's no longer the point. And what's all this nonsense about going to the country again next year?

HORSHAM. [*Mildly.*] After consulting me, Percival said at Bristol . . .

BLACKBOROUGH. [*Quite unchecked.*] I know. But if we pursue a thoroughly safe policy, and the bye-elections go right . . there need be no vote of censure carried for three or four years. The Radicals want a rest with the country, and they know it. And one has no right, what's more, to go wantonly plunging the country into the expenses of these constant general elections. It ruins trade.

FARRANT. [*Forlornly sticking to his point.*] What has all this to do with Trebell?

HORSHAM. [*Thoughtfully.*] Farrant, beyond what you've told us, Percival didn't recommend me to throw him over.

FARRANT. No, he didn't . . that is, he didn't exactly.

HORSHAM. Well . . he didn't?

FARRANT. I'm trying to be accurate. [*Obviously their nerves are now on edge.*] He said we should find him tough to assimilate—as he warned you.

> HORSHAM, *with knit brows, loses himself in thought again.* BLACKBOROUGH *quietly turns his attention to* FARRANT.

BLACKBOROUGH. Farrant, you don't seriously think that . . outside his undoubted capabilities . . Trebell is an acquisition to the party?

FARRANT. [*Unwillingly.*] Perhaps not. But if you're going to chuck a man . . don't chuck him when he's down.

BLACKBOROUGH. He's no longer down. We've got him O'Connell's promise, and jolly grateful he ought to be. I think the least we can do is to keep our minds clear between Trebell's advantage and the party's.

CANTELUPE. [*From the distant music-stool.*] And the party's and the Country's.

BLACKBOROUGH. [*Countering quite deftly.*] Cantelupe, either we think it best for the country to have our party in power or we don't.

FARRANT. [*In judicious temper.*] Certainly, I don't feel our responsibility towards him is what it was ten minutes ago. The man has other careers besides his political one.

BLACKBOROUGH. [*Ready to praise.*] Clever as paint at the Bar—best Company lawyer we've got.

CANTELUPE. It is not what he loses, I think . . but what we lose in losing him.

He says this so earnestly that HORSHAM *pays attention.*

HORSHAM. No, my dear Charles, let us be practical. If his position with us is to be made impossible it is better that he shouldn't assume it.

BLACKBOROUGH. [*Soft and friendly.*] How far are you actually pledged to him?

HORSHAM *looks up with the most ingenuous of smiles.*

HORSHAM. That's always such a difficult sort of point to determine, isn't it? He thinks he is to join us. But I've not yet been commanded to form a cabinet. If neither you —nor Percival—nor perhaps others will work with him . . what am I to do? [*He appeals to them generally to justify this attitude.*]

BLACKBOROUGH. He no longer thinks he's to join us . . it's the question he left us to decide.

He leaves HORSHAM, *whose perplexity is diminishing.* FARRANT *makes an effort.*

FARRANT. But the scandal won't weaken his position with us now. There won't be any scandal . . there won't, Blackborough.

HORSHAM. There may be. Though I take it we're all guiltless of having mentioned the matter.

BLACKBOROUGH. [*Very detached.*] I've only known of it since I came into this house . . but I shall not mention it.

FARRANT. Oh, I'm afraid my wife knows. [*He adds hastily.*] My fault . . my fault entirely.

BLACKBOROUGH. I tell you Rumour's electric.

HORSHAM *has turned to* FARRANT *with a sweet smile and with the air of a man about to be relieved of all responsibility.*

HORSHAM. What does she say?

FARRANT. [*As one speaks of a nice woman.*] She was horrified.

HORSHAM. Of course. [*Once more he finds refuge and*

comfort on the hearthrug, to say, after a moment, with fine resignation.] I suppose I must let him go.

CANTELUPE. [*On his feet again.*] Cyril!

HORSHAM. Yes, Charles?

> *With this query he turns an accusing eye on* CANTE-LUPE, *who is silenced.*

BLACKBOROUGH. Have you made up your mind to that?

FARRANT. [*In great distress.*] You're wrong, Horsham. [*Then in greater.*] That is . . I t h i n k you're wrong.

HORSHAM. I'd sooner not let him know to-night.

BLACKBOROUGH. But he asked you to.

HORSHAM. [*All show of resistance gone.*] Did he? Then I suppose I must. [*He sighs deeply.*]

BLACKBOROUGH. Then I'll get back to Aylesbury.

> *He picks up his motor-cap from the table and settles it on his head with immense aplomb.*

HORSHAM. So late?

BLACKBOROUGH. Really, one can get along quicker at night if one knows the road. You're in town, aren't you, Farrant? Shall I drop you at Grosvenor Square?

FARRANT. [*Ungraciously.*] Thank you.

BLACKBOROUGH. [*With a conqueror's geniality.*] I don't mind telling you now, Horsham, that ever since we met at Shapters I've been wondering how you'd escape from this association with Trebell. Thought he was being very clever when he crosed the House to us! It's needed a special providence. You'd never have got a cabinet together to include him.

HORSHAM. [*With much intention.*] No.

FARRANT. [*Miserably.*] Yes, I suppose that intrigue was a mistake from the beginning.

BLACKBOROUGH. Well, good-night. [*As he turns to go he finds* CANTELUPE *upright, staring very sternly at him.*] Good-night, Cantelupe.

CANTELUPE. From what motives have we thrown Trebell over?

BLACKBOROUGH. Never mind the motives, if the move is the right one. [*Then he nods at* HORSHAM.] I shall be up again next week if you want me.

> *And he flourishes out of the room; a man who has done a good hour's work.* FARRANT, *who has been mooning depressedly around, now backs towards the door.*

FARRANT. In one way, of course, Trebell won't care a damn. I mean he knows as well as we do that office isn't worth having . . he has never been a place-hunter. On the other hand . . what with one thing and the other . . Blackborough is a sensible fellow. I suppose it can't be helped.

HORSHAM. Blackborough will tell you so. Good-night.

> *So* FARRANT *departs, leaving the two cousins together.* CANTELUPE *has not moved, and now faces* HORSHAM *just as accusingly.*

CANTELUPE. Cyril, this is tragic.

HORSHAM. [*More to himself than in answer.*] Yes . . most annoying.

CANTELUPE. Lucifer, son of the morning! Why is it always the highest who fall?

> HORSHAM *shies fastidiously at this touch of poetry.*

HORSHAM. No, my dear Charles, let us, above all things, keep our mental balance. Trebell is a most capable fellow. I'd set my heart on having him with me . . he'll be most awkward to deal with in opposition. But we shall survive his loss, and so would the country.

CANTELUPE. [*Desperately.*] Cyril, promise me there shall be no compromise over this measure.

HORSHAM. [*Charmingly candid.*] No . . no unnecessary compromise, I promise you.

CANTELUPE. [*With a sigh.*] If we had done what we

have done to-night in the right spirit! Blackborough was almost vindictive.

HORSHAM. [*Smiling without amusement.*] Didn't you keep thinking . . I did . . of that affair of his with Mrs. Parkington . . years ago?

CANTELUPE. There was never any proof of it.

HORSHAM. No . . he bought off the husband.

CANTELUPE. [*Uneasily.*] His objections to Trebell were —political.

HORSHAM. Yours weren't.

CANTELUPE. [*More uneasily still.*] I withdrew mine.

HORSHAM. [*With elderly reproof.*] I don't think, Charles, you have the least conception of what a nicely balanced machine a cabinet is.

CANTELUPE. [*Imploring comfort.*] But should we have held together through Trebell's bill?

HORSHAM. [*A little impatient.*] Perhaps not. But once I had them all round a table . . Trebell is very keen on office, for all his independent airs . . he and Percival could have argued the thing out. However, it's too late now.

CANTELUPE. Is it?

> *For a moment* HORSHAM *is tempted to indulge in the luxury of changing his mind; but he puts Satan behind him with a shake of the head.*

HORSHAM. Well, you see . . Percival I can't do without. Now that Blackborough knows of his objections to the finance he'd go to him and take Chisholm and offer to back them up. I know he would . . he didn't take Farrant away with him for nothing. [*Then he flashes out rather shrilly.*] It's Trebell's own fault. He ought not to have committed himself definitely to any scheme until he was safely in office. I warned him about Percival . . I warned him not to be explicit. One cannot work with

men who will make up their minds prematurely. No, I
shall not change my mind. I shall write to him.

> *He goes firmly to his writing desk, leaving* CANTE-
> LUPE *forlorn.*

CANTELUPE. What about a messenger?

HORSHAM. Not at this time of night. I'll post it.

CANTELUPE. I'll post it as I go.

> *He seeks comfort again in the piano, and this time
> starts to play, with one finger, and some hesitation,
> the first bars of a Bach fugue.* HORSHAM'S *pen-nib
> is disappointing him, and the letter is not easy to
> phrase.*

HORSHAM. But I hate coming to immediate decisions.
The administrative part of my brain always tires after
half an hour. Does yours, Charles?

CANTELUPE. What do you think Trebell will do now?

HORSHAM. [*A little grimly.*] Punish us all he can.

> *On reaching the second voice in the fugue* CANTE-
> LUPE'S *virtuosity breaks down.*

CANTELUPE. All that ability turned to destructiveness . .
what a pity! That's the paradox of human activities . .

> *Suddenly* HORSHAM *looks up, and his face is lighted
> with a seraphic smile.*

HORSHAM. Charles . . I wish we could do without
Blackborough.

CANTELUPE. [*Struck with the idea.*] Well . . why not?

HORSHAM. Yes . . I must think about it. [*They both
get up, cheered considerably.*] You won't forget this, will
you?

CANTELUPE. [*The letter in* HORSHAM'S *hand accusing
him.*] No . . no. I don't think I have been the cause of
your dropping Trebell, have I?

> HORSHAM, *rid of the letter, is rid of responsibility,
> and is his charming, equable self again. He com-
> forts his cousin paternally.*

HORSHAM. I don't think so. The split would have
come when Blackborough checkmated my forming a cabinet. It would have pleased him to do that . . and he
could have, over Trebell. But now that question's out of
the way . . you won't get such a bad measure with Trebell in opposition. He'll frighten us into keeping it up to
the mark, so to speak.

CANTELUPE. [*A little comforted.*] But I shall miss one
or two of those ideas . .

HORSHAM. [*So pleasantly sceptical.*] Do you think
they'd have outlasted the second reading? Dullness in the
country one expects. Dullness in the House one can cope
with. But do you know, I have never sat in a cabinet yet
that didn't greet anything like a new idea in chilling
silence.

CANTELUPE. Well, I should regret to have caused you
trouble, Cyril.

HORSHAM. [*His hand on the other's shoulder.*] Oh . .
we don't take politics so much to heart as that, I hope.

CANTELUPE. [*With sweet gravity.*] I take politics very
much to heart. Yes, I know what you mean . . but that's
the sort of remark that makes people call you cynical.
[HORSHAM *smiles as if at a compliment, and starts with*
CANTELUPE *towards the door.* CANTELUPE, *who would not
hurt his feelings, changes the subject.*] By the bye, I'm
glad we met this evening! Do you hear Aunt Mary wants
to sell the Burford Holbein? Can she?

HORSHAM. [*Taking as keen, but no keener, an interest
in this than in the difficulty he has just surmounted.*] Yes,
by the will she can, but she mustn't. Dear me, I thought
I'd put a stop to that foolishness. Well, now, we must
take that matter up very seriously.

　　　They go out talking, arm in arm.

THE FOURTH ACT

At TREBELL'S again; later the same evening.

*His room is in darkness but for the flicker the fire makes
and the streaks of moonlight between the curtains.
The door is open, though, and you see the light of
the lamp on the stairs. You hear his footstep, too.
On his way he stops to draw back the curtains of
the passage-way window; the moonlight makes his
face look very pale. Then he serves the curtains of
his own window the same; flings it open, moreover,
and stands looking out. Something below draws his
attention. After leaning over the balcony, with a
short "Hullo" he goes quickly downstairs again. In
a minute* WEDGECROFT *comes up.* TREBELL *follows,
pausing by the door a moment to light up the room.*
WEDGECROFT *is radiant.*

TREBELL. [*With a twist of his mouth.*] Promised, has
he?

WEDGECROFT. Suddenly broke out, as we walked along,
that he liked the look of you, and that men must stand by
one another nowadays against these women. Then he
said good-night and walked away.

TREBELL. Back to Ireland and the thirteenth century.

WEDGECROFT. After to-morrow.

TREBELL. [*Taking all the meaning of to-morrow.*] Yes.
Are you in for perjury, too?

WEDGECROFT. [*His thankfulness checked a little.*] No
. . not exactly.

TREBELL *walks away from him.*

TREBELL.   It's a pity the truth isn't to be told, I think. I suppose the verdict will be murder.

WEDGECROFT.   They won't catch the man.

TREBELL.   You don't mean . . me?

WEDGECROFT.   No, no . . my dear fellow.

TREBELL.   You might, you know. But nobody seems to see this thing as I see it. If I were on that jury I'd say murder, too, and accuse . . so many circumstances, Gilbert, that we should go home . . and look in the cupboards. What a lumber of opinions we inherit and keep!

WEDGECROFT.   [*Humouring him.*] Ought we to burn the house down?

TREBELL.   Rules and regulations for the preservation of rubbish are the laws of England . . and I was adding to their number.

WEDGECROFT.   And so you shall . . to the applause of a grateful country.

TREBELL.   [*Studying his friend's kindly, encouraging face.*] Gilbert, it is not so much that you're an incorrigible optimist . . but why do you subdue your mind to flatter people into cheerfulness?

WEDGECROFT.   I'm a doctor, my friend.

TREBELL.   You're a part of our tendency to keep things alive by hook or crook . . not a spark but must be carefully blown upon. The world's old and tired; it dreads extinction. I think I disapprove . . I think I've more faith.

WEDGECROFT.   [*scolding him.*] Nonsense . . you've the instinct to preserve your life as everyone else has . . and I'm here to show you how.

TREBELL.   [*Beyond the reach of his kindness.*] I assure you that these two days while you've been fussing around O'Connell—bless your kind heart—I've been waiting events, indifferent enough to understand his indifference.

WEDGECROFT.   Not indifferent.

TREBELL. Lifeless enough already, then. [*Suddenly a thought strikes him.*] D'you think it was Horsham and his little committee persuaded O'Connell?

WEDGECROFT. On the contrary.

TREBELL. So you need not have let them into the secret?

WEDGECROFT. No.

TREBELL. Think of that!

> *He almost laughs; but* WEDGECROFT *goes on quite innocently.*

WEDGECROFT. Yes . . I'm sorry.

TREBELL. Upsetting their moral digestion for nothing.

WEDGECROFT. But when O'Connell wouldn't listen to us we had to rope in the important people.

TREBELL. With their united wisdom. [*Then he breaks away again into great bitterness.*] No . . what do they make of this woman's death? I saw them in that room, Gilbert, like men seen through the wrong end of a telescope. D'you think if the little affair with Nature . . her offence and mine against the conveniences of civilization . . had ended in my death, too . . then they'd have stopped to wonder at the misuse and waste of the only force there is in the world . . come to think of it, there is no other . . than this desire for expression . . in words . . or through children. Would they have thought of that and stopped whispering about the scandal?

> *Through this* WEDGECROFT *has watched him very gravely.*

WEDGECROFT. Trebell . . if the inquest to-morrow h a d put you out of action . .

TREBELL. Should I have grown a beard and travelled abroad, and after ten years timidly tried to climb my way back into politics? When public opinion takes its heel from your face it keeps it for your finger-tips. After twenty years to be forgiven by your more broad-minded friends and tolerated as a dotard by a new generation . . .

WEDGECROFT. Nonsense. What age are you now . . forty-six . . forty-seven?

TREBELL. Well . . let's instance a good man. Gladstone had done his best work by sixty-five. Then he began to be popular. Think of his last years of oratory.

He has gone to his table, and now very methodically starts to tidy his papers, WEDGECROFT *still watching him.*

WEDGECROFT. You'd have had to thank Heaven for a little that there were more lives than one to lead.

TREBELL. That's another of your faults, Gilbert . . it's a comfort just now to enumerate them. You're an anarchist . . a kingdom to yourself. You make little treaties with Truth and with Beauty, and what can disturb you? I'm a part of the machine I believe in. If my life as I've made it is to be cut short . . the rest of me shall walk out of the world and slam the door . . with the noise of a pistol shot.

WEDGECROFT. [*Concealing some uneasiness.*] Then I'm glad it's not to be cut short. You and your cabinet rank and your disestablishment bill!

TREBELL *starts to enjoy his secret.*

TREBELL. Yes . . our minds have been much relieved within the last half hour, haven't they?

WEDGECROFT. I scribbled Horsham a note in a messenger office and sent it as soon as O'Connell had left me.

TREBELL. He'd be glad to get that.

WEDGECROFT. He has been most kind about the whole thing.

TREBELL. Oh, he means well.

WEDGECROFT. [*Following up his fancied advantage.*] But, my friend . . suicide whilst of unsound mind would never have done . . The hackneyed verdict hits the truth, you know.

TREBELL. You think so?

WEDGECROFT. I don't say there aren't excuses enough in this miserable world, but fundamentally . . no sane person will destroy life.

TREBELL. [*His thoughts shifting their plane.*] Was she so very mad? I'm not thinking of her own death.

WEDGECROFT. Don't brood, Trebell. Your mind isn't healthy yet about her and——

TREBELL. And my child.

> *Even* WEDGECROFT'S *kindness is at fault before the solemnity of this.*

WEDGECROFT. Is that how you're thinking of it?

TREBELL. How else? It's very inexplicable . . this sense of fatherhood. [*The eyes of his mind travel down— what vista of possibilities. Then he shakes himself free.*] Let's drop the subject. To finish the list of shortcomings, you're a bit of an artist, too . . therefore, I don't think you'll understand.

WEDGECROFT. [*Successfully decoyed into argument.*] Surely an artist is a man who understands.

TREBELL. Everything about life, but not life itself. That's where art fails a man.

WEDGECROFT. That's where everything but living fails a man. [*Drifting into introspection himself.*] Yes, it's true. I can talk cleverly, and I've written a book . . but I'm barren. [*Then the healthy mind re-asserts itself.*] No, it's not true. Our thoughts are children . . and marry and intermarry. And we're peopling the world . . not badly.

TREBELL. Well . . either life is too little a thing to matter, or it's so big that such specks of it as we may be are of no account. These are two points of view. And then one has to consider if death can't be sometimes the last use made of life.

> *There is a tone of menace in this which recalls* WEDGECROFT *to the present trouble.*

WEDGECROFT. I doubt the virtue of sacrifice . . or the use of it.

TREBELL. How else could I tell Horsham that my work matters? Does he think so now? . . not he.

WEDGECROFT. You mean if they'd had to throw you over?

Once again TREBELL *looks up with that secretive smile.*

TREBELL. Yes . . if they'd had to.

WEDGECROFT. [*Unreasonably nervous, so he thinks.*] My dear fellow, Horsham would have thought it was the shame and disgrace if you'd shot yourself after the inquest. That's the proper sentimental thing for you so-called strong men to do on like occasions. Why, if your name were to come out to-morrow, your best meaning friends would be sending you pistols by post, requesting you to use them like a gentleman. Horsham would grieve over ten dinner-tables in succession, and then return to his philosophy. One really mustn't waste a life trying to shock polite politicians. There'd even be a suspicion of swagger in it.

TREBELL. Quite so . . the bomb that's thrown at their feet must be something otherwise worthless.

FRANCES *comes in quickly, evidently in search of her brother. Though she has not been crying, her eyes are wide with grief.*

FRANCES. Oh, Henry . . I'm so glad you're still up. [*She notices* WEDGECROFT.] How d'you do, Doctor?

TREBELL. [*Doubling his mask of indifference.*] Meistersinger's over early.

FRANCES. Is it?

TREBELL. Not much past twelve yet.

FRANCES. [*The little gibe lost on her.*] It was Tristan to-night. I'm quite upset. I heard just as I was coming away . . Amy O'Connell's dead. [*Both men hold their breath.* TREBELL *is the first to find control of his and give the cue.*

TREBELL. Yes . . Wedgecroft has just told me.

FRANCES. She was only taken ill last week . . it's so extraordinary. [*She remembers the doctor.*] Oh . . have you been attending her?

WEDGECROFT. Yes.

FRANCES. I hear there's to be an inquest.

WEDGECROFT. Yes.

FRANCES. But what has been the matter?

TREBELL. [*Sharply forestalling any answer.*] You'll know to-morrow.

FRANCES. [*The little snub almost bewildering her.*] Anything private? I mean . .

TREBELL. No . . I'll tell you. Don't make Gilbert repeat a story twice . . He's tired with a good day's work.

WEDGECROFT. Yes . . I'll be getting away.

> FRANCES *never heeds this flash of a further meaning between the two men.*

FRANCES. And I meant to have gone to see her to-day. Was the end very sudden? Did her husband arrive in time?

WEDGECROFT. Yes.

FRANCES. They didn't get on . . he'll be frightfully upset.

> TREBELL *resists a hideous temptation to laugh.*

WEDGECROFT. Good-night, Trebell.

TREBELL. Good-night, Gilbert. Many thanks.

> *There is enough of a caress in* TREBELL'S *tone to turn* FRANCES *towards their friend, a little remorseful for treating him so casually, now as always.*

FRANCES. He's always thanking you. You're always doing things for him.

WEDGECROFT. Good-night. [*Seeing the tears in her eyes.*] Oh, don't grieve.

FRANCES. One shouldn't be sorry when people die, I know. But she liked me more than I liked her . . [*This time* TREBELL *does laugh, silently.*] . . so I somehow feel in her debt and unable to pay now.

TREBELL. [*An edge on his voice.*] Yes . . people keep on dying at all sorts of ages, in all sorts of ways. But we seem never to get used to it . . narrow-minded as we are.

WEDGECROFT. Don't you talk nonsense.

TREBELL. [*One note sharper yet.*] One should occasionally test one's sanity by doing so. If we lived in the logical world we like to believe in, I could also prove that black was white. As it is . . there are more ways of killing a cat than hanging it.

WEDGECROFT. Had I better give you a sleeping draught?

FRANCES. Are you doctoring him for once? Henry, have you at last managed to overwork yourself?

TREBELL. No . . I started the evening by a charming little dinner at the Van Meyer's . . sat next to Miss Grace Cutler, who is writing a *vie intime* of Louis Quinze, and engaged me with anecdotes of the same.

FRANCES. A champion of her sex, whom I do not like.

WEDGECROFT. She's writing such a book to prove that women are equal to anything.

He goes towards the door, and FRANCES *goes with him.* TREBELL *never turns his head.*

TREBELL. I shall not come and open the door for you . . but mind you shut it.

FRANCES *comes back.*

FRANCES. Henry . . this is dreadful about that poor little woman.

TREBELL. An unwelcome baby was arriving. She got some quack to kill her.

These exact words are like a blow in the face to her, from which, being a woman of brave common sense, she does not shrink.

TREBELL.   What do you say to that?

She walks away from him, thinking painfully.

FRANCES.   She had never had a child. There's the common-place thing to say . . Ungrateful little fool! But . .

TREBELL.   If you had been in her place?

FRANCES.   [*Subtly.*] I have never made the mistake of marrying. She grew frightened, I suppose. Not just physically frightened. How can a man understand?

TREBELL.   The fear of life . . do you think it was . . which is the beginning of all evil?

FRANCES.   A woman must choose what her interpretation of life is to be . . as a man must, too, in his way . . as you and I have chosen, Henry.

TREBELL.   [*Asking from real interest in her.*]   Was yours a deliberate choice, and do you never regret it?

FRANCES.   [*Very simply and clearly.*] Perhaps one does nothing quite deliberately and for a definite reason. My state has its compensations . . if one doesn't value them too highly. I've travelled in thought over all this question. You mustn't blame a woman for wishing not to bear children. But . . well, if one doesn't like the fruit one mustn't cultivate the flower. And I suppose that saying condemns poor Amy . . condemned her to death . . [*Then her face hardens as she concentrates her. meaning.*] and brands most men as . . let's unsentimentally call it i l l o g i c a l, doesn't it?

He takes the thrust in silence.

TREBELL.   Did you notice the light in my window as you came in?

FRANCES.   Yes . . in both as I got out of the cab. Do you want the curtains drawn back?

TREBELL.   Yes . . don't touch them.

He has thrown himself into his chair by the fire.
She lapses into thought again.

FRANCES.   Poor little woman,

TREBELL. [*In deep anger.*] Well, if women will be little and poor . .

> *She goes to him and slips an arm over his shoulder.*

FRANCES. What is it you're worried about . . if a mere sister may ask?

TREBELL. [*Into the fire.*] I want to think. I haven't thought for years.

FRANCES. Why, you have done nothing else.

TREBELL. I've been working out problems in legal and political algebra.

FRANCES. You want to think of y o u r s e l f.

TREBELL. Yes.

FRANCES. [*Gentle and ironic.*] Have you ever, for one moment, thought in that sense of anyone else?

TREBELL. Is that a complaint?

FRANCES. The first in ten years' housekeeping.

TREBELL. No, I never have . . but I've never thought selfishly, either.

FRANCES. That's a paradox I don't quite understand.

TREBELL. Until women do they'll remain where they are . . and what they are.

FRANCES. Oh, I know you hate us.

TREBELL. Yes, dear sister, I'm afraid I do. And I hate your influence on men . . compromise, tenderness, pity, lack of purpose. Women don't know the values of things, not even their own value.

> *For a moment she studies him wonderingly.*

FRANCES. I'll take up the counter-accusation to-morrow. Now I'm tired and I'm going to bed. If I may insult you by mothering you, so should you. You look tired and I've seldom seen you.

TREBELL. I'm waiting up for a message.

FRANCES. So late?

TREBELL. It's a matter of life and death.

FRANCES. Are you joking?

TREBELL.   Yes. If you want to spoil me, find me a book
to read.

FRANCES.   What will you have?

TREBELL.   Huckleberry Finn. It's on a top shelf towards the end somewhere . . or should be.

> *She finds the book. On her way back with it she
> stops and shivers.*

FRANCES.   I don't think I shall sleep to-night. Poor
'Amy O'Connell!

TREBELL.   [*Curiously.*]   Are you afraid of death?

FRANCES.   [*With humorous stoicism.*]   It will be the
end of me, perhaps.

> *She gives him the book, with its red cover; the '86
> edition, a boy's friend, evidently. He fingers it
> familiarly.*

TREBELL.   Thank you. Mark Twain's a jolly fellow. He
has courage . . comic courage. That's what's wanted.
Nothing stands against it. You be-little yourself by laughing . . then all this world and the last and the next grow
little, too . . and so you grow great again. Switch off
some light, will you?

FRANCES.   [*Clicking off all but his reading lamp.*]   So?

TREBELL.   Thanks. Good-night, Frankie.

> *She turns at the door, with a glad smile.*

FRANCES.   Good-night. When did you last use that nursery name?

> *Then she goes, leaving him still fingering the book,
> but looking into the fire and far beyond. Behind
> him, through the open window, one sees how cold
> and clear the night is.*
>
> *At eight in the morning he is still there. His lamp
> is out, the fire is out, and the book laid aside. The
> white morning light penetrates every crevice of the
> room and shows every line on* TREBELL'S *face. The*

spirit of the man is strained past all reason. The
door opens suddenly, and FRANCES *comes in, trou-*
bled, nervous. Interrupted in her dressing, she has
put on some wrap or other.

FRANCES. Henry . . Simpson says you've not been to
bed all night.

He turns his head and says, with inappropriate
politeness——

TREBELL. No. Good morning.

FRANCES. Oh, my dear . . what is wrong?

TREBELL. The message hasn't come . . and I've been
thinking.

FRANCES. Why don't you tell me? [*He turns his head*
away.] I think you haven't the right to torture me.

TREBELL. Your sympathy would only blind me towards
the facts I want to face.

SIMPSON, *the maid, undisturbed in her routine,*
brings in the morning's letters. FRANCES *rounds on*
her irritably.

FRANCES. What is it, Simpson?

MAID. The letters, Ma'am.

TREBELL *is on his feet at that.*

TREBELL. Ah . . I want them.

FRANCES. [*Taking the letters composedly enough.*]
Thank you.

SIMPSON *departs, and* TREBELL *comes to her for his*
letters. She looks at him with baffled affection.

FRANCES. Can I do nothing? Oh, Henry!

TREBELL. Help me to open my letters.

FRANCES. Don't you leave them to Mr. Kent?

TREBELL. Not this morning.

FRANCES. But there are so many.

TREBELL. [*For the first time lifting his voice from its*
dull monotony.] What a busy man I was.

FRANCES. Henry . . you're a little mad.

TREBELL.   Do you find me so? That's interesting.

FRANCES.   [*With a ghost of a smile.*] Well . . maddening.

> *By this time he is sitting at his table; she near him,
> watching closely. They halve the considerable post
> and start to open it.*

TREBELL.   We arrange them in three piles . . personal
. . political . . and preposterous.

FRANCES.   This is an invitation . . the Anglican League.

TREBELL.   I can't go.

> *She looks sideways at him as he goes on mechan-
> ically tearing the envelopes.*

FRANCES.   I heard you come upstairs about two o'clock.

TREBELL.   That was to dip my head in water. Then I
made an instinctive attempt to go to bed . . got my tie off,
even.

FRANCES.   [*Her anxiety breaking out.*] If you'd tell me
that you're only ill . . .

TREBELL.   [*Forbiddingly commonplace.*] What's that
letter? Don't fuss . . and remember that abnormal conduct is sometimes quite rational.

> FRANCES *returns to her task with misty eyes.*

FRANCES.   It's from somebody whose son can't get into
something.

TREBELL.   The third heap . . Kent's . . the preposterous. [*Talking on with steady monotony.*] But I saw it
would not do to interrupt that logical train of thought
which reached definition about half past six. I had then
been gleaning until you came in.

FRANCES.   [*Turning the neat little note in her hand.*]
This is from Lord Horsham. He writes his name small
at the bottom of the envelope.

TREBELL.   [*Without a tremor.*] Ah . . give it me.

> *He opens this as he has opened the others, carefully*

putting the envelope to one side. FRANCES *has
ceased for the moment to watch him.*

FRANCES. That's Cousin Robert's handwriting. [*She
puts a square envelope at his hand.*] Is a letter marked
private from the Education Office political or personal?

By this he has read HORSHAM'S *letter twice. So
he tears it up, and speaks very coldly.*

TREBELL. Either. It doesn't matter.

In the silence her fears return.

FRANCES. Henry, it's a foolish idea . . I suppose I have
it because I hardly slept for thinking of her. Your trouble is nothing to do with Amy O'Connell, is it?

TREBELL. [*His voice strangled in his throat.*] Her
child should have been my child, too.

FRANCES. [*Her eyes open, the whole landscape of her
mind suddenly clear.*] Oh, I . . no, I didn't think so . .
but . . . .

TREBELL. [*Dealing his second blow as remorselessly as
dealt to him.*] Also I'm not joining the new Cabinet, my
dear sister.

FRANCES. [*Her thoughts rushing now to the present—
the future.*] Not! Because of . . ? Do people know?
Will they . . ? You didn't . . ?

As mechanically as ever he has taken up COUSIN
ROBERT'S *letter, and, in some sense, read it. Now he
recapitulates, meaninglessly, that his voice may just
deaden her pain and his own.*

TREBELL. Robert says . . that we've not been to see them
for some time . . but that now I'm a greater man than
ever I must be very busy. The vicarage has been painted
and papered throughout, and looks much fresher. Mary
sends you her love and hopes you have no return of the
rheumatism. And he would like to send me the proof
sheets of his critical commentary on First Timothy . . for
my alien eye might possibly detect some logical lapses.

Need he repeat to me his thankfulness at my new attitude
upon Disestablishment . . or assure me again that I have
his prayers. Could we not go and stay there only for a
few days? Possibly his opinion——

> *She has borne this cruel kindness as long as she can,
> and she breaks out . .*

FRANCES. Oh . . don't . . don't!

> *He falls from his seeming callousness to the very
> blankness of despair.*

TREBELL. No, we'll leave that . . and the rest . . and
everything.

> *Her agony passes.*

FRANCES. What do you mean to do?

TREBELL. There's to be no public scandal.

FRANCES. Why has Lord Horsham thrown you over,
then . . or hasn't that anything to do with it?

TREBELL. It has to do with it.

FRANCES. [*Lifting her voice; some tone returning to
it.*] Unconsciously . . I've known for years that this sort
of thing might happen to you.

TREBELL. Why?

FRANCES. Power over men and women, and contempt
for them! Do you think they don't take their revenge
sooner or later?

TREBELL. Much good may it do them!

FRANCES. Human nature turns against you . . by instinct . . in self-defence.

TREBELL. And my own human nature!

FRANCES. [*Shocked into great pity by his half articu-
late pain.*] Yes . . you must have loved her, Henry . . in
some odd way. I'm sorry for you both.

TREBELL. I'm hating her now . . as a man can only
hate his own silliest vices.

FRANCES. [*Flashing into defence.*] That's wrong of
you. If you thought of her only as a pretty little fool . .

Bearing your child . . all her womanly life belonged to
you . . and for that time there was no other sort of life
in her. So she became what you thought her.

TREBELL.   That's not true.

FRANCES.   It's true enough . . it's true of men towards
women. You can't think of them through generations as
one thing and then suddenly find them another.

TREBELL.   [*Hammering at his fixed idea.*]   She should
have brought that child into the world.

FRANCES.   You didn't love her enough.

TREBELL.   I didn't love her at all.

FRANCES.   Then why should she value your gift?

TREBELL.   For its own sake.

FRANCES.   [*Turning away.*]   It's hopeless . . you don't
understand.

TREBELL.   [*Helpless; almost like a deserted child.*]   I've
been trying to . . all through the night.

FRANCES.   [*Turning back, enlightened a little.*]   That's
more the trouble then than the Cabinet question?

> *He shakes himself to his feet and begins to pace the
> room, his keenness coming back to him, his brow
> knitting again with the delight of thought.*

TREBELL.   Oh . . as to me against the world . . I'm
fortified with comic courage. [*Then turning on her like
any examining professor.*]   Now which do you believe . .
that Man is the reformer, or that the Time brings forth
such men as it needs, and, lobster-like, can grow another
claw?

FRANCES.   [*Watching this new mood carefully.*]   I believe that you'll be missed from Lord Horsham's Cabinet.

TREBELL.   The hand-made statesman and his hand-made
measure! They were out of place in that pretty Tory
garden. Those men are the natural growth of the time.
Am I?

FRANCES.   Just as much. And wasn't your bill going to

be such a good piece of work? That can't be thrown
away . . wasted.

TREBELL. Can one impose a clever idea upon men and
women? I wonder.

FRANCES. That rather begs the question of your very
existence, doesn't it?

He comes to a standstill.

TREBELL. I know.

*His voice shows her that meaning in her words and
beyond it a threat. She goes to him, suddenly shaking with fear.*

FRANCES. Henry, I didn't mean that.

TREBELL. You think I've a mind to put an end to that
same?

FRANCES. [*Belittling her fright.*] No . . for how unreasonable . . .

TREBELL. In view of my promising past. I've stood for
success, Fanny; I still stand for success. I could still do
more outside the Cabinet than the rest of them, inside, will
do. But suddenly I've a feeling the work would be barren. [*His eyes shift beyond her; beyond the room.*]
What is it in your thoughts and actions which makes them
bear fruit? Something that the roughest peasant may
have in common with the best of us intellectual men . .
something that a dog might have. It isn't successful clev-
erness.

She stands . . his trouble beyond her reach.

FRANCES. Come, now . . you've done very well with
your life.

TREBELL. Do you know how empty I feel of all virtue
at this moment?

*He leaves her. She must bring him back to the
plane on which she can help him.*

FRANCES. We must think what's best to be done . .
now . . and for the future.

TREBELL. Why, I could go on earning useless money at the Bar . . think how nice that would be. I could blackmail the next judgeship out of Horsham. I think I could even smash his Disestablishment Bill . . and perhaps get into the next Liberal Cabinet and start my own all over again, with necessary modifications. I shan't do any such things.

FRANCES. No one knows about you and poor Amy?

TREBELL. Half a dozen friends. Shall I offer to give evidence at the inquest this morning?

FRANCES. [*With a little shiver.* They'll say bad enough things about her without your blackening her good name.
　　　Without warning, his anger and anguish break out again.

TREBELL. All she had . . all there is left of her! She was a nothingness . . silly . . vain. And I gave her this power over me!
　　　He is beaten, exhausted. Now she goes to him, motherlike.

FRANCES. My dear, listen to me for a little. Consider that as a sorrow and put it behind you. And think now . . whatever love there may be between us has neither hatred nor jealousy in it, has it, Henry? Since I'm not a mistress or a friend, but just the likest fellow-creature to you . . perhaps.

TREBELL. [*Putting out his hand for hers.*] Yes, my sister. What I've wanted to feel for vague humanity has been what I should have felt for you . . if you'd ever made a single demand on me.
　　　She puts her arms round him; able to speak.

FRANCES. Let's go away somewhere . . I'll make demands. I need refreshing as much as you. My joy of life has been withered in me . . oh, for a long time now. We must kiss the earth again . . take interest in common things, common people. There's so much of the world

we don't know. There's air to breathe everywhere. Think
of the flowers in a Tyrol valley in the early spring. One
can walk for days, not hurrying, as soon as the passes are
open. And the people are kind. There's Italy . . there's
Russia, full of simple folk. When we've learned to be
friends with them we shall both feel so much better.

TREBELL. [*Shaking his head, unmoved.*] My dear sister . . I should be bored to death. The life contemplative
and peripatetic would literally bore me into a living death.

FRANCES. [*Letting it be a fairy tale.*] Is your mother
the Wide World nothing to you? Can't you open your
heart like a child again?

TREBELL. No, neither to the beauty of Nature nor the
particular human animals that are always called a part of
it. I don't even see them with your eyes. I'm a son of the
anger of Man at men's foolishness, and unless I've that to
feed upon . . . ! [*Now he looks at her, as if for the first
time wanting to explain himself, and his voice changes.*]
Don't you know that when a man cuts himself, shaving, he
swears? When he loses a seat in the Cabinet he turns
inward for comfort . . and if he only finds there a spirit
which should have been born, but is dead . . what's to be
done then?

FRANCES. [*In a whisper.*] You mustn't think of that
woman . . .

TREBELL. I've reasoned my way through life . . .

FRANCES. I see how awful it is to have the double blow
fall.

TREBELL. [*The wave of his agony rising again.*] But
there's something in me which no knowledge touches . .
some feeling . . some power which should be the beginning of new strength. But it has been killed in me unborn
before I had learnt to understand . . and that's killing me.

FRANCES. [*Crying out.*] Why . . why did no woman

teach you to be gentle? Why did you never believe in any
woman? Perhaps even I am to blame.

TREBELL.   The little fool, the little fool . . why did she
kill my child? What did it matter what I thought her?
We were committed together to that one thing. Do you
think I didn't know that I was heartless and that she was
socially in the wrong? But what did Nature care for
that? And Nature has broken us.

FRANCES.   [*Clinging to him as he beats the air.*] Not
you. She's dead, poor girl . . but not you.

TREBELL.   Yes . . that's the mystery no one need believe
till he has dipped in it. The man bears the child in his
soul as the woman carries it in her body.

> *There is silence between them, till she speaks, low
> and tonelessly, never loosing his hand.*

FRANCES.   Henry, I want your promise that you'll go on
living till . . till . .

TREBELL.   Don't cry, Fanny, that's very foolish.

FRANCES.   Till you've learnt to look at all this calmly.
Then I can trust you.

> TREBELL *smiles, but not at all grimly.*

TREBELL.   But, you see, it would give Horsham and
Blackborough such a shock if I shot myself . . it would
make them think about things.

FRANCES.   [*With one catch of wretched laughter.*] Oh,
my dear, if shooting's wanted . . shoot them. Or I'll do
it for you.

> *He sits in his chair just from weariness. She stands
> by him, her hand still grasping his.*

TREBELL.   You see, Fanny, as I said to Gilbert last night
. . our lives are our own and yet not our own. We understand living for others and dying for others. The first is
easy . . it's a way out of boredom. To make the second
popular we had to invent a belief in personal resurrection.
Do you think we shall ever understand dying in the sure

and certain hope that it really doesn't matter . . that God is infinitely economical and wastes perhaps less of the power in us after our death than men do while we live?

FRANCES. I want your promise, Henry.

TREBELL. You know I never make promises . . it's taking oneself too seriously. Unless indeed one has the comic courage to break them, too. I've upset you very much with my troubles. Don't you think you'd better go and finish dressing? [*She doesn't move.*] My dear . . you don't propose to hold my right hand so safely for years to come. Even so, I still could jump out of a window.

FRANCES. I'll trust you, Henry.

She looks into his eyes and he does not flinch. Then, with a final grip, she leaves him. When she is at the door he speaks more gently than ever.

TREBELL. Your own life is sufficient unto itself, isn't it?

FRANCES. Oh, yes. I can be pleasant to talk to, and give good advice through the years that remain. [*Instinctively she rectifies some little untidiness in the room.*] What fools they are to think they can run that government without you!

TREBELL. Horsham will do his best. [*Then, as for the second time she reaches the door.*] Don't take away my razors, will you? I only use them for shaving.

FRANCES. [*Almost blushing.*] I half meant to . . I'm sorry. After all, Henry, just because they are forgetting in personal feelings what's best for the country . . it's your duty not to. You'll stand by and do what you can, won't you?

TREBELL. [*His queer smile returning, in contrast to her seriousness.*] Disestablishment. It's a very interesting problem. I must think it out.

FRANCES. [*Really puzzled.*] What do you mean?

He gets up with a quick movement of strange

> *strength, and faces her. His smile changes into a*
> *graver gladness.*

TREBELL. Something has happened . . in spite of me.
My heart's clean again. I'm ready for fresh adventures.

FRANCES. [*With a nod and answering gladness.*] That's
right.

> *So she leaves him, her mind at rest. For a minute*
> *he does not move. When his gaze narrows it falls*
> *on the heaps of letters. He carries them carefully*
> *into* WALTER KENT'S *room, and arranges them as*
> *carefully on his table. On his way out he stops for*
> *a moment; then with a sudden movement bangs the*
> *door.*
>
> *Two hours later the room has been put in order. It*
> *is even more full of light and the shadows are hard-*
> *er than usual. The doors are open, showing you*
> KENT'S *door still closed. At the big writing table, in*
> TREBELL'S *chair, sits* WEDGECROFT, *pale and grave, in-*
> *tent on finishing a letter.* FRANCES *comes to find him.*
> *For a moment she leans on the table silently, her*
> *eyes half closed. You would say a broken woman.*
> *When she speaks, it is swiftly, but tonelessly.*

FRANCES. Lord Horsham is in the drawing room . .
and I can't see him, I really can't. He has come to say he
is sorry . . and I should tell him that it is his fault, partly.
I know I should . . and I don't want to. Won't you go
in? What are you writing?

> WEDGECROFT, *with his physicianly pre-occupation,*
> *can attend, understand, sympathise, without looking*
> *up at her.*

WEDGECROFT. Never mind. A necessary note . . to the
Coroner's office. Yes, I'll see Horsham.

FRANCES. I've managed to get the pistol out of his
hand. Was that wrong . . oughtn't I to have touched it?

WEDGECROFT. Of course you oughtn't. You must stay
away from the room. I'd better have locked the door.

FRANCES. [*Pitifully.*] I'm sorry . . but I couldn't bear
to see the pistol in his hand. I won't go back. After all,
he's not there in the room, is he? But how long do you
think the spirit stays near the body . . how long? When
people die gently, of age or weakness . . . But when the
spirit and body are so strong and knit together and all
alive as his . . .

WEDGECROFT. [*His hand on hers.*] Hush . . hush!

FRANCES. His face is very eager . . as if it still could
speak. I know that.

> MRS. FARRANT *comes through the open doorway.*
> FRANCES *hears her steps, and, turning, falls into her*
> *outstretched arms, to cry there.*

FRANCES. Oh, Julia!

MRS. FARRANT. Oh, my dear Fanny! I came with Cyril
Horsham . . I don't think Simpson even saw me.

FRANCES. I can't go in and talk to him.

MRS. FARRANT. He'll understand. But I heard you
come in here . .

WEDGECROFT. I'll tell Horsham.

> *He has finished and addressed his letter, so he goes*
> *out with it.* FRANCES *lifts her head. These two are*
> *in accord, and can speak their feelings without dis-*
> *guise or preparation.*

FRANCES. Julia, Julia . . isn't it unbelievable?

MRS. FARRANT. I'd give . . oh, what wouldn't I give to
have it undone!

FRANCES. I knew he meant to . . and yet I thought I
had his promise. If he really meant to . . I couldn't
have stopped it, could I?

MRS. FARRANT. Walter sent to tell me, and I sent round
to . . .

FRANCES. Walter came soon after, I think. Julia, I was

in my room . . it was nearly breakfast time . . when I
heard the shot. Oh . . don't you think it was cruel of him?

MRS. FARRANT.   He had a right to. We must remember
that.

FRANCES.   You say that easily of my brother . . you
wouldn't say it of your husband.

They are apart by this. JULIA FARRANT *goes to her
gently.*

MRS. FARRANT.   Fanny . . will it leave you so very
lonely?

FRANCES.   Yes . . lonelier than you can ever be. You
have children. I'm just beginning to realise . . .

MRS. FARRANT.   [*Leading her from the mere selfishness
of sorrow.*] There's loneliness of the spirit, too.

FRANCES.   Ah, but once you've tasted the common joys
of life . . once you've proved all your rights as a man or
woman . . .

MRS. FARRANT.   Then there are subtler things to miss.
As well be alone like you, or dead like him, without them
. . I sometimes think.

FRANCES.   [*Responsive, lifted from egoism, reading her
friend's mind.*] You demand much.

MRS. FARRANT.   I wish that he had demanded much of
any woman.

FRANCES.   You know how this misery began? That
poor little wretch . . she's lying dead, too. They're both
dead together now. Do you think they've met . . ?

*JULIA grips both her hands, and speaks very stead-
ily, to help her friend back to self control.*

MRS. FARRANT.   George told me as soon as he was told.
I tried to make him understand my opinion, but he thought
I was only shocked.

FRANCES.   I was sorry for her. Now I can't forgive
her, either.

MRS. FARRANT. [*Angry, remorseful, rebellious.*] When will men learn to know one woman from another?

FRANCES. [*With answering bitterness.*] When will all women care to be one thing rather than the other?

> *They are stopped by the sound of the opening of* KENT'S *door.* WALTER *comes from his room, some papers from his table held listlessly in one hand. He is crying, undisguisedly, with a child's grief.*

KENT. Oh . . am I in your way . . ?

FRANCES. I didn't know you were still here, Walter.

KENT. I've been going through the letters, as usual. I don't know why, I'm sure. They won't have to be answered now . . will they?

> WEDGECROFT *comes back, grave and tense.*

WEDGECROFT. Horsham has gone. He thought perhaps you'd be staying with Miss Trebell for a bit.

MRS. FARRANT. Yes, I shall be.

WEDGECROFT. I must go, too . . it's nearly eleven.

FRANCES. To the o t h e r inquest?

> *This stirs her two listeners to something of a shudder.*

WEDGECROFT. Yes.

MRS. FARRANT. [*In a low voice.*] It will make no difference now . . I mean . . still nothing need come out? We needn't know why he . . why he did it.

WEDGECROFT. When he talked to me last night, and I didn't know what he was talking of . . .

FRANCES. He was waiting this morning for Lord Horsham's note . . .

MRS. FARRANT. [*In real alarm.*] Oh, it wasn't because of the Cabinet trouble . . you must persuade Cyril Horsham of that. You haven't told him . . he's so dreadfully upset as it is. I've been swearing it had nothing to do with that.

WEDGECROFT. [*Cutting her short, bitingly.*] Has a time

ever come to you when it was easier to die than to go on living? Oh . . I told Lord Horsham just what I thought.

He leaves them, his own grief unexpressed.

FRANCES. [*Listlessly.*] Does it matter why?

MRS. FARRANT. Need there be more suffering and re-proaches? It's not as if even grief would do any good. [*Suddenly, with nervous caution.*] Walter, you don't know, do you?

WALTER *throws up his tear-marked face, and a man's anger banishes the boyish grief.*

WALTER. No, I don't know why he did it . . and I don't care. And grief is no use. I'm angry . . just angry at the waste of a good man. Look at the work undone . . think of it! Who is to do it! Oh . . the waste . . !

ever come to you when it was easier to die than to go on living? Oh . . ." I told Lord Horsham just what I thought.

He leaves them, his own grief unexpressed.

FRANCES [listening]. Does it matter why?

MRS. FARRANT. Need there be more suffering and reproach? It's not as it even grief would do any good. [Suddenly with nervous reaction.] Walter, you don't know, do you?

WALTER turns on her his tear-marked face, and a man's anger dominates the brutal cry.

WALTER. No, I don't know why he did it . . . and I don't care. And grief is no use. I'm angry . . . just angry at the waste of a good man. Look at the work undone . . . think of it! Who is to do it! Oh . . . the waste . . . !

"The Marrying of Ann Leete" was produced by the Stage Society, at the Royalty Theatre, on the evening of January 26th, 1902.

ANN LEETE	*Miss Winifred Fraser*
LORD JOHN CARP	*Julian Royce*
GEORGE LEETE	*Kenneth Douglas*
MR. DANIEL TATTON	*J. Malcolm Dunn*
LADY COTTESHAM	*Miss Henrietta Watson*
CARNABY LEETE	*H. A. Saintsbury*
JOHN ABUD	*C. M. Hallard*
THE REV. DR. REMNANT	*Howard Sturge*
MRS. OPIE	*Miss Helen Rous*
DIMMUCK	*George Trollope*
MR. TETGEEN	*A. E. George*
LORD ARTHUR CARP	*Charles V. France*
MR. SMALLPEICE	*J. Y. F. Cooke*
SIR GEORGE LEETE	*Arthur Grenville*
MR. CROWE	*Sydney Paxton*
LADY LEETE	*Miss Bessie Page*
MRS. GEORGE LEETE	*Miss Florence Neville*
THE REV. MR. TOZER	*Ivan Berlin*
MR. PRESTIGE	*Howard Templeton*
MRS. PRESTIGE	*Mrs. Gordon Gray*

"The Voysey Inheritance" was first played at the Court Theatre, a Vedrenne-Barker performance, on the afternoon of November 7th, 1905.

Mr. Voysey	*A. E. George*
Mrs. Voysey	*Miss Florence Haydon*
Trenchard Voysey, K.C.	*Eugene Mayeur*
Honor Voysey	*Miss Geraldine Olliffe*
Major Booth Voysey	*Charles Fulton*
Mrs. Booth Voysey	*Miss Grace Edwin*
Christopher	*Harry C. Duff*
Edward Voysey	*Thalberg Corbett*
Hugh Voysey	*Dennis Eadie*
Mrs. Hugh Voysey	*Miss Henrietta Watson*
Ethel Voysey	*Miss Alexandra Carlisle*
Denis Tregoning	*Frederick Lloyd*
Alice Maitland	*Miss Mabel Hackney*
Mr. Booth	*O. B. Clarence*
The Rev. Evan Colpus	*Edmund Gwenn*
Peacey	*Trevor Lowe*
Phœbe	*Miss Gwynneth Galton*
Mary	*Mrs. Fordyce*

"Waste" was produced by the Stage Society at the Imperial Theatre, Westminster, on the evening of November 24th, 1907.

LADY DAVENPORT	*Miss Amy Coleman*
WALTER KENT	*Vernon Steel*
MRS. FARRANT	*Miss Beryl Faber*
MISS TREBELL	*Miss Henrietta Watson*
MRS. O'CONNELL	*Miss Aimée De Burgh*
LUCY DAVENPORT	*Miss Dorothy Thomas*
GEORGE FARRANT	*Frederick Lloyd*
RUSSELL BLACKBOROUGH	*A. Holmes-Gore*
A FOOTMAN	*Allan Wade*
HENRY TREBELL	*Granville Barker*
SIMPSON	*Miss Mary Barton*
GILBERT WEDGECROFT	*Berte Thomas*
LORD CHARLES CANTELUPE	*Dennis Eadie*
THE EARL OF HORSHAM	*Henry Vibart*
EDMUNDS	*Trevor Lowe*
JUSTIN O'CONNELL	*J. Fisher White*